THE ARCTIC FOX

The
ARCTIC FOX

Bush Pilot of the North Country

DON C. BRAUN

with John C. Warren

toExcel

San Jose New York Lincoln Shanghai

The Arctic Fox
Bush Pilot of the North Country

Published by toExcel
an imprint of iUniverse.com, Inc.

For information address:
iUniverse.com, Inc.
620 North 48th Street
Suite 201
Lincoln, NE 68504-3467
www.iuniverse.com

Originally published by Back Bay Press

ISBN: 0-595-00329-X

Printed in the United States of America

To my sons

Christopher, Charles and Joel

ACKNOWLEDGMENTS

Don and I started working on this project in February of 1992 when he was confined to a hospital bed in Minneapolis and the doctors assigned to his case were about to send him home to die after giving up trying to reverse his failing health.

So, I want to thank all the Braun relatives who strongly suggested that we collaborate on this book in the 11th hour of Don's life. Thanks also to Bob Cesnik, M.D., Don's personal physician back home in St. Cloud, for keeping the Arctic Fox going for over a year after his hospital discharge so we could tape record and transcribe all of Don's stories and personal reflections before his death on Good Friday, April 9, 1993.

My heartfelt thanks to Christopher, Charles and Joel, Don's three sons, for their support and help with this project, and for Jackie Braun's loving attention to all of Don's need in the twilight of his life.

Max Ward, of course, is an integral part of the Don Braun story, and his thoughtful Foreword is very appropriate and appreciated. Special thanks, too, to all those who carefully reviewed drafts of the manuscript to ensure its accuracy. Max and his wonderful wife, Marjorie, provided many excellent suggestions in addition to their enthusiastic support. Max's good friend and gifted Canadian author Walter Stewart gave generously of his time, professional advice and encouragement to this project.

Thanks also to Art Morrow for his numerous suggestions and contributions of personal photographs and writings; to Don's brothers and sisters, and brother-in-law and fellow pilot Vern Reller, for reviewing the manuscripts and offering encouragement all along the way; and to Don's friend, Moe Lynn.

The beautiful cover design was the work of my talented daughter, Shanna Goudy, who also produced the maps on the inside covers. The cover drawing is printed with the permission of Falkins McIntosh – Reed Stenhouse, a Wardair insurer who commissioned the work several years ago and generously provided limited edition prints to Don and his family and friends at Wardair. My thanks to Mr. Stenhouse for use of this very special drawing.

I am also indebted to Linda Hanner, an author and publisher, who patiently guided me through the many steps of publication; and to my editor, Carol Frick, whose knowledge, skill, good sense and excellent suggestions magically turned my manuscript into a book. Carol is a remarkable person for whom I have the highest regard.

I especially want to thank my wife, Mary Jo, for all of the encouragement and support she has given this project. She loved and admired her Uncle Don. And you will, too, when you read this remarkable story.

— *John C. Warren*

FOREWORD

The North of Canada is a wondrous land. It can be inspiring, beautiful and beguiling. It can also be cruel, desolate, soul-destroying and unforgiving. A certain breed of man was required to accept the challenges and hardships of Northern flying when the aircraft was relatively primitive. Don Braun was just such a man.

There was just a handful of good bush pilots in Don's time, and before his time. Don's background of skills, plus his resourcefulness and temperament, made him an honoured member of the few. Excellence in airmanship and aircraft handling was taken for granted by

those who flew in the Arctic; but the additional skill of finding one's way and surviving in the harsh elements of midwinter in Arctic wastes was essential to achieving fame and respect in the Arctic. Don carned that fame and respect throughout the North. So often people would say, "Only Don could do that," or "We must have Don for this particular trip."

I remember hearing an irregular engine sound while standing on the dock one day. I looked up to observe an Otter approaching Yellowknife Bay from the north. Sure enough, it was Don, bringing an Otter back with one cylinder out. He had removed the push rods from an unserviceable cylinder, plugged the housings so as not to lose oil, and flown back to base on six of the seven cylinders. Such was the skill of one who had cut his teeth overhauling and repairing engines of all types.

Flying machines were Don's life. He understood them from the ground up. I remember observing Don with great delight upon his first exposure to Wardair's Boeing 727. He studied the wing trailing edge devices during take-off, rushed forward to observe the wing leading edge, then back to the trailing edge as the flaps were being retracted. He didn't have to be told what was happening. He knew that the wing had been dramatically changed and replaced with a lift drag device. He sat quietly for a long time, digesting this transition.

As is so often the case during those busy formative years of an air service, Don and I were too busy to spend the time together that we would have liked. On a trip to a camp just 53 miles north of Yellowknife, we were so busy chatting that we flew over our destination and on north for an extra 20 minutes or so before realizing where we were. Those at the mine site were completely astonished to hear the aircraft fly by the camp and the sound fade away. Needless to say, it took a long time for the local mirth over that incident to be forgotten.

It seems that we race through the years assuming life will go on forever. It is not until we "remember" that the reality of life sinks home. I begrudge having to just "remember" that wonderful friend, Donald C. Braun, but I feel sure he is flying with eagles.

— *Maxwell W. Ward*

CONTENTS

ONE   Three Days in an Igloo 1

TWO   The Glider 13

THREE   Setting Up Shop in Harlem 22

FOUR   The War Years as a Royal Canadian
Air Force Pilot 35

FIVE   Snare River Bush Pilot 55

SIX   Retreat to the Farm, Return to
the North 73

SEVEN   Life with Max in Yellowknife 85

EIGHT   Ice Roads in the Barren Lands 103

NINE   Back in the Igloo 117

TEN   High Arctic Flights 128

ELEVEN   The Bristol Freighter 145

TWELVE   The North Pole Landing, 1967 165

THIRTEEN   Return to the Pole, 1969 184

FOURTEEN   The Arctic Fox 201

FIFTEEN   Fire-Bombing and Other Crazy Stunts   204

SIXTEEN   Many Searches, Few Rescues 212

SEVENTEEN   Time to Call It Quits 223

EIGHTEEN   Just One More Flight 230

EPILOGUE   Final Log Entry: A Personal Reflection . 243

CHAPTER ONE

THREE DAYS IN AN IGLOO

*"As a matter of fact, I enjoyed trips alone.
Even in the Arctic islands when I was flying
the old single-engine Otter and all I had was
some extra gas and maybe sandwiches for the
day, that never bothered me in the least. I
always figured I was prepared to stay if
forced to land and shut down."*

I started out in the dark, flying the Otter northwest out
of the village of Coppermine which is located one hundred miles above the Arctic Circle on the north coast of
Canada's Northwest Territories. It was November 24,
1958, and my mission was to take a Christmas load of
supplies to an Arctic weather station on Banks Island.
The boys at Sachs Harbour got their supplies at the end
of November because after that it was continuously pitch
black and we couldn't fly that far north again in a single
engine until early spring.

Banks Island is the westernmost island in the Arctic
Archipelago, and Sachs Harbour is located on the west
coast of the barren 23,000-square-mile rock plateau, a
distance of 374 miles from Coppermine. There were no
airstrips at Sachs Harbour, so you had to pick a place to
land and you needed some daylight to do that. We would
take off in the dark, fly most of the way in the dark, and
try to reach the station during the brightest part of the
day, which would be twilight around noon. The sun
never came up that time of year, never above the horizon.
There was a little hillside near the weather station that
was smooth and when you could see it you could land,
coast down the hill and end up right by the back door of
the building, if everything went just right.

The Otter's big 600-hp Pratt & Whitney nine-cylinder
radial engine was tough and loud, like most radials. It
was a reliable old workhorse of an engine, and the throb-
bing sound of it in the cockpit was somehow reassuring
as I left the coast behind and headed out over the straits
toward Victoria Island against a fairly strong headwind.
We always flew up the west side of Victoria Island so we
wouldn't have as much open water to cross. The open
water of Amundsen Gulf between Banks Island and the
coast was black and looked just awful, with the wind always blowing and white caps churning this particular
time of year. When you're flying single engine, the minute
you get out over that dirty black water, everything seems
to go wrong. If nowhere else, in your mind. The engine
somehow always sounds like it's going to give you trouble
when you're flying across that kind of open water. The
less of it you have to cover the better, so I flew across
where it was only 30 miles and about 20 minutes to Victoria Island. After hugging the coast of the island, I
pushed across another strait toward Banks. By this time
I was about 200 miles out of Coppermine and now the
headwind had become much stronger. In fact, I had such
a headwind at this point that I began to wonder if I was
going to make it to Sachs Harbour. So I took the Otter
down low, even though I was still over the strait, and
made my way across the black water ever so slowly at
about 600 feet.

Just a few hours earlier at Coppermine, Father
LaPointe had remarked that he thought the weather
looked kind of bad. The kindly but rugged Order of Mary
Immaculate priest had once again put me up for the night
at his mission. "Really, I think you're taking off into a bad
situation. You should stay a day," he said. "No, Father," I
replied. "I've delayed this trip long enough. I waited four
days for weather at Wardair headquarters in Yellowknife
before I could even start out yesterday for Coppermine."
I explained to the good Father that this being the weather
station's only supply load before Christmas, all the crew's

Christmas gifts were on board the Otter. Even a Christmas tree.

There were six personnel at the station and the government usually rotated two crew members at a time so no one served more than a year in such an isolated post. For some reason they weren't going to change any personnel this trip. More Christmas parcels for the men arrived each day I waited and I kept adding them to the load and pulling something else off. I even began throwing off emergency gear because flying alone tends to make you think you're invincible. We carried a Mount Logan tent, which was a small nylon tent in which we always wrapped a snow knife. It's a big, long knife with a serrated edge for sawing through even the hardest packed snow. Off went the tent and, inadvertently, the snow knife with it. I never thought of the snow knife and I had never built an igloo before in my life anyway, so what was I going to do with a snow knife?

I threw my jack out, too. We would carry a jack to pry the Otter loose if the plane's skis became frozen down in the snow overnight. Also tossed was my extra gasoline for the blow pots used to heat the Otter's engine on very cold mornings, and white gas for my little stove. That made room for several dozen eggs for Father LaPointe's mission. I always brought him fresh eggs. Or when we were put up for the night by someone who liked whiskey or rum, we brought some along as payment for our stay. If they wanted fruit, we brought some along. With the priests it was either eggs or fruit, or whatever we could haul. We stayed at both Catholic and Anglican missions, and often at the posts of the Royal Canadian Mounted Police — "Mounties" for short. Just throw a little extra in your load for these friendly people because they always seemed to have a spare bed or space on the floor for you. So I had the eggs, the Christmas tree and over a ton of gifts and supplies all aboard and tied down as I lifted off from Yellowknife for Coppermine and Sachs Harbour on

November 23 after a four-day wait. I was happy to be on my way at last.

Father LaPointe had fried some of the eggs for me at breakfast before I left for Banks Island. The eggs were for the mission and not for me, I'd protested, but he persisted. He then handed me a sackful of Arctic char, about half a dozen, and I said, "Oh, Father, I'm never going to eat these!" He pointed at the sky and said, "You never know."

I glanced at the sackful of char on the floor of the cockpit, then turned my attention once again to the headwind problem and the slow progress the old Otter was making across the strait. When you make landfall on Banks Island there are a couple of reference points to look for, and when I came off the straits to Banks I made landfall at Victory Point and then came around almost due west and saw DeSalis Bay in the late morning twilight. DeSalis Bay is on the southeast shore of Banks Island, approximately 84 miles east of Sachs Harbour. The bay is almost completely enclosed, which makes the water freeze over nice and smooth like a lake down south instead of all chopped up with ridges. It was a good landing area if you needed to land.

The island itself rose up from the frozen bay to perhaps 600 to 800 feet of solid rock with a little scrub and no trees. There was a very broad valley coming down through the hills to the bay and running through the center of the valley was Sand Creek. I radioed Sachs Harbor and told them my location and that I would arrive in about an hour, maybe less if the headwinds subsided. I was getting low on fuel because of bucking these terrific headwinds, so I was staying low and proceeding up this valley well off to one side so I could make a turn toward the creek and get out if anything should happen.

I hadn't even gotten the microphone back on the holder when suddenly the Otter was caught in a downdraft the likes of which I've never experienced in all my

life. The Otter was going down so fast that when I hung
the mike on the holder, it just proceeded to go right up
against the ceiling along with the load behind me. I immediately turned to get the hell out of there. With full
power and trying to hold speed I was still going down to
within 100 feet of the ground. I was definitely going to
plow right into the ground when the next thing I knew
the Otter was going straight up at about the same rate.
Up we went, even higher than I had been in normal
flight. Just like an express elevator, only 100 mph. And
the top end was the same, with an abrupt stop and then
another plunge back down while the whole load flew up
against the ceiling again. This happened about three
times in a minute or two.

We would always tell the young fellows new to the North
Country that they really didn't have to worry about
severe turbulence in the North. Nice, smooth flights,
except for a line of thunderstorms now and then. Although I didn't know it at the time, the Otter was caught
in what they call rotor winds. A very strong wind blowing
across the rough terrain of the island had slammed into
the smooth sidewall of the Sand Creek valley and then
bounced upward with enough force to create an area of
low pressure, causing the wind to rotate over and back
down into the sidewall and up again. That's what I had
run into, and why I had never hit the ground. I would
run into one side and then the other, going up and down
in the process.

The turbulence was so severe that I actually didn't
think the wings would stay on the airplane. I looked several times to see if they were still there. It took two men
with a large bar to stretch the heavy bungee cords and
hook them to the landing skis of the Otter, yet with each
change of direction the skis would go up and down with
such force the whole plane would shudder. Loads inside
an Otter can be hard to tie down, but I had tied the load
forward quite well. Even so, each time we changed direction everything would hit the ceiling or the floor. I had

the Christmas tree for the boys at Sachs Harbour on top of the load, and that tree had every branch on the upper and lower sides smashed right off. It was just flat.

I was maybe five to seven miles into the island when all of this happened, and it quit just as suddenly as it began. Of course by this time I was so shaken that all I could think of was to get on the ground because I didn't know if I had damaged the aircraft. I knew, however, that the Otter probably didn't have enough gas in her to continue against those headwinds even if I could get around the rotor winds and attempt to make Sachs Harbour. As I flew back toward DeSalis Bay I radioed Sachs Harbour that I would be putting down in the bay and not to send out a search party for me. Once the Otter was well out over the bay, I turned back toward the island and landed into what I thought was the wind. Even on the bay the wind was moving in toward the rugged hills of the island, so I actually came in downwind. The old Otter is very docile and gently turned itself into the wind as it slowed. It was on ice and there was no way to control it.

My first thought was that I had better get the aircraft tied down because I'm here for the night. There's no two ways about it. It was now well into the afternoon with little twilight remaining. You either get to where you're going or you land someplace and wait until the next day. And I had landed near the shore so there were some big snowdrifts to use if I needed to build an igloo. I didn't know how long I might be there.

There was a three-inch ice auger aboard the Otter that we used to drill ice bridges for lashing down our aircraft. On each side of the plane you'd drill a pair of holes at 45-degree angles that met about 12 inches or so under the ice. Then you would feed a rope through and tie the wings down. I shut down the Otter, climbed out and before I got the first hole drilled the wind shifted and started to pick up. I climbed back into the Otter and started her up to keep the aircraft from blowing away. I

turned into the wind, kept the engine running, got out
and drilled an ice bridge right next to the left ski where
I could jump back in if the plane started to move away.
With the ski lashed down, I shut the Otter down again,
which was a mistake. Before I could drill an ice bridge
for the right wing the darn thing began to pivot on the
one ski as the wind blew even harder. I got back in and
started the engine again, keeping the throttle just as
close as you could so the aircraft wouldn't go forward or
backward. With the engine running, I tied the right wing
down, then the left. Finally, I shut her down for the
night.

It was getting to be a real Arctic storm, a surface
storm where you couldn't see anything for ten yards in
any direction because of ground drift. I got the engine
tent out and struggled for the longest time just to get it
over the engine because it was a big heavy piece of canvas and the storm made it almost impossible to climb on
the steps around the aircraft. Finally I was able to get it
all laced up around the engine but I couldn't anchor it to
the ground with snow because it was blowing so hard. I
had hoped to sleep in the tent under the engine but there
was no way, so I doubled it back up around the engine
and climbed into the Otter and spent a miserable night
half propped up in the cockpit with the frozen load in a
temperature of about 10 or 15 below. I didn't sleep much
that night, just dozed.

The next morning when it got a little gray — as I say,
there are just about three hours of twilight that time of
year — I thought storm or no storm, I'm going to try to
build an igloo because I can't sleep in that damn cabin
anymore if it's going to keep storming like this. Then I
found I didn't have the snow knife. But I did have a
square-nosed shovel which I would use instead of the
aircraft jack to dig the Otter's skis out from the snow and
ice in the event they should freeze down.

I had seen the Eskimo people — more properly called
Inuit today since "Eskimo" is a Cree Indian word mean-

ing "raw meat eaters" — build igloos, which was fortunate. Contrary to popular belief, you don't simply stack
chunks of snow on top of each other one tier at a time. It
doesn't work that way. Once you get part way up you
can't start another tier without the whole works falling
in. So an igloo is really built like a snail shell. You start
with a tapered block that's quite short and gradually
increase the height of each block around the first tier
until your last block in the tier is full block height of
about 14 inches. Once you have this spiral then you
have something to set the next block up against so it will
stay there. Then you put full blocks around the spiral
and continue in this manner, coming up like a scroll
rather than a single layer of blocks. Eventually you end
up with just a hole in the top and you can cover that
with a single large block. You then pack snow into the
seams and smooth the whole thing over.

The storm had let up a bit so I could at least see to
find the right kind of snow for an igloo and get this
project started. Naturally I didn't want to build it any
bigger than I had to, seeing that I was kind of handi-
capped on tools. So I built it six feet in diameter because I
thought, well, what the heck, I'm about six feet tall. It
took me a couple of hours to complete the task, and by
the time it was dark again I had a nice snug place to
crawl into with my sleeping robe, the little stove, some
Royal Canadian Air Force C-rations and my syrup can
for carrying drinking water.

We carried good sleeping robes, usually Arctic five-star
robes that were really a blanket with a down filling
stitched in and a canvas outer shell that was fairly impervious to water. But on the ice you did have to have a
ground sheet to keep from getting wet, and the one I had
wasn't all that good. The little Coleman stove was a
single-burner with a small tank that, fortunately, was
full of gas. It would burn about six hours, so I could
burn it for a half-hour at a time for a couple of days and
still have gas. I always carried fresh water in the winter.

In the summer you just drank out of the lakes in the North Country because the water was good enough. Even though it contained my drinking water, the syrup can also came in real handy for keeping me warm.

I'd light the stove long enough to heat the syrup can, throw it into the bottom of that robe and go to sleep. Then about four or five hours later I'd wake up because I was getting cold, mostly due to the poor ground sheet than anything else. I'd light the stove, heat the can again, throw it back into the robe and go back to sleep. With 22 hours of darkness you weren't doing a hell of a lot except keeping warm and sleeping. I didn't eat much, but every once in a great while I would start up the stove and cook some oatmeal or whatever else they had in those C-ration packages, or maybe some pemmican. Whatever I decided would be a delicious repast.

You had to be careful, though, not to get things too warm inside the igloo. If that happens you might glaze the inside, and then it would lose its insulating qualities. You've got to keep the temperature down to around 20 to 25 degrees. So you keep the stove out near the middle and actually open the top of the igloo just a bit when you're cooking or heating water. When you're dressed for 20 or 30 below and you get into an igloo, your body heat soon brings it up to 20 above or so, and it's really quite comfortable.

When I first crawled into the igloo and out of that damned wind, it dawned on me that nearly a whole day had gone by since landing on the bay. The weather had improved only slightly, with the outside temperature a rather balmy 10 below but the wind blowing so hard it made for a wind chill down in the minus 50 below range. One of the last things I did before retreating to the relative calm and warmth of my new igloo was to heat up the Otter's radio system with a blow pot and contact Sachs Harbour. I confirmed my location and that everything was okay. I didn't need to be rescued at this point. It was a short conversation. I didn't want to use the battery any

more than necessary. I would have to get the Otter started
on that battery later.

The blow pots we used to heat our engines were similar to an old plumber's blow pot. They had a large base
filled with gasoline and a coiled burner that would va-
porize and burn the gas in a tall flame out of the top. We
would make a baffle for the flame so the heat came out
of the sides as well. You would sit under the engine tent
with a couple of blow pots after a long shutdown in cold
weather to get the oil and engine warmed up for starting. North Country pilots were dependent on them.

When I heated up the radios and the inverter, which
were located in the back of the Otter, I was careful to
keep the cabin door open as a precaution against frost
build-up in the equipment. The aircraft's batteries drove
a 12-volt motor which in turn drove a 120-volt generator. The inverter would convert that 12 volts to 120 or
220 volts when you were transmitting because 12 volts
isn't enough to power a long-range transmitter. The inverter ran only when you were speaking and would start
when you pressed the mike button. I would discover the
next day that frost from the blow pot had frozen up the
inverter and it wouldn't turn any more. I was tempted to
try thawing it out, but then it would be wet and I might
blow something. That wouldn't help my battery any, so I
didn't do anything about it. Let them worry for once, I
thought. They didn't worry, though.

The first night in that six-foot igloo I had my head up
against the sloping wall while I was sleeping. My breath
would form long streamers of frost hanging from the
wall. Every time I woke up I would be looking straight
into a bunch of frost, and the first little move would
bring it all down in my face. So the next day I decided
some home improvements were in order and I added a
porch entrance to the igloo, like you see in pictures. I
had simply been using a block of snow that I pulled in
place when I entered, but the porch gave me an extra

couple of feet to stretch my legs and get my head away
from that wall.

Then I got real ambitious. We always carried an axe in
the airplane and luckily I hadn't thrown it out with everything else. I finished off the top of the igloo by hacking
out a slab of ice from the bay and setting it on top so I
now had a skylight. I had a real nice igloo by the time it
was finished.

The second night in the igloo I got downright comfortable. It was about 20 below outside but the wind wasn't
blowing nearly as hard and I was beginning to feel quite
at home. You always undressed before getting into the
sleeping robe, especially if any of your clothing was at all
damp. I undressed down to my Norwegian underwear,
the kind with the diamond net weave and fairly large
holes. It not only provides a layer of insulation but it has
the one advantage of breathing. You could go outside and
work like a horse and not get sweaty. I fired up the little
stove to heat up the syrup can of water and promptly fell
sound asleep.

Pow! When that syrup can blew it woke me with such
a start. The whole inside of the igloo was just a red glow
from the little stove and all the steam. I thought, geez,
I've gone to hell for sure. The water had started to boil
and the plastic cap on top sealed itself to the can from
the heat until finally the pressure blew the top off. At
first I couldn't imagine what had happened or even
where I was. But then I realized it was just a small accident and all I had done was lost my sleeping robe heater.

I settled back into the sleeping robe hoping the steam
would not glaze the inside of the igloo too badly, though I
was pretty sure this would be my last night here and it
probably didn't matter that much. My thoughts began to
drift back to my boyhood on the farm in Minnesota
where I was thrilled by the early barnstormers and
dreamed of someday being a pilot. I never in my wildest
dreams could have imagined that 35 years later I would

be a bush pilot forced down and stuck in an igloo in the middle of nowhere some 350 miles above the Arctic Circle. Or that just nine years after this igloo episode, on May 6, 1967, I would be the first pilot to land a wheel-equipped aircraft at the North Pole.

All alone in that igloo, I really felt at peace and thankful I didn't have any passengers with me. I probably would have felt an obligation to take better care of them than myself despite complaining and whining that this is wrong or that is wrong. You're simply trying to survive, not have everything lovely. I just could never understand guys who flew in the North Country and then got all panicky when they were in trouble or went down someplace. What were they thinking when they decided to fly up here, anyway?

The wind had quieted down and I remember trying to look for stars through my improvised skylight. My thoughts again returned to when I was just a kid, maybe six, seven or eight years old, and once in a while you'd see an old biplane chugging across the sky. And I would think, gee, what a wonderful way to go.

Chapter Two

THE GLIDER

*"I think Dad thought it was absolutely crazy. I
should be helping more with the farm work
and not being such a bad example for my two
brothers. Ma spent most of her time praying. I
can just imagine my father seeing me up there.
Especially once I started getting that home-
built glider up 600 or 800 feet over the farm."*

I was born at home, the oldest of three brothers and
five sisters, and christened Donald Conrad Braun. The
year was 1913, and our farmstead was located on the
west side of the Mississippi River just south of St. Cloud,
Minnesota. We were a close bunch of kids because our
ages covered only about a 17-year span. We're all eight
still alive as of this writing. They're pretty special, brothers and sisters both. I guess we're a family we can really
be proud of. My mother deserves a lot of credit for that.
She prayed so hard for all of us that we just about had
to turn out right.

It would have been terrible not to be good after she
prayed so hard.

The land for the farm was acquired in 1864 under the
Homestead Act, and we have several copies of the original deed signed by Abraham Lincoln. The first house was
a log cabin. It was replaced in 1886 by the farmhouse I
grew up in and live in today. Most of the farm property
has been developed for housing, but standing in the front
yard you can still see the road where I learned to fly.

When I was real little, before I got into mechanical
things, the Beaver Islands down in the river were my
favorite place. That's where I spent my spare time, and at
that time the fishing was still good. The explorer Zebulon

Pike named the islands, I guess because there were a lot
of beaver in those days. I would go there when I had time
off from farm work, which was usually Sundays. Satur-
days, of course, were just like any other day on the farm.
But on Sundays I spent my time down on those islands.
They were real intriguing to me.

They were still running logs on the river, and in the
spring a small flat-bottom steamboat would work its way
up river and use its whistle to communicate with the log
drivers. You could hear it coming for half a day, it was so
loud. The boat had a small pile driver on it and they
drove pilings to keep the logs in the main stream. But
there were always logs that had slipped away into the
side streams and the men would try to work them back
into the main log raft. It was always something to look
forward to in spring.

The old steam tractors used to whistle and toot, too.
You could hear them for several hours before they got to
the farm. They'd be coming up the road, but why they
tooted I honestly don't know. There were only a few
steam tractors in the area, so we'd hire them to do all the
threshing and silo filling. The other farmers in the neigh-
borhood would come and help. And then, of course, we'd
go and help them.

A cow yard with a slope like ours was a pure menace
to those big iron wheels. They'd slip and skid all over the
place. And they always had to be careful that the tractor
wasn't upwind of the threshing because sparks from the
old steam engine could easily ignite the straw piles. You
could lose the whole darned works and maybe the farm,
too.

We had an old three-horse gasoline engine out in a
shed near the farmhouse that ran a generator for our 32-
volt lighting system. I remember Dad didn't get angry at
us kids very often, but he would get angry at something
else and take it out on us. If the generator wouldn't start
in the winter, and it often didn't, you had to be careful if
you were out in the shed with him because he would

eventually get mad enough to start throwing his tools. You'd better not be in the way.

That old engine used to pump the water, too. There was a tank up in the attic of our house and you always had to watch it because the overflow pipe wasn't big enough. If you caught it right when it started to overflow you were okay. But if you didn't, you had water all over the attic and running down the downstairs walls. We also pumped all the water for cooling the milk and the surplus went out to a big stock tank in the yard for the cattle. That was the only water supply we had in those days until we got a pressure system.

My dad was full of virtue, with one exception. He used to get real annoyed at a piece of machinery like the generator. And he had a bad habit of trying to repair machinery while it was running. I don't know why he never lost a finger or hand. He often had the skin knocked off his knuckles from trying to do things when he was angry.

Although I loved my father and respected his decisions without question, I honestly deplored the way Dad fixed machinery. It was just terrible. You stood there and watched him and wondered what the hell he was doing. He was great with bailing wire and stuff like that. But tools, no. He'd pitch tools in every direction and then get angry because he didn't know where they were.

I was different. Everything had to be in the right place. When I built something it was supposed to be the best, although it was probably barely average. Yet it was the best I could do as a kid, and somehow I know my father always appreciated that.

One day, an old Standard biplane landed in the field right in front of our farm home. It pulled up by the end of a row of evergreens and two fellows got out. I remember the pilot had a leather helmet and goggles, and I think a leather jacket. He wanted to know if they could tie the airplane overnight and, of course, I was only too happy to have it there. I spent the rest of that evening and early the next morning looking at that airplane close up, inspecting every part.

The two men had gone to town and brought some extra gas back with them. They poured it in and pretty soon they were gone. But it so impressed me as a kid that you could just go and fly. I thought, boy, that's what I'm going to do someday.

After that biplane had stopped over at the farm I started building a lot of model airplanes the way most kids did back then. They were just rubber-band powered. No gas motors or anything like they have now. I was also developing an interest in mechanics and I built a little contraption that was supposed to be my first car. It was powered by an old two-cylinder engine with great big flywheels on it. It had a straight belt to the rear axle and when you cranked it up you had to jump on the brake or it got away from you. No gears. One speed forward. No reverse.

My next project was a powered ice boat with a pusher prop attached to a Model T engine. You could get it up to 40 or even 50 mph along the side streams of the river. I usually stayed on the side streams because the ice on the main stream was never considered safe. The engine was a little cranky starting, though. It had upright stacks and I would put a little ether into them, give it a crank and away we went. It was a two-person operation because I needed someone to close the throttle right away so I could jump in.

One afternoon I asked my sister Marge to stand up front by the cockpit and I carefully instructed her to close the throttle right away when the engine fired. The minute it fired, what did she do? She stepped away. I couldn't get around the prop soon enough to get in and away it went down the river. It finally hit an island, bounced a couple of times and then flipped over. The impact broke the prop and I still have it hanging in my shop. It was hand-carved out of a solid chunk of fir.

Not laminated. Which is probably why it cracked. I sure gave her hell but she said, "Well, I wasn't going to just stand there while that thing was going!" I said that was the whole idea! If I ever brought it up she would always tell the story her way.

We had fun with that ice boat for a winter or two. Then I built a Model T racer in my own very limited way. I also collected old motorcycles. I'd get them in baskets, bring them home and put them back together to see if I could get them running. The thing I didn't understand at the time were magnetos. They were probably the weakest point in all motors back then. Condensers were built right into the magnetos. So when the condenser would go bad, the magneto was useless and I was just about finished right there. Very few places in town would repair or even look at them. But anything mechanical I could usually patch together and get it to run.

One of the motorcycles was an old Excelsior. My two brothers, Jim and Bob, pushed that darn thing all around the yard with me on it but it just wouldn't go. I even got the hired man to join in. His name was Floyd and he was partly deaf, but he always liked to be out in the yard with us in the evening. I thought maybe if I helped push it would go, so I had Floyd get on the machine and told him that if it started he should be sure to get the throttle cranked clear to the outside so the motorcycle would slow down and stop. Then we could start it again.

Well, that thing took right off. Poor old Floyd, he didn't even hear the engine start. And when it took off his arms came inward and opened the throttle instead of closing it. He was hanging half off the back of that thing when it went roaring into the evergreens and there was all kinds of crashing as he went through each row of trees. There was a barbed wire fence on the far side of the trees and the motorcycle hit the fence with a great big screech. But old Floyd wasn't hurt a darn bit. He just came wandering

back out, dazed but unhurt. We thought we'd killed him
for sure because we were always getting him into
trouble.

By the time I was 17 in 1930, I had managed to get a
couple of rides in some people's biplanes. Sven Peterson
had one and took me up. I also had another ride from
someone down at the old Cable Airport south of St.
Cloud. It was the greatest feeling being up there, so I
decided to build an airplane.

My choice was a Pietenpol Air Camper, which was a
very popular home-built at the time. It was powered by
either a Model T or a Model A engine, but the preferred
engine was the Model A. You bought the plans and then
the wood from the aircraft supply houses and built it
according to the plan's specifications. It was all wood,
and you built up the two outside fuselage halves first. I
got that far and also built the tailplane, but decided I'd
never have enough money to finish it with an engine and
all. The Model T would need quite a few modifications
before you could fly, so I just gave up and sold the
pieces. Then I started to build a glider.

This friend of mine, Ray Russell, had just built a
glider, a Standard Mead with a 32-foot wing span. It was
the first glider in town to my knowledge. I actually started
to learn to fly in that glider. Sven Peterson and his
brother leased some land on the north side of St. Cloud
and that was what is now the town's airport. Ray had his
glider there while I was building mine.

We'd put the nose of Ray's glider on a brick or a piece
of two-by-four and he would let me sit in it and try to
keep the wings level in a good, stiff breeze. I didn't leave
the ground, but you could actually try to turn a little out
of the wind and still keep it balanced because then the
air would change over the wings. I got to be pretty good
at this and thought I was so damn smart.

My first attempt at flight was in Ray's glider, and when
I came off the ground behind the tow car there was a bit
of a crosswind. Immediately this thing was not only going

forward but it was going sideways, too. Well, I tripped off right away because I sure as heck didn't want to go in that direction. It really amazed me so much that I was going sideways as well as forward. But gradually I started getting the hang of it and learned to fly straight and a little higher until I was really flying it!

I borrowed Ray's plans to build my glider, a Standard Mead design, but added two more feet to the wing span. It was finished in 1932 and we towed it with my dad's car. My two kid brothers were too young to fly the glider, so they were my tow car drivers. We would tow the glider out of the yard and right down the field road. I used a thousand feet of braided clothesline and a couple hundred feet of rope for the tow line. The braided line was so there wouldn't be a sharp snap on the nose of the glider when the car hit bumps on the road.

With 1,200 feet of tow rope I was able to get up to where the tow car was directly below me and the line would come up from behind, it had such a big bow in it. I'd be up as high as 800 or 900 feet on that 1,200 feet of line, sitting right above the tow car. Then I'd trip off and sail around for a while, come back and try to land in the yard so we'd be ready to do it again. I never stayed up more than three or four minutes.

There would always be a few people lined up along the road when you flew the glider. And you'd talk to them as you'd go by because with the glider there was no noise.

One beautiful summer evening I was talking to these people on the ground and forgot about the big oak tree with the dead limb that stuck out over the field road. The tow car always had to move over just a little and I normally did likewise so as not to hit that damn tree. The tow cable caught under the limb when I didn't go around and it started to pull me right down toward the ground. I was able to hit the release and pull away just in time.

I swung out over the field and then made too sharp a turn. I sailed into a railroad embankment and over-turned. That was the only time in the glider that I landed

when I didn't plan on it, and I was thankful the damage
was very slight. Just a cracked wing tip. If I'd known
more about flying I could have taken advantage of the
east winds to get some lift up the hillside, but I didn't
know any of those things. I only knew a few basics.

The main one was: Don't stall it.

I often wondered why my mother was always in the
farmhouse when I was out flying the glider. I can't remember her ever coming out to watch. With that crash I
knew it was because she must have worried so.

After graduating from Cathedral High School in May
1931, I stayed on the farm and helped out by doing
chores and fixing things. I also delivered milk around
town. There was this one particularly cute gal in school
named Marie Nolen, but I hadn't seen her for a year or so
after graduation. She got a job as a fountain clerk at
Clock's Tick Tock Cafe and it just so happened I delivered milk there. We delivered the milk through the back
door and I would always try to find some reason to get up
to the front. We never had any real reason to go up there,
but I'd find some excuse. And I finally got up enough
nerve to ask Marie for a date. I had dated a few others,
but nothing serious. Marie was the main one and I remember we used to talk for hours about our future. She
was going to be a nurse, but I wasn't sure what I wanted
to do with my life.

Then in the spring of 1934 I learned of an apprenticeship position in aircraft maintenance being offered by the
Alexander Eaglerock aircraft factory out in Colorado
Springs. I was a pretty good mechanic and my love for
flying that old glider convinced me I should apply for the
spot. I would work without pay for an entire year, and
you had to pay your own expenses. At the end of the
year, if you qualified, you received an aircraft mechanic's
certificate or license.

I had saved a little money and Dad said he would try
to send something each week. I can remember it was five

dollars, which was all Dad could afford, and I feel now that it was very fortunate they could send me anything during the Depression.

None of the motorcycles I put together would be trustworthy on the nearly 1,200 miles of roads to Colorado Springs. Before I went west I purchased an old 1928 Indian, which would be more reliable and provide a softer ride than the others.

I rode that motorcycle all the way to Colorado, and in those days it was still half gravel clear across Nebraska and beyond. It just about shook me to pieces. But I made it.

CHAPTER THREE

SETTING UP SHOP IN HARLEM

*"Mr. Schumacher, who ran the airport on
Harlem Avenue, didn't think I had enough
flying time to be piloting all these planes, a
point which he made clear to me many times
those first couple of years. But I thought I
had enough to test every machine that came
through our shop. And I did."*

The original Alexander Eaglerock was a biplane that
was quite well known back in 1934 for its ability to take
off and land at fairly high altitudes considering the poor
engines they had in those days. It had an immense
amount of wing compared to most of the old biplanes.
The Alexander Eaglerock factory in Colorado Springs had
gone broke building the "Bullet," a low-wing monoplane
with retractable landing gear and a top speed of 150
mph. When I arrived to begin my year-long apprenticeship all that remained were four of the original workmen.
They were busy overhauling the old Eaglerocks and also
building the Alexander Flyabout, a little two-place high-
wing monoplane.

As it turned out, my apprenticeship was in both rebuilding aircraft and in building new aircraft. That was
my training as a mechanic, and I got my mechanic's
certificate on my first writing after the year ended. We
learned woodworking, cable splicing, welding and fabric
work. Everything that went into building and rebuilding
the old aircraft. Air frame work, aluminum welding and
that sort of thing.

The family that owned the factory also owned a small
film outfit in town that made runners for the advertise-
ments before featured films. To earn some extra money
to supplement what Dad sent from home, I would rewind

film for 50 cents an hour three nights a week. So, three days a week I worked eight hours as an apprentice, learning as we worked, and another eight hours in the basement rewinding film and watching the old chain link boilers that heated the buildings. That made for one heck of a long day.

Marie was in nursing school at St. Cloud Hospital while I was out in Colorado, and her graduation was nearing when my apprenticeship ended in the spring of 1935. We kept in touch mostly by mail during that year apart and I was now determined to make it back to St. Cloud for her graduation. I did make it, but the trip was a nightmare from the start.

A friend of mine at the factory, John Anderson, from Liberty, Nebraska, nearly killed himself on a Henderson motorcycle he had bought. I bought what was left of it and salvaged the engine because I had cracked the piston in the Indian. I found a 1924 frame, cut it way down, mounted the Henderson engine on it and started back home.

I was riding through the rain at night somewhere in Nebraska and fell asleep, ending up in a ditch that was so muddy the bike stayed right side up. But I couldn't budge it, so I sat there in the rain for an hour or more until a car came along and pulled me out. The old Henderson had those big footboards, and when they got stuck in the mud that was it. You just sat there.

After riding all night I stopped to get some gas in the morning with the little money I had left. I went inside the station to sit down while the attendant was filling the tank and I fell sound asleep as soon as I hit the chair. The guy let me sleep for several hours and then told me he didn't have the heart to wake me.

That evening I rode into the Twin Cities with a nearly empty gas tank and stopped at my Uncle Art Braun's house. I borrowed 50 cents from him to get a couple of gallons of gas for the final 75-mile leg of my trip home for

Marie's graduation, which was the very next morning. I
think I slept through most of the ceremony.

My stay back on the farm was a short one. I had ap-
plied for work at Stinson Aircraft in Detroit and it wasn't
long before they called and offered me a job. In no time at
all I was on the road to Detroit with not much more than
a change of clothes and a few dollars.

Stinson Aircraft was founded in 1926 and had become
successful with its early Detroiter and Reliant series of
monoplanes. I started out by welding wing spar fittings
for the last of the Reliant series, the SM8A, which was a
four-place straight-wing Stinson with wooden spars and
a 225-hp Lycoming radial up front. Then they changed
the design to an all-metal wing with a fabric cover. The
wing started out narrow, then broadened out. They called
it the Gullwing Stinson and I helped with the changeover,
rebuilding jigs and other equipment.

My year at Stinson was good experience but the pay,
even at top wages of 75 cents an hour, was terrible. I was
welding doorposts for another company every night I
could stand it, just to survive in the big city. My enter-
tainment was going to Polish weddings. The Stinson factory was located out on the west end in the Polish section
and a good many young Polish fellows worked there.
There was a wedding nearly every weekend. They always
started on Friday night and lasted until Sunday night.

The pay was so bad that you were always looking for a
place that paid maybe five cents more when you got to
the top. It took me about a year to work my way up from
beginner to top wager at Stinson, and then I was off to
Chicago and a job with American Airlines that paid a few
cents more an hour.

American Airlines in late 1935 was hardly a big company. I remember the company picnic at a park on the
Fox River and the president running around with a scis-
sors snipping off people's neckties. I think his name was
J.L. Smith. His office and the operations offices were all
in the same hangar with the airplanes. One day we got

word that one of the company's planes was returning with an engine fire and within two minutes everybody in the organization knew it and was running to see the aircraft coming in on fire.

When I joined American they were still flying the old twin-engine Curtiss Condor, which was an all fabric-covered biplane that carried about eight passengers in the cabin and a couple of pilots up front. It was a nice flying airplane and it looked good in the air. They also flew the Stinson Model A low-wing tri-motor, which was smaller than the Condor and only carried six passengers. With three engines and just six passengers, it was a pretty dumb design in my opinion.

Although I was just a welder, what really was exciting to me at the time was the fact American had the very first DC-2s. And while I was with them they received their first DC-3, which we thought was a monster of an aircraft. A truly revolutionary plane, which of course it was. You just couldn't believe there was such an airplane as the DC-3 because of its size, all-metal construction and streamlined shape.

During those months with Stinson in Detroit and American Airlines in Chicago I became determined to quit working for someone else and set up an aircraft repair shop of my own. I got to know a fellow at Associated Aircraft, which was a complete aircraft parts company located just a few hangars down from American where I worked. His name was Marcellas Foos and he told me Associated would help me out if I wanted to start a shop at a general aviation airfield in southwest Chicago called Harlem Airport.

So, at the tender age of 24 and with the approval and encouragement of a man named Fred Schumacher, who owned Schumacher Flying Service, Inc., and basically ran the airfield, I constructed a shop building at Harlem Airport and went into business for myself. After I was in the business about six months Marcellas said he wanted to get into a business of his own, so he bought in for very little and we became partners. It was a good thing, too, because I had come to the conclusion it was going to be tough going it alone. Besides, Marcellas knew the parts business real well and he was also very capable at keeping the books. It was a nice combination since that left me free to work on the aircraft, which is all I really wanted to do.

We called the business B & F Aircraft Service. Braun and Foos. And it's still in business today although it's now operated by some nephews of a partner Marcellas eventually took in after I had sold him my share to join the war effort in 1941. But they still call it B & F Aircraft Supply, Inc., because of the reputation. B & F has a big display at the air show in Oshkosh, Wisconsin, every year and they sell parts for all types of home-built airplanes.

Harlem Avenue runs north and south along the west side of Chicago, and we used the building I put up at Harlem Airport for our service center. Later we purchased a second building down in Oaklawn, about four miles away. We used it for rebuilding engines and storing our stock. I also turned a small office area in the Oaklawn building into my living quarters.

Most days I would be working ten, twelve or more hours at the Harlem shop on a wide variety of small aircraft. Evenings and weekends would be spent at the Oaklawn shop rebuilding engines. It was a good life and I enjoyed it. What I really enjoyed most, however, was flying the aircraft after I worked on them. Test flying them, so to speak.

I really never soloed in a powered aircraft until I started working on them at Harlem in 1936. There simply wasn't enough time or extra money for flight lessons while I was working in Detroit or for American Airlines.

Yet all the aircraft we repaired had to be test flown when we finished before turning them back to their owners. I started taking planes up with little more than my glider experience and a few rides in powered ma-

chines to go by. The owners of the aircraft would sometimes give me pointers about flying their planes and the
rest usually wasn't hard to figure out.

Mr. Schumacher, who ran the airport, didn't think I
had enough flying time to be piloting all these planes, a
point which he made clear to me many times those first
couple of years. But I thought I had enough to test every
machine that came through our shop. And I did.

In this manner I was able to fly many, many different
aircraft. When I left B & F in 1941, I had nearly 500
flying hours in 45 different types of aircraft.

One of them was a Laird Speedwing, a stubby-winged
biplane with a 330-hp engine in it. It was a highly ma-
neuverable little plane, but also very tricky to land. The
Speedwing was the commercial version of the Laird racing plane, and a lady named Opal Lassiter Anderson
owned and piloted this particular one.

Opal would fly the Speedwing at airshows in the region, but she wouldn't fly it cross-country because she
never liked to land at an airport she didn't know. So I
would fly the Speedwing to the site of the airshow late
Friday or early Saturday. Opal would meet me with her
car, drive me home, then drive back to the airshow. All
because she was afraid of that plane on landings. Of
course, most people were, and for good reason.

One time she had a Navy pilot fly it back to Harlem
Airport for her after an airshow. He landed and dumped
it right over on its back by using the brakes too hard.
Nose first, right over on its back. It was touchy. A real
ground-looping little devil, that Speedwing.

Opal was one of the early 99s, a national organization
of women pilots that included Amelia Earhart among its
members. Women's pilot clubs are still called The 99s,
but I'm not sure why.

Then there was Cornelius Coffee, one of the first
blacks in the early years of aviation in the Chicago area.
He's quite a famous person in aviation circles and even

to this day you read something about him in the news
every once in a while. Coffee had the hangar right next
door to us at Harlem and he was a real good friend.

He was one of the finest guys you could know, a good
mechanic, a good instructor and good with other people
no matter how obnoxious they might be. Most of all he
was a very patient kind of fellow.

One day I was working in the shop and I heard this
Piper Cub go by time after time. I could tell he was getting
lined up to land but after a minute or two I'd hear the
engine throttle up again and he'd go by the hangar. This
went on for about 20 minutes, and I thought what the
hell is going on out there anyhow.

I looked out the door and here is this Cub trying to hit
a little grassy spot off the runway. Now you have to understand that Harlem didn't have paved runways. It was
built on gumbo, so when the field got wet the only places
you could land were a few grassy spots away from the
runways. The runways became greased skating rinks as
soon as they got a little wet and you dared not use them.
Well, by this time Coffee was out watching, too, because
the guy happened to be one of Coffee's students and this
was only the second time he had been up on his own.

After another two or three circuits, when this poor fellow was about 30 feet in the air, he just quit flying out of
desperation and the Cub went up on one wing and
stalled. It came down hard and crumpled the right wing
and nose. Coffee dashed across the field at a full run to
the site of the wreck but I thought, geez, I don't want to
see a lot of blood and gore. So I went on over, but I wasn't
hurrying.

When I got there, I could see the guy lying in the grass
and mud ahead of the airplane with Coffee standing over
him. He lay face down and didn't move. Finally Coffee
bent down, half rolled the poor guy over and put his hand
under his head.

"Are you all right, boy?" Coffee asked. The young man opened his eyes, looked up at Coffee and said, "Yeah, but I'm just too disgusted to move."

He got up and walked back to the hangar with us. Coffee's Cub was all crumpled up in a heap, but I never heard Coffee say a harsh word to that fellow. In fact, he didn't say much at all.

It was about this time, around 1937, that I acquired my first real airplane, a small high-wing monoplane known as the American Eaglet. It was a basket case and we got it in parts. The Eaglet had two open cockpits beneath the wing and was originally powered by a 45-hp Szekely engine. Just before the war the Eaglets were fitted with a 40-hp Continental A40 engine, but mine had the old Szekely.

Somebody had wrecked the fuselage and I had to rebuild it completely. The engine also needed a lot of work, but eventually I restored the Eaglet to the way it looked originally. A year later I completely rebuilt it again, this time streamlining the Eaglet by making a full cowling for the engine instead of the engine sticking out. I topped off the cowling with a spinner around the prop and also fabricated coverings for the open wheel struts. It was really a nice looking little airplane by the time I was done. I thought it was a shame the aircraft manufacturers back then gave so little attention to streamlining.

Over the next couple of years B & F also acquired an old four-place Stinson SM8A high-wing monoplane that I flew mostly on weekends around the Chicago area. It had a 220-hp Lycoming radial engine. And we also owned a Waco 9, a three-place biplane powered by a 90-hp Curtiss OX5 eight-cylinder water-cooled engine.

For most of 1937 and 1938, however, the Eaglet was my transportation home to the farm in St. Cloud and, with increasing frequency, up along the west shore of Lake Michigan to West Allis near Milwaukee where Marie was now working as a nurse at the Veterans Administration Hospital.

Marie and I were married at St. Cloud on June 4, 1938. I flew up to St. Cloud in the Eaglet a few days before the wedding and spent the better part of a day giving rides to my brothers and sisters and their friends. The field I was using was very sandy, but it was fairly close to the farm. I didn't realize it at the time, but the sand was getting into the wheel bushing and grinding down the axle.

Late in the day my father's sister, Clara Braun, who never married and was affectionately called Aunt Brownie by everyone, climbed into the Eaglet cockpit for a ride. The take-off went okay but when I touched down, the wheel just folded up and the axle dug into the sand. I held it as long as I could, but the darned thing slowly went over. As this story is told and retold at Braun family gatherings, I freed myself from the cockpit and immediately proceeded to inspect the Eaglet for damage while leaving poor Aunt Brownie hanging upside down in the other cockpit. According to our family, I left Aunt Brownie in this position for too long a time. If you ask me, she wasn't upset at all. I think she was just wondering what was going on.

The wing and rudder weren't damaged a bit, but the wooden prop was completely splintered so I put on another one and repaired the axle in no time at all. After the wedding, Marie and I spent a couple of days in St. Cloud and then took off in the Eaglet for Chicago. It was quite a trip.

We got started late, naturally. The little Eaglet cruised around 75 mph at the most and the gas tank only held eight gallons, so its range was maybe 350 miles. We had to land at Madison for gas at one of the outlying fields. They hadn't cut the grass for so darned long that when we got loaded with a full tank plus all our luggage and Marie in the second cockpit, I just couldn't get off the ground because the grass was too high for our weight.

While I was racing up and down the field trying to take off, some fellow on a motorcycle stopped to watch all the commotion. I finally asked him if he would take Marie over on his motorcycle to another field about ten miles away. Then I would come over and pick her up. He agreed.

Away went Marie on the back of that motorcycle, and being 100 pounds lighter I was now able to take off and fly over to the other field where we resumed our trip to Chicago.

With all this fooling around it was getting late in the day and I figured we would have barely enough gas to make it from Madison to Harlem Airport. We ran into a series of thunderstorms and I had to fly around them, then we ran into headwinds. The sky was starting to get dark and the next thing I knew we were running out of gas over the north side of Chicago.

The gas gauge in the little Eaglet was just a piece of wire on a cork float that would bob out of the top of the gas tank in front of the windshield. It was so dark by now that I couldn't see it, so I reached around the windshield and felt where it was. Boy, it was getting down real low and was just about ready to disappear into the tank. We still had about 20 miles to Harlem Airport so I decided we had to land in the dark and hope for the best. I had just passed a radio tower that was quite visible because of its lights, so I turned and lined up on it. I knew the area we were over was mostly open fields, and you could see their outline. But you couldn't tell in early June whether the fields were grass, oats or corn. I picked out a field and as I got closer it appeared to be grass with a row of trees right before it.

I kept the lights on the tower in my sights until I saw the trees go flashing under us, then I pulled the power and settled into the field. We no sooner dropped in than we stopped rather abruptly in the middle of a field of oats.

We were safely down but Marie was not pleased with me to say the least and the Eaglet wouldn't budge from that oat field. So I walked over to the farmhouse and asked if they had a phone. I told them I was out in their oat field with an airplane, but that didn't seem to register with the farmer for some reason. After calling Foos to come and get us, I told the farmer we were going to make some tracks through his oats in the morning getting the plane out of the field. He said that was okay, just don't tramp down a lot of it.

Foos finally came and we took Marie to the nearest railroad station so she could return to Milwaukee and her job. Then I went to bed. Foos and I got up around five a.m. and returned to the farm with a can of gas. We pushed the Eaglet as far as we could, then towed it out the rest of the way with our car. We made it to an old gravel road, gassed it up and I took off for Harlem Airport.

It wasn't long before Marie was able to join me in Chicago, and we set up housekeeping in the converted office area of our Oaklawn building where I had been living. It wasn't fancy, but the price was right and it was quite convenient for work.

Everything seemed to be going well, although we weren't making much money running an aircraft repair business during the Great Depression. We were strictly a hand-to-mouth operation, which meant we didn't get paid until the job was finished. We hired a young fellow and explained this to him, but he quit in the middle of a job before we had money to pay him the $25 we owed him for his time. We let him go with the understanding we would give him five dollars a week until he was paid up.

Well, he waited only about a week before calling the sheriff and complaining that we owed him money and wouldn't pay. A couple of sheriff's deputies came out to the repair shop and said we owed this money, and I said I knew we did but we had an agreement with him. They said that just wouldn't hold water, so they took me over to the Cicero jail where all the gangsters were held at that time. I spent the entire night in jail while my partner, Foos, was running around trying to raise $500 bail. As the senior partner, I was the one that had to go to jail.

In those days $500 was a fortune, but Foos finally raised it and bailed me out the next morning. Just think of it, I spent one night in a stupid jail cell in Cicero. For owing $25. We went to court and I think they allowed us to go ahead with the original arrangement.

We had a regular crew that worked with us through thick and thin during the late 1930s and 1940. Even my kid brother Jim and Marie's oldest brother, Julius, came down from St. Cloud and worked for us in the shop. They'd all wait just like Foos and I did for our money once a job was completed. It seemed like were broke about half the time. We paid Jim and the kid that put me in jail and the other mechanic's helpers about 75 cents an hour. It wasn't much, but then at Stinson in Detroit a few years earlier I was paid a top welder's wage of 78 cents an hour.

By the spring of 1941 I was certain our country was going to war. Foos had a draft deferment because of a heart problem or something like that. But I was eligible for the draft, and with six or more years of aircraft mechanics experience behind me I was sure they would ignore my 500 hours of flying time and grab me as a mechanic.

I wanted to fly. And about this time Canada happened to be looking for pilots for the Commonwealth of Nations air training program. As part of the war effort, Canada had become one big training field for pilots from all nations of the British Commonwealth. They recruited 22 pilots from the Chicago area alone prior to the U.S. entry into World War II, and I ended up being one of them. Marie was able to get her job back at the V.A. Hospital in West Allis. She would work there until I could send for her to join me in Canada.

I sold my share of B & F to my good friend and partner, Marcellas Foos. As for the little Eaglet, I sold that to my brother Jim and another young fellow. We were in the process of putting a Salmson nine-cylinder engine in it, a small 40-hp French-built model that was only 22 inches across. Jim and his friend flew it with the new engine for a time, then sold it to some guy who landed in an orchard and took both wings completely off. It was never rebuilt as far as I know.

It's a shame I wasn't able to recover that little Salmson engine. But by this time I was up in Canada and my life was about to change more than I could ever realize or appreciate.

CHAPTER FOUR

THE WAR YEARS AS A ROYAL CANADIAN AIR FORCE PILOT

"There was a 400-foot ceiling over Fort Nelson. As we came down through the soup I had to keep adding power continuously because the weight of the ice was building up all over the aircraft. I said to Bounce, 'You know, we're going to have to make it in the first time because we're never going to make it around again.' He nodded in agreement."

In the spring of 1941 I found myself in the old Toronto exhibition grounds which had been turned into a massive induction center for all the young men coming from everywhere in the world to join the British Commonwealth training scheme.

I use the term "scheme" because when I signed up in Chicago it was in response to a call for young men willing to volunteer a few months of their time to train pilots and navigators in Canada. My understanding was that I would go to Canada and get some flying time as a civilian in the training program, then return to the U.S. and join the Army Air Corps as a pilot instead of as a mechanic. Well, it didn't work out that way.

As soon as I arrived in Toronto they began pressuring us to join the Royal Canadian Air Force. Within 10 days I was in the RCAF instead of flying as a civilian. I didn't even have time to tell Marie what I had done. When I did, of course, it was a big shock to her.

The training scheme in Canada was really desperate for pilots and they promised us commissions as officers if we had some flying time. They were training the British, Canadians, Australians, New Zealanders and all the

freedom fighters that came to Canada from countries that
had been overrun by the Nazis, and it would be my job to
help train them. After six weeks of training we were commissioned, with the understanding that we could return
to the States any time we wanted to, provided the U.S.
went to war.

The whole thing appealed to me at the time. I was liable
to be drafted in the U.S. as an airplane mechanic, but in
Canada my 500 hours of flying time in nearly 50 different
aircraft counted for something. You could enter the RCAF
as a Pilot Officer and fly right away. You got a patch on
your shoulder that read which country you were from.
You kept your citizenship whether you were a Yank, an
Aussie, a Pole or a Brit, yet you had to pledge allegiance
to the Queen as far as orders went.

During my stint in the RCAF I had many offers to transfer back to the U.S. Army Air Corps, but the Canadians
treated me so well that I felt I would be letting them
down if I left. They gave us training in many different
aircraft, and while it was rushed, I was proud to be stationed out at Rivers, Manitoba, as an RCAF Pilot Officer
helping to train astronavigators after only four months of
being in Canada.

If I was easy to train, it was probably because I had
flown so many different aircraft at Harlem Airport and
they didn't have to spend much time on me.

We trained in the North American SN-J, which was the
U.S. Navy's version of the Army's AT-6 Harvard, an advanced fighter trainer with a stubby low-wing and a big,
noisy 450-hp Pratt & Whitney engine on the front. Then
we trained in the Fairey Battle to get an idea of how a
bigger airplane flew. It was a six-ton fighter bomber with
a 1200-hp Rolls Royce engine up front. It had a bombar-
dier-gunner in the belly and four firing guns, but it was
slow and cumbersome so they used it only for training.
Fairey was a British aircraft manufacturer, and the old
Battle was a nice airplane to fly. It had a wonderful
sounding 12-cylinder Rolls.

Quite often I think about the fact my early flying escapades at Harlem Airport made me really airsick the first couple of hundred hours, but I kept going back up and eventually overcame the problem. Without that flying time, I probably would have washed out of pilot training in the military in the first 50 hours, especially in the U.S.

I was posted at Rivers, Manitoba, for about eight months and most of that time was spent piloting the old twin-engine Avro Ansons during astronavigating training sessions. The Anson was like a greenhouse with wings on it. They were mostly fabric-covered with a thin veneer of wood over the wings and tailplane. The only metal was around the nose and the engine cowlings, otherwise it was just windows, fabric and some wood veneer.

The astronavigation flights lasted about three and a half hours and my crew normally consisted of an astronavigation instructor and three students. If there were clouds we had to be above them, naturally, because the whole idea was to navigate by the stars at night or the sun during the day and somehow get home. Navigating by the heavenly bodies was often used on bombing runs and it was a mighty cold business at such altitudes.

The old Ansons didn't have much in the way of real radio communications equipment, just a little two-way radio that usually froze up so solid in the extreme cold of the cabin that we carried a portable radio navigation box with us at all times to help us find the way home on a radio beacon. I always had two pairs of gloves with me, one pair on my hands and the other stuffed inside my clothing. When your hands got so cold you couldn't move them anymore, you changed gloves. Your feet froze; everything else froze.

How those three navigation students could work on their calculations in that cold I'll never know. The students were directly behind me in three little compartments where they couldn't copy from each other. The instructor would go back and work with them during the flight, but they had to sit there for the entire trip with

their gloves on doing their plotting. They were lost about
two-thirds of the time when they were brand new. You
would fly their course and hope to hell they weren't
more than about 30 miles off so you could find your way
back home with the radio navigation box. You had to be
within 30 miles of your home station to use it.

Many nights I flew home on the hum of my radio navigation box when the boys took us way the hell off course
somewhere. The instructor would ask the students to
decide which set of their figures to give me, and I had to
follow the course they gave me even though I knew it was
wrong. I knew exactly where we were supposed to go every
flight, but if they gave me a course that was 10 degrees off
I had to fly it because they had to be proven wrong.

I wasn't on the flight, but one of my favorite stories is
about the navigation instructor who left his seat next to
the pilot and went back to talk with his students. Just
as he leaned down over one of the student's desks the
windshield directly in front of his empty cockpit seat
exploded and a white owl — a great big white owl — flew
past him and slammed into the back bulkhead of the
Anson where it made a sizable dent. Lucky the navigator
had left his seat and bent down, or he would have been
just as dead as that owl.

They took the remains of the owl to a taxidermist and
he was able to patch it together. It decorated the mantle
at headquarters in Rivers for quite some time.

The carcass of an old Anson was also on display at
Rivers for a short time to demonstrate what hail could
do to one of those flying baskets if you were unlucky or
foolish enough to fly one into a summer thunderstorm.
The wooden leading edges of the wings and tailplane are
about an eighth of an inch thick at the most, and they
were so perforated it was a miracle the pilot was able to
bring her in.

That was one thing that scared the hell out of you in
an Anson — running into a thunderstorm at night. In

those days you had little or no warning, and we were told that if we ran into one we should get the heck out of it as quickly as we could.

I can remember one night I ran into just a bit of hail, but it rattled like crazy because of all the windows and fabric on the Anson. It sounded like a severe, pounding hailstorm and I made such a quick turn to get out of it that I toppled the gyroscopes in my flight instruments. When you don't have many hours of instrument time, and I didn't at that point, panic sets in in one hell of a hurry. But I got out of it and was able to reset the gyros and continue on. The old Anson was a very easy airplane to fly, and for that I was thankful.

In late 1941 the decision was made to move the astro-navigation school to Pennfield Ridge, New Brunswick, and by early 1942 I was stationed there as one of the "older" pilots in our group. We were still flying our navigation training flights in the Ansons, and those of us with more hours in the program were also making a daily submarine patrol flight out over the Bay of Fundy.

The Bay of Fundy lies between southern Nova Scotia on the east and New Brunswick on the west, and it's famous for having some of the highest tides in the world. There had been sightings of German U-boats right up to the mouth of the bay, and we carried two 500-pound depth charges in the old Ansons during our patrols of the bay and beyond. We never spotted a thing.

Those winter months of early 1942 at Pennfield Ridge were miserable. We lived in summer cottages on a lake. The cottages were uninsulated and so cold we valued our few lights bulbs as much for their heat as for their light. The Pennfield Ridge Station stayed open for only eight or nine months before it was closed because we had so much trouble with fog rolling in. Our aircraft would be scattered all over the countryside or out over the water and it just wasn't a good place to train navigation students. Mercifully, they moved our entire opera-

tion back to Rivers, Manitoba, and I happily flew one of
the Ansons back.

No sooner had I arrived when I was sent to Number
Eight Repair Depot at Trenton, Ontario, where I spent a
few days before being posted out west to Number Ten
Repair Depot at Calgary, Alberta. My job would be to
test fly all the aircraft that were assembled or rebuilt at
the depot. I guess that made me a test pilot.

Actually, it wasn't much different from my test flying
days at Harlem Airport in Chicago, except now I was
testing aircraft somebody else had mostly worked on.
And that always made me a little nervous. The aircraft
that came through the depot were mostly training types,
a lot of de Havilland Tiger Moths and the old Stearman
PT-17 biplane with a 220-hp Continental radial that you
still see around today, and even a few of the big old
Fairey Battles with huge Rolls Royce Merlin engines.
They were used for bombardier training and night bombing practice. I also tested the old Cessna T-50 Crane,
which was a low-wing basket-type with a pair of nine-
cylinder 245-hp Jacobs radial engines on it, enough to
simulate a larger twin-engine aircraft for training. We
also had a lot of aircraft in live storage and each one had
to be flown 20 minutes a week.

Then I would get to test some pretty fancy aircraft once
in a while. The Bristol Blenheim aircraft was one of them,
a twin-engine with 1,600 hp on each side. It wasn't very
large, but was quite a powerful little plane. It didn't last
too long because it was designed early in the war and fell
by the wayside as more advanced aircraft took its place.

I also flew a thing called the Fleet Fort, which was the
world's most deadly aircraft in the opinion of most pilots, including this one. It was designed to take the
place of the North American series of secondary single
engine trainers and was made by an outfit called Canadian Car and Foundry, a name that sounds as if they
shouldn't be building airplanes.

It was a terrible design. They tried to use it as a secondary trainer but lost so many student pilots it was decided the plane would be used solely for training wireless radio operators. Experienced pilots would fly the thing from the front cockpit and the student radio operator would sit in the back practicing their codes and whatever else they had to know to operate on the silent side. But they still kept killing people in the darn thing.

The Fleet Forts were being assembled at the depot at Calgary and I tested most of them.

I remember the first time I took off in a Fleet Fort. They had great big soft balloon tires, some of the first nylon tires, and when they would sit in the hangar for a couple of days or a week they would develop big flat spots. The loud thumping sound of the tires down the runway at take-off was bad enough. But in the air the flat spots made the plane shake so violently you couldn't see the instrument panel or anything.

And that was only the first problem.

The Fleet Fort took off at about 90 mph and cruised at 110 mph, so you had only a 20-mph range between stall and cruising speeds. If you looked at them sideways they'd go into a snap roll. All you had to do was pull back on the stick and you were into an inverted stall.

They were so bad you couldn't even dive them fast enough to complete a loop. You would always fall off somewhere. I used to try and chase the Tiger Moths stationed nearby, but they would turn away with ease while I would turn upside down and continue pretty much straight ahead when I tried to turn with them. They were just hopeless. Many young men were killed horsing around in the Fleet Fort, diving at some farmer's house or barn just for the thrill of it and ending up buried in the farmer's yard. They didn't realize or perhaps forgot that pulling up from a high-speed dive in that damn thing usually ended in a stall, a roll and going in. That's all there was to it.

Of course even in a gentle old plane like the Cessna Crane you could find yourself in the damnedest predicaments. The T-50 Crane was one of the first secondary twin-engine trainers used in the States and Canada to train pilots going on to larger twins. It wasn't much of an airplane, mostly built of wood, wire, steel tubing and fabric.

I was flying a Crane back east to Number Eight Repair Depot where I was being posted after spending most of the summer and fall of 1942 at the depot in Calgary. When you were being transferred, if there was an aircraft that needed to go your way, they usually let you take it. It was an easy, cheap way for the RCAF to get the aircraft where they wanted it. And it saved me from having to take the train to Trenton, Ontario.

At some point in the flight I decided to enjoy a cigar, so I lit one up and cracked the side window to vent the smoke. Wouldn't you know it, the rear door on that old Crane decided to pop open. The suction was just terrific and — presto! — the cigar was gone and I didn't know where.

It might have flown out the window or it might have been sucked out the rear door. Or it might have hit the far back wall and gone out.

Or, it might still be lit and rolling around somewhere under the floorboards. There I sat, alone, waiting for that wooden Crane to catch fire and trying to figure a way to shut the back door. I decided to slow the plane down as much as I could, right near a stall, then leave my seat and try to slam the door shut. It turned out to be a real circus act. I got her going really nice and slow, but every time I reached the door the nose would go up and she would damn near stall. I'd have to reach back, get hold of the wheel and bring her back somewhere near level flight before going for the door again. Finally about the third time I got that stupid door shut, but not until the Crane was just about completely stalled out.

All this time I was keeping an eye out for the cigar and either the sight or smell of smoke. Back in my seat, I spent the next half-hour before landing thinking about

that damn cigar. It was pure torture because I thought
sure as hell that old Crane was going to be on fire any
minute. As it turned out, the plane never did catch on
fire and we never did find the cigar.

My stay at Trenton depot was a short one. I had re-
peatedly requested overseas assignment but they said I
was too old. Instead, I was assigned to the North West
Air Command and my new job would be flying personnel
and supplies along the Northwest Staging Route. In
January 1943, then, I moved back to Alberta, only this
time I was stationed farther north at Edmonton.

Word had it the staging route was considered a "plum"
assignment and pilots were likely to be with the Air
Command for some time. I was also earning more with a
recent promotion to Flight Lieutenant, so Marie and I at
long last began planning for the day she would join me
at Edmonton and we could live together as a married
couple once again. Nearly two years had passed since
our parting in Chicago, and we longed to be with each
other more than anything else.

After a couple of months I found an apartment and
Marie took the train from St. Cloud to Edmonton. We
were together for the rest of the war, and we were never
happier.

The Northwest Staging Route stretched all the way from
Edmonton to Alaska. We serviced the airstrips along the
route since the Japanese had reached the Aleutian Islands and everyone was worried about the possibility of
an invasion. In fact, we later flew runs in a Norseman
"bush" airplane, as well as the Lockheed, all the way
down the Mackenzie River to Fort Simpson and Norman
Wells and other places where survey work was being
done to establish another line of airfields farther east of
the staging route in case Japanese forces made landfall
and cut off the recently completed Alcan Highway.

We were flying about half a dozen commandeered
Lockheed 10s. They were the first Lockheed Electras, a
10-place twin-engine airliner first introduced around

1934. They were similar to the old 247-D, the very first
Boeing airliner. The Lockheeds had been civilian aircraft
and the Canadian government had commandeered them
for us. They were real beauties, with all-metal bodies
and a pair of 420-hp Pratt & Whitney engines and a top
speed of over 200 mph. I later learned that many of the
younger pilots, particularly those in training, thought we
were the elite. We didn't think so at the time, but the
younger men, including a chap by the name of Max Ward,
really envied us and thought flying those Lockheeds
along the staging route was just about the best job anybody could get.

During my nearly three years on the staging route I
made hundreds of flights with a number of different
copilots. One of them, a fellow named Pat Ivey, became a
good friend through the years and he was with me on
one flight I will never forget.

We were flying the run from Edmonton to Norman
Wells along the Mackenzie River rather than the staging
route to Alaska, and for some reason we were going up
at night. We usually tried to schedule our flying during
daylight hours, but this one was to be at night. Our first
leg took us north from Edmonton to Fort Smith, which
sits on the Alberta-Northwest Territories border and is
situated on the Slave River. Pat and I refueled the Lockheed at Fort Smith, which would give us plenty of fuel to
make Norman Wells nearly 700 miles to the northwest
where Imperial Oil's most northerly oil wells were located.

Enroute to Norman Wells we would be passing over
some of the most beautiful but rugged and desolate
country known to man. We would pass over a little place
called Wrigley where they had a small airstrip but no
radio facilities, and also over Fort Simpson which, like
Norman Wells, had radio communications unless its
diesel generator quit. Radio facilities along the routes we
flew were mostly powered by diesel and if the engine quit
they would have to go out and start up a backup unit by
hand before the radio could come back on line. There

could be delays of 45 minutes or more with no radio at these small airstrips, especially if the backup diesel didn't start right away.

It was late November or early December as I recall, and as Pat and I proceeded up the Mackenzie the weather got worse. A heavy overcast developed and we had to fly on top of it where it was very nice but you didn't know what the hell was ahead or below. After a time I figured we were probably close to Fort Simpson, which would mean we still had 250 miles to go before reaching Norman Wells, so I called Fort Simpson on our radio. A young man was giving the weather report and he went on and on for the longest time before I finally spoke to him.

We were well past Fort Simpson by the time I was able to inform the young man of our position and destination. We learned later he had information that Norman Wells radio was off the air, but he apparently forgot to communicate this to us. Or if he did we never heard it because by now we were too far away and our communication was busting up pretty badly.

Flying above the overcast I remember so clearly the sight of Sugarloaf Mountain sticking up through the clouds in front of us. It was a big, round mound of rock alongside the river, and it meant we were now about halfway between Fort Simpson and Norman Wells. Little Wrigley would be just behind us, invisible and silent beneath the overcast. The sight of old Sugarloaf also meant we could start trying to make radio contact with Norman Wells. But try as we might, there was nothing coming out of Norman Wells on that radio and we couldn't understand why. Just about this time our fuel ran out in one tank.

What the hell is going on here, I thought and probably said out loud. We were still supposed to have plenty of fuel in this airplane. Since I didn't know exactly what the problem was, and because we couldn't make any contact with Norman Wells, I decided we had better turn tail and get the hell back to Fort Simpson.

We switched on a reserve tank and began to cross-flow fuel to keep both engines going, then turned and went back. Luckily the overcast began to disappear as we headed south and we could see the lights of Fort Simpson from about 40 miles away. I was taking the Lockheed up high because I was worried we were going to run out of gas and we would have to glide as far as possible if that happened. There was a nice, big lake about 10 miles before Fort Simpson and I thought if worse comes to worst we could take a chance on it being frozen enough to support us.

As we neared Fort Simpson the fuel gauges were showing all but empty, just hitting the bottom of the pegs and bouncing a little. I pulled the throttles way back and started a fairly fast descent because we were up high and I was going to come straight in. With so little fuel left I wasn't planning on making any circuits of the field.

We made it in. I taxied into the yard, shut down the Lockheed, walked into the small office and asked what in the world happened to the radio at Norman Wells. The young man with the long weather forecast apologized and said, "Honestly, I just plainly forgot to tell you they were shut down for maintenance."

We checked the aircraft over and found our problem was a blown fuel line. In those days the aircraft engines had copper gas lines, and to join two lines you inserted an aluminum sleeve into each end, pushed them together and covered the joint with a piece of rubber hose. A clamp holding the fuel line in place had broken off and the joint had worked itself apart with all the vibration. The gas just poured out all the while we headed back to Fort Simpson, and because we had cross-fed the gas from the reserve tank, all of our tanks were dry by the time we landed.

In fact, when we fueled up the Lockheed after repairing the gas line we put in all but one gallon of the total tankage of the aircraft. One gallon was all we had slopping around in there somewhere.

Another thing I'll never understand is why we didn't catch fire. The engine exhaust ran right alongside the spray of fuel coming from the blown line. Several years ago Pat and I were reminiscing about that flight and he said, "You know, Don, that's the only time in my life when I ever offered you a cigarette and you took it. I knew immediately we were in trouble."

The Lockheed 10 was a wonderful old plane, but the windshield was prone to frost up pretty bad when you were flying in the soup. Sometimes we'd be carrying VIPs in the back, so we would have the cockpit door closed and just sit at the controls not doing much of anything for hours on end. It got boring real fast, so we actually didn't mind the soup and a little bit of frost because we'd play Xs and Os on the windshield. It helped pass the time.

I remember one time the frost became ice and darn near ended our careers. My copilot on this trip was a rather heavyset young man named Bounce Weir. He was a great big guy and we always used to argue about whose half of the cockpit he was using because the Lockheed cockpit was very narrow and Bounce was pretty broad at the bottom. We were flying the same old Lockheed 10, but this time we were going up the staging route along the Alcan Highway toward Alaska. Luckily we didn't have any passengers, only a light load of freight. As we approached Fort Nelson in the northeast corner of British Columbia, we started to run into an overcast. There had been weather forecasts indicating icing conditions, so we took the Lockheed up to about 11,000 feet in an attempt to avoid the overcast and ice.

The overcast became worse despite our higher altitude, so I decided we would land at Fort Nelson and wait until conditions improved. We would have to depend on the radio beacon from our navigation range finder to help bring us in. The beacon would bring us over the airstrip and we would turn and go back about three minutes where we would then make a procedural turn and begin final approach.

There was a 400-foot ceiling over Fort Nelson. As we came down through the soup I had to keep adding power continuously because the weight of the ice was building up all over the aircraft. I said to Bounce, "You know, we're going to have to make it in the first time because we're never going to make it around again." He nodded in agreement.

I made the procedural turn about three minutes out and got everything lined up for our landing. But by now the windshield was so heavily iced up we couldn't see a thing. I told Bounce to take over for a few minutes so I could scrape some of the ice off the windshield.

Fortunately the Lockheed 10 had sliding side windows, and I was able to take an ice scraper and reach out through the side window in an attempt to scrape a hole in the ice covering the windshield. It was icing up so fast, however, that my effort was in vain. A few seconds after clearing a hole it would frost over and I would be flying blind again, except for what little I could see through the opening in my side window. Finally I gave up and told Bounce I would try and land by laying my head against the side window and peeking out through the opening in it.

By this time we were running almost full power to maintain enough speed to keep the old gal in the air. Bounce was calling off our air speed and I caught a glimpse of the Connus Islands as we passed over them, which was a good sign that we were right on track. We were down to about 120 mph with the gear and flaps out, running full power and not able to climb an inch more. It was actually a controlled descent, but we were lined up right and everything went well as I pressed against the side window to catch sight of the runway.

When we hit the runway, we hit hard. The ice flew off the Lockheed and through the props. It battered the wings and fuselage. It was just like landing in a storm of ice chunks, but we made it.

On the ground at Fort Nelson it was warm enough to melt most of the ice off the old Lockheed in about an hour or so. The ice in some places was up to three-quarters of an inch thick, and I remember looking at the Lockheed sitting there in a great big puddle of water and ice. Most planes wouldn't carry that much ice, and we were fortunate to be carrying a light load. This all happened in a 12- or maybe 14-minute letdown, just a very short period of time.

While I was busy flying, Marie had made friends with some of the young ladies her age in Edmonton and we began to socialize with their families and circle of friends. We were fond of two gals in particular, May and Josephine Connelly, along with their brother, Bill. Their father ran a funeral parlor. The Connelly sisters and Bill became close friends and we kept in touch with them over the years. May and Jo never married, and they still live together in Edmonton. Every time I pass through the city I try to stop by for a visit. If I'm staying over, the Connelly sisters always insist on putting me up for the night. What wonderful friends they are.

Thanks to Marie, my social life was quite a bit more civilized than most of the RCAF boys. Marie felt the airmen were a wild bunch, which was pretty near the truth, so I didn't spend much time with them in the bar recounting stories after each flight. Actually, I didn't mind at all because some of the senior officers had rather inflated opinions of themselves and I just wasn't interested in trying to act impressed.

No, instead of spending my time in the officers' club I hooked up with a young corporal and we raced Model Ts at fairgrounds and rodeos all across southern Alberta during the summers of 1943 and 1944.

We raced a circuit that ran from Edmonton south some 280 miles to Lethbridge near the Montana border. We raced at all the small towns and even at big ones like Calgary. The races were held on a third- to a half- mile

oval dirt tracks. Altogether there were about 30 of us in
the circuit, and our Model Ts were highly modified. The
competition under the hood was just as fierce as on the
track.

First you completely stripped the old Ford, then
underslung the frame so it rode about four inches lower
than normal. The Model T didn't have springs the long
way, just transverse springs, so we'd snub the inner side
of the frame with a strap to keep it fairly level in the
hard turns. We'd split the intakes in half, bore them out
and polish them, then weld them back together so you'd
have a better flow. A few of us welded longitudinal fins
about an inch and a half deep in the oil pan to help cool
the oil. I rigged up a half-inch external oil line to bring
oil from the transmission housing forward to the front of
the engine. It provided a deep flow of oil all the way back
through the engine. I even coiled the line so the oil
would cool on its way forward.

The end result of all our modifying was a Model T that
could turn a half-mile track in just about 30 seconds,
which meant we were hitting 60 mph on the oval. We
timed our racer down and back on a mile-long straightaway one time and averaged just over 70 mph. Not bad
for a Model T.

Driving the old Model T racer at 60 mph was a thrill a
minute. You were strapped into an open seat perched
atop a wide-open frame, a perfect target for all the dirt,
mud and debris that cars in front of you could kick up
during a race. The old wooden spoke wheels were a particular menace. They'd last only so long before flying
apart in a turn. If you happened to be behind someone
when it happened, watch out! The rear outside wheels
were particularly prone to fail. During a race,whenever
the fellow in front of me had wooden wheels, I would
also keep a sharp eye on that wheel in a turn. Wire
wheels for the Model Ts were hard to find, but we would
use them whenever we could for safety's sake as well as
for better performance.

I never had a serious accident, but there were a few close calls and one really embarrassing incident at Calgary where the oval was made of glacial silt. It got very dusty and was hard on engines, so they would wet it down before each race. And when they did, it was extremely slippery during the first few laps.

It was a qualifying race with about 24 cars on the track lined up in six rows. I was second from the inside in the second row. Coming out of the first turn on the first lap, barely past the grandstand and not even up to full speed, the fellow in front of me started to skid out. I got out of his way, but it was so slippery that when I tried to correct I started going sideways.

There was a big archway on the back side of the track and I did everything possible to steer my racer through it. I almost made it, except for one post.

I hit the post pretty much head on, but at an angle so the old Model T half climbed up the darn thing. I sat there at about a 45-degree angle for a few embarrassing seconds until it fell back down almost in slow motion. It was all bent out of kilter, so we took our racer back home and tied one corner to a telephone pole and the other corner to our pickup truck. We kept yanking and yanking until we got the frame straight again. The Model T racers usually had to be overhauled between every race, so it just meant a little extra work and we would be ready to race again.

We'd drive the Model T to meets 50 or 75 miles away so the bearings and rings and whatever else we replaced would be properly broken in by the time we reached the track. On longer distances we would ship the car by train, but mostly we drove our racer and old pickup truck cross country. Just me, the corporal and sometimes Marie.

I never was one to worry about promotions, which probably explains why they were few and far between. I held the rank of Flight Lieutenant during most of my three years on the staging route, and while some of the senior pilots like myself were angling for a permanent command, I just wanted to fly. On many occasions I was sent up to the various stations along the route as temporary O.C., or Officer Commanding, at places like Fort Nelson or Whitehorse. It was a lousy job, but they were short stints and before too long I would be back in Edmonton with Marie, which was just fine with me.

Rank never did impress me, but how in the world I was promoted to Squadron Leader barely six months after standing down our old man is something I still wonder about.

It was early 1945 and I had just returned from a training course back East. The first thing the boys told me was that they were having trouble with our commanding officer taking over — flying from the left seat in the Lockheeds, and he wasn't that sharp anymore. I said that would never happen in any aircraft in my command because I'd let him know he couldn't sit in my seat.

Well, it wasn't 24 hours before our C.O. needed a lift somewhere and our Lockheed just happened to be going in his direction. I had sent my copilot, Larry Hall, over to get a weather briefing while I did my walk around the aircraft to check it out. The C.O. came up to me and said, "I'll be doing the flying today, Braun." I didn't say a word.

He asked where my copilot was and I told him he was getting a weather briefing. "Well, he won't be going with us today," the C.O. said. "Oh, yes he will," I responded, adding, "You may not need him but I need him because this is my first flight since getting back from the East Coast."

He didn't take that very well and things deteriorated real fast. The C.O. climbed aboard the Lockheed and proceeded to sit in the left seat. I climbed in and said to him, "I had no idea how badly you were going to need a copilot because he'll be going with you." He asked what I meant by that remark and I politely explained, "If you're the captain of this aircraft, then there's no point in my remaining on board because you need a copilot, not me."

He stormed out of the left seat and brushed past me, muttering, "I'll see you later. You'll hear about this, Braun." Fine, I thought, and climbed into my seat while Hall, who was now aboard wondering what the hell was going on, climbed into his.

I could just imagine the old man's embarrassment, but I had made up my mind to stand him down and that was it. He sat in the back of the old Lockheed for the entire trip and never said another word, not even a thanks at the end of the flight.

That was the last time I flew him for about six months, which is when my promotion to Squadron Leader came through. I always figured my giving the old man hell would kill my promotion. But it didn't, and I still don't know why. A short time later, in August of 1945, I was notified that . . . *"His Majesty, The King, has conferred upon you the Air Force Cross."* It was an honor and a complete surprise to this farm boy from Minnesota to rate such a thing.

During my nearly five years in the RCAF flying different aircraft, I encountered many situations and conditions that tested and honed my skills as a pilot. The runs up and down the Northwest Staging Route, and the secondary route along the Mackenzie River, were my first real experience in Northern flying. But nothing compared to what I learned about bush flying before the war was over.

Every so often they had some of us fly survey crews in and out of those small villages and posts where airstrips were being planned along the Mackenzie River. That's where I was introduced to the wonderful old Noorduyn Norseman, the first of the real bush planes.

The Norseman in its day was as advanced as the de Havilland Otter was when it came along in 1951. It was just plainly so superior to everything else that was

being used for bush flying when it was first introduced in
1936, and that was still the case when I first flew it in
1943. We were flying the latest model, the Mark VI,
which was slightly larger and heavier than the earlier
Mark IV version. The Norseman was not docile and slow
like the Otter on take-off and landing. It took off at
about 65 mph and landed at about the same speed. But
there was nothing else at the time that could bring in a
half-ton payload to a remote landing area quite like the
Norseman. It was powered by a big 550-hp Wasp nine-
cylinder radial engine and I simply loved flying the darned
thing any chance I could get.

We had several RCAF Norsemen assigned to the survey work. Each of us had a survey crew that we moved
around the countryside and kept supplied. Our aircraft
were maintained by a couple of mechanics, and for a
time we were based out of Norman Wells to the far north.

Bush flying the North Country in the Norseman was
an entirely different experience than flying over it at
12,000 feet in the Lockheed 10. In bush flying you fly
through mountain passes and up river valleys, across
the tops of forests and through the morning mist. God
willing, you land and take off wherever you can.

It was the airplane — the bush plane, really — that
made life tolerable, sometimes profitable and certainly
more civilized in the North Country. In the cockpit of the
old Norseman I felt a part of this land, not simply a trav-
eler passing high over it.

I wanted to stay in the North Country and make it my
home.

CHAPTER FIVE

SNARE RIVER BUSH PILOT

*"The powder man nodded he was ready and I
ran over to the Norseman and started it up
while he set a 10- or 12-minute fuse so we
could get far away. We took off and circled
about a mile away, waiting for the dynamite
to blow up. And when it blew it was the
damnedest explosion I ever saw."*

On Tuesday, October 2, 1945, Air Vice-Marshal T. A.
Lawrence, C.B., A.O.C., of the North West Air Command
announced my retirement from the RCAF, and the October 2 issue of the *Edmonton Journal* newspaper carried
the story: *An American flier who came to Canada from
Chicago to join the RCAF, and who has been in Edmonton
with the North West Air Command since January 1943, is
retiring into civilian life. He is Sqdn. Ldr. Don Braun, A.F.C.,
office commanding No. 6 communications flight...* My official
discharge date was November 17, 1945.

With my RCAF days at an end and no immediate prospects for a flying job, I made a deal with one of our ser-
geants to start a trucking business out of Edmonton. We
called it T & B Van Lines. Toutant and Braun. Lloyd
Toutant was his name, and our aim was to truck into
northern Alberta because Tout knew the area up around
High Prairie. His folks lived there.

Even as winter approached I thought it was quite an
idea and was convinced we would get into the trucking
business in a big way. The trouble was, the roads and the
weather didn't cooperate.

After the war there was little effort to improve the roads
in the North, and in the spring we would be banned from
the roads entirely. Most of the roads were gumbo and
we'd drag along in second and third gear for hundreds of

miles when they were wet. Instead of eight or 10 miles to
a gallon, our trucks were getting maybe four. And we
were going through engines and tires like crazy. Tout and I
tried very hard to make it go. We just about killed ourselves during 1946 and had little to show for it.

One of the real coincidences in my life happened while
I was in the trucking business. I had made a delivery to
High Prairie and was headed back to Edmonton along a
six-mile detour in the road. It had rained in the area and
the detour had turned into even worse gumbo than we
had been fighting all year on the regular roads.

Do you think I could keep that van on top of that road?
Hell, no. No matter how hard I'd try it would start to ease
off the road and then I'd have to climb out, cut some brush
and put it under the rear wheels. I'd get back on track for
a few hundred yards or so and repeat the same thing.

I was about two-thirds of the way along this detour
and once again down on all fours in the gumbo, stuffing
branches under the tires, when lo and behold, here comes
a Jeep from the other direction. I thought, good gosh,
what a Godsend. I hope this guy will be willing to turn
around and pull me through the rest of the detour. That's
all I need, just a little bit of help from a four-wheel drive.

The Jeep pulled up and the driver got out and sloshed
through the gumbo back to the rear of the van where I
was stuffing branches. I looked up and there was my kid
brother Jim standing over me!

He said, "What the hell are you doing under there?" I
told him my problem and he told me to hop back in the
van. Jim hitched his Jeep to my truck and pulled me
through the detour to the regular road in low gear.

Can you imagine my surprise at running into my kid
brother in the middle of nowhere, stuck in the gumbo?
I didn't even know he was anywhere in Canada at the
time. As it turned out, he was on that particular stretch
of road because he was in the U.S. Air Force with a DC-4
crew that was doing some work after the war on the

staging route. The Jeep had a winter top welded on it and it wouldn't fit through the rear door of the DC-4, so Jim had to drive it to Dawson Creek where he would meet up with the rest of the crew. In those days there was only one road to Dawson Creek and it went through High Prairie.

Jim had passed through Edmonton, but not without stopping by our house and visiting Marie. She told him I was up north making a delivery, so he knew I was on the road but he didn't know if he would meet up with me. Our chance encounter took place somewhere between the town of Athabasca and Lesser Slave Lake, a couple of hundred miles north of Edmonton.

Several years later Jim told me he ran into an Indian farther up the road, after we had parted company. The man had an old patched-together car that somehow had ended up in the ditch, and he asked Jim if he would try to pull it out with the Jeep. Jim said he didn't think it would work, but he would try if that's what the fellow wanted. So they hooked a chain on the thing but it wouldn't budge even after Jim gave it a few good tugs.

The Indian told Jim to back up and take a run at it. Jim told him it would probably come apart, which of course it did. He went roaring down the road with just a front axle trailing behind the Jeep.

Meantime, my old RCAF friend and sometimes copilot, Pat Ivey, had stayed in the Edmonton area after the war. Pat was determined to keep flying and he thought the crop-dusting business would be just the ticket. He had joined up with our old squadron leader, the fellow I replaced, and they were going to start a business. Because Pat had remained active as a pilot in the area, he was approached in late 1946 by the people building a hydro-electric dam about 95 miles northwest of Yellowknife on the Snare River. They wanted Pat to be the project pilot and fly personnel and supplies between Yellowknife and the dam site.

Pat turned them down because he planned to crop-dust, but he sent the man doing the recruiting over to see if I would be interested. The man's name was Archie McEachren, and as I recall he didn't have to do much selling to sign me on. Archie was a manager for the company building the dam, Northern Construction, and at the time he recruited me he was sharing a room at the Yellowknife Hotel with a young bush pilot who had recently arrived on the scene with his own airplane to start a charter flying service.

The pilot was Max Ward, who had also served in the RCAF in western Canada and would later become my close friend, my boss and, eventually, head of Canada's largest charter airline, Wardair Canada.

Archie said Northern Construction and the Mannix engineering company would provide housing for Marie and me at the project site. And I would be flying a beautiful old Mark IV Norseman that had been rebuilt by the Alberta government. It seems Alberta was going into the air business for some reason or another and they had two Norseman Mark IVs, PAA and PAB, that had both been completely rebuilt. Northern Construction and Mannix had purchased PAB and I would be flying it for the next couple of years until the project was completed.

I remember telling my trucking partner, Tout, "Boy, if you'll take this thing over you can have it just for what it cost me, maybe less, because I'm going back to flying." I sold out and Tout went on to become quite successful with a fleet of semis. Pat Ivey went on to a crop-dusting career in California, even dusting at night with some guy on the ground marking the field with a light, all of which I couldn't understand since Pat really never had very good eyes. I wouldn't have done it.

Pat had always regretted that he didn't take the Snare River job, and he shared that regret plus many fond memories during our last visit together in the summer of 1990. Pat, like me, was a motorcycle nut, and he rode his bike all the way from Chico, California, where he and his lovely wife, Natalie, had settled, to visit me in St. Cloud. A mutual friend from the old days, George Potter, drove down from Edmonton and that made it a really nice reunion.

On the return trip, somewhere in Montana, George turned north for Edmonton and Pat waved goodbye while continuing west on his motorcycle. Just out of Missoula, Pat pulled off the road, got his bike on its stand and then fell to the ground, spilling his nitro pills all over the place.

He never got up again. Pat was dead, right there, of a heart attack.

In early 1947, just around my 34th birthday, Marie and I left Edmonton for the Snare River project mostly because Pat Ivey wanted to be a crop duster. We lived in a construction camp only 225 miles south of the Arctic Circle. The buildings were made of lumber from a nearby island where the company had set up a sawmill. There was a large two-story bunk house for the 80-man construction crew and a small single-story staff house where Marie and I had a room. Then there were a couple of larger houses for the upper echelon. Marie was employed in the office. It was all very primitive by today's standards, but we managed.

The Northern Canada Power Commission had contracted with Northern Construction and Mannix Company to build the hydroelectric dam to supply power for Yellowknife and the region's mining operations. One of the large mining companies already owned and operated a small hydroelectric facility about 12 miles north of Yellowknife, and the Snare River project was proposed by another big mining firm. The government stepped in and said, no, we're not going to have privately owned power in the Northwest Territories. The project would be publicly owned and operated so Yellowknife and the mines would have equal access to the power.

Prospecting for hard rock gold in the Yellowknife area
started in the 1890s and continued somewhat fitfully over
the years until there was a big strike in 1934. Up until
that time Yellowknife was little more than an Indian
settlement and a ramshackle outpost for prospectors
and adventurers. It was named for the Yellowknife Indians and was situated along Back Bay on the east side of
the North Arm of Great Slave Lake, one of two great
lakes in the Northwest Territories.

Great Slave Lake is an immense body of water, nearly
11,000 square miles and just over 2,000 feet deep. That
makes it larger than Lake Erie and deeper than Lake
Superior. The other great inland sea of the far North,
Great Bear Lake up on the Arctic Circle, is a bit larger
than Great Slave Lake but not nearly as deep.

Yellowknife boomed until the war, and then it was all
but ignored until there was an even larger strike in 1944
and Yellowknife again grew like crazy once the war was
over. The biggest mining operations belonged to Giant
Yellowknife Mines and Consolidated Mining and Smelting, but the countryside was littered with small operators.

The Yellowknife docks along Back Bay were a beehive of
activity both winter and summer. Mining was an around-
the-clock, 365-day-a-year business, and aircraft were
the best way to move people and supplies in and out
since there was no road to Yellowknife at this time. Work
on the Snare River hydro project was also year-round,
and starting with my first flight on February 6, 1947, I
soon found myself flying the Norseman into Yellowknife
almost daily for mail, equipment and fresh food supplies
for the crew. Yellowknife was a rough-and-tumble sort of
frontier town, but I liked it more with each visit.

I also flew Archie and some of the other management
people between the project site and Yellowknife quite a
bit. Project design and management were provided by
the Montreal Engineering Company, and their chief was
George Eckenfelder, a fine guy who became a good
friend. He was single at the time, but later married a

great gal, Alice, and today they make their home out on Vancouver Island. Alice is really outgoing, as if she's known you for the last 50 years when you meet her for the first time. On a recent visit she made a lunch that was just unbelievable. Baked fish and everything, like Thanksgiving, only better.

Another engineer I hauled around was Bill Stuart. I would tie his canoe to the Norseman's floats and we would fly to different places where Bill could study the feasibility of diverting smaller rivers into the Snare to increase the flow for future dams. And eventually they did put in additional dams and hydroelectric plants based on Bill's good work.

Then there was Bun Russell, a government hydrographer on the project who had us fly into streams and rivers throughout the North Country to measure flows for possible hydro development. I say "us" because there was another bush pilot Russell sometimes hired when my workload got heavy or I had the old Norseman shut down for its 100-hour maintenance check.

It was Max Ward, of course, the handsome young Canadian determined to make his fortune in the flying business out of Yellowknife.

Max was a native of Edmonton, and although his father was a career railroad man, all Max ever wanted to do was fly. After his stint with the RCAF, Max was bound and determined to be a bush pilot. He arrived in Yellowknife in the fall of 1946 with a brand new de Havilland Fox Moth biplane. There weren't many built and the engine was one of those British inverted things that burned as much oil as gasoline. They tended to run out of oil before they ran out of gas and a lot of them fell out of the air. Max had purchased his Fox Moth for $10,000, including floats and skis, but not before he busted it up on the way home from the de Havilland plant near Toronto.

Max attempted to land the Fox Moth at a small airstrip at Kenora after dark, which he knew he shouldn't have done. They had been grading the runway and left a windrow of gravel down the center when they quit work for the day. Max landed in it.

When I arrived on the scene in early 1947 Max was calling himself and his repaired Fox Moth the Polaris Charter Company, and Northern Construction, Mannix and the Montreal engineering people were using his services regularly. Even after I was hired we continued to use Max on the days I was shut down or when work piled up. The Fox Moth was much smaller than the Norseman, but Max made up for it with determination and long hours.

Max was a hard-driving type of fellow, working from sunrise to sunset seven days a week. He was doing all right until the authorities shut him down for operating without a license. It was the first of Max's many encounters with the Canadian government in trying to run a charter air service, but it didn't stop him. He quickly hooked up with a man in Yellowknife who held a license but was just about retired, and Max was back in business in his Fox Moth on a 50-50 basis.

I would always shut the Norseman down for a 100-hour check, although a lot of people in the North would fly their aircraft all winter long and then take them down to Edmonton for a complete overhaul in the spring. Not us. We'd shut down, summer or winter, every 100 hours. It would take our engineer, Bert Stevenson, and me a day and a half to complete the job, and I always worked right with him. We would change the plugs and the oil, drain and clean the sumps, drain the fuel tanks until we were sure there was no water in them, patch any little fabric holes in the belly. Whatever had to be done.

Northern Construction, Mannix and Montreal Engineering almost insisted on an airplane a day so they would get their mail and keep the guys in camp happy with fresh food. When I was shut down Max would come in with the Fox Moth and often bring his beautiful wife, Marjorie, and their first little girl, Gai, along for the ride.

Marjorie was also from Edmonton, but she was new to the North, like Marie. Gai was just a toddler, barely old enough to walk, and Marjorie would carry her around the camp in a packboard on her back while Max went about his business. Marie and I got to know Max and his wife through these visits but we really didn't socialize. There just wasn't time and, besides, we were stuck out in a construction camp nearly 100 miles by air from Yellowknife.

Flying for the hydro project kept me coming and going almost daily during my year and a half at the Snare River camp. Like Max, I was a hard driver and put in long days. Unlike Max, I was a lot more relaxed and easygoing. Yet each of us, in our own way, was discovering what being a bush pilot in the North Country was all about.

It meant long days, irregular hours and often little or no notice. It meant flying at the convenience of others in all kinds of weather. It meant loading and unloading heavy payloads that belonged to someone else. It meant knowing how to live and work in extreme cold; how to read the weather and the condition of snow and ice. It meant knowing every nut and bolt in your aircraft so you could do maintenance and repairs in the field. It meant knowing the country well enough to fly almost anywhere in the North; being smart enough to read the country.

But most of all being a bush pilot meant being able to take off and land just about anywhere, usually in a minimum of space. That meant you had to be able to handle aircraft equipped with floats and skis, not just wheels.

There are line pilots who only go where the schedule goes, such as flying for a scheduled airline. There are wheel pilots who are only qualified to fly aircraft with wheels. And then there are bush pilots. Bush pilots fly anytime, anywhere, usually relying on a combination of skill, brains and instinct to keep flying by the seat of their pants to a bare minimum.

The only flight I had ever made in an aircraft equipped with something other than wheels was when I bolted some skis on my little Eaglet during a snowstorm in Chicago years earlier and was the only plane flying when the storm let up. During my RCAF years they had me fly a Norseman with skis out of Edmonton. My first trip was to an Indian village on the west end of Lake Athabasca to pick up a little girl who was badly burned. They told me to land on the mudflats in front of the village since it was just after freeze-up and the ice on the lake wasn't thick enough. I honestly didn't know what I was doing at that point because it had been so long since the Chicago storm and the Norseman was a completely different — and much bigger — aircraft than the tiny Eaglet. But I got away with it and brought the child back to Edmonton. Later, when we began flying the survey crews up the Mackenzie River during the war, I was checked out on floats in an RCAF Norseman. Each flight on skis and floats prepared me for the Snare River job and my later years as a bush pilot for Wardair.

One of the first lessons learned bush flying a Norseman in the RCAF days was to drain the oil from the aircraft after shutdown in cold weather, then heat it up the next morning by placing the pail of oil in a bucket of water that sat atop an airtight stove. When the oil was warm I would pour it back into the Norseman and crank it up even at 40 below zero Fahrenheit. It worked every time, although I have to admit there were times I was so tired and cold at the end of the day that draining the oil was the last thing I wanted to do. But if I needed to fly again before spring, there was no question. I just did it. I continued to practice this winter ritual while flying for the Snare River project in the old Norseman-PAB.

The Snare River hydro project consisted of an earth-filled dam some 66 feet high that was built around a solid rock island. The main tunnel and the exciter tunnel were drilled right through the rock in the middle of the river, with the powerhouse located behind them. It was a huge undertaking, and its remote location with no road access made it a real challenge to get all the supplies and heavy equipment to the construction site. The tonnage was far in excess of what aircraft could handle, and the motorized freight barges used on Great Slave Lake in the summer could only ferry some of the supplies needed, and then only as far as Old Fort Rae at the end of the North Arm of the big lake.

Most of the supplies and heavy equipment for the project had to be hauled to the site in the winter during freeze-up by the same means used to supply Yellowknife back then: Cat trains.

A Cat train consisted of a large Caterpillar-type tractor pulling a line of extra heavy duty sleighs. They were like farm sleighs, but instead of hauling a ton or two of hay they carried a minimum load of 10 tons per sleigh. A typical Cat train pulled about seven or eight sleighs, or a payload of roughly 80 tons of everything imaginable — steel, cement, cables, tools, gasoline, fuel oil, spare parts, turbine blades, motors, food stocks, office supplies, household items and who knows what else. The last sled in the train usually carried a caboose with sleeping and eating quarters for the crew.

They always needed a little push to get started, but once a Cat train got rolling it was quite a sight to behold as it moved slowly out of Hay River on the south shore of Great Slave Lake. The first Cat train to make the dangerous crossing was in 1938. Each season the trains would proceed north about four or five miles per hour in groups of three to Yellowknife on a designated route or "ice road" across the frozen lake, a distance of about 140 miles. Those with payloads intended for the hydro project would continue on past Yellowknife and head northwest up the North Arm to Rae and a staging area for the final leg of the trip. The trains moved 24 hours a day, stopping only for repairs or because of a storm. Crews normally consisted of four men per train, two Cat "skinners" or drivers, a brakeman and an observer. Men who could take care of themselves under the worst of circumstances were carefully recruited for the crews.

I watched many a Cat train during the winter of 1947–
48, usually from the air. You could just about count on a
train breaking down or going through the ice during its
200-mile run from Hay River to the dam site. Once the
train started its run, my job included flying out almost
daily to check its location and how the crew was doing
moving up the lake. Often I would fly ahead and check
the condition of the ice road, looking for low spots or
pressure ridges in the ice. The Cat trains usually waited
until just after Christmas to begin their runs, when the
ice was 30 or more inches thick, but pressure ridges
were a real danger no matter how thick the ice.

In the process of the ice forming on the lake, pressure
ridges would develop in just about the same places year
after year as the ice expanded and contracted with
changes in temperature. The ridges would get bigger with
each warm spell, often rising up more than 10 feet high
and several miles long. When it turned cold the ice would
crack along the pressure ridges and pose a further danger to the Cat skinners.

A small "pathfinder" Caterpillar-type tractor with a
driver wise in the ways of lake ice would go out in advance of the season's first trains to prepare the roadbed
in the ice. The men would plow aside any snow and deal
with pressure ridges. They would blast through the pressure ridges with dynamite and then use the small tractor
to chisel a path through the ridge and lay a bed of heavy
timbers for the Cat trains to cross once the planking was
frozen solid in place. I would fly new timber planking in
when they busted up what they carried along, and then
fly the broken timber out. The pathfinder tractor often
pulled a small sleigh that carried fresh cut saplings
along with the usual gear. The saplings would be placed
on the ice to mark the trail ahead for the Cat trains that
followed.

Even with a carefully prepared ice road there were
times when a big Cat or one of the sleighs would go
through the ice and sink to depths of a thousand feet or

more. But a much more common problem was mechanical failure. The old tractors in those days always had
something going wrong. The rear drives, particularly,
were a problem. So I would have to fly out rear drives
and they'd change them right out on the lake no matter
what the temperature. The crew would throw a tent over
the disabled tractor and put an airtight heater inside. I'd
fly in firewood for the airtight if the Cat train was too far
out on the lake.

When the Cat trains hauling supplies for the hydro
project reached Rae, everything had to be broken down
and rearranged for the more difficult and perilous 50-
mile traverse of smaller lakes and portages to the construction site. They had a big staging area at Frank
Channel near Rae on the shore of North Arm.

The men would unload the sleighs and then carefully
reload them with lighter payloads tied as securely as
possible. While a Cat train would haul 80 tons across
the lake, it could safely haul only about half that
amount over the rough portages. Crews used Cats to
compact snow in all the low spots along the portages
and try to establish a half decent snow road to the
camp, but even so the payloads had to be lightened and
the length of the trains cut back. Sleighs and payloads
could be lost and men injured or worse if a tractor
couldn't hold its sleighs going down a portage. The
sleighs would smash into each other, then the tractor
and crew.

One of the damnedest jobs I had that winter was
hauling in extra sleighs for the portage runs. We did it
piece by piece, in the Norseman. There were a bunch of
old sleighs a few miles from the staging area, maybe 15
or 20, that had been abandoned during the war years.
Several of us flew over and dismantled about 10 of them
since some were busted up and not worth salvaging.
Two of us could barely lift one runner and the bolsters
connecting the runners were still heavier. It took many
round trips in the old Norseman to bring all the pieces

over for 10 complete sleighs, but we did it. And in the middle of winter, too, with the temperature often 40 below zero Fahrenheit or colder.

Besides the harsh conditions old Mother Nature would throw at us, another danger on the Snare River project was man-made: dynamite. They used tons of it on the project and in the summer of 1946, a year before construction was scheduled to start, about 20 tons of dynamite was barged across Great Slave Lake from Hay River. The dynamite barge went up North Arm past Rae, then moved up several rivers and connecting lakes where it was unloaded on the north end of Slemon Lake. From there the dynamite would be hauled by sleigh the rest of the way to the dam site in the winter.

By the time they got around to moving it, however, the spring thaw was already underway and the dynamite had started to gel and ooze out of the cases from sitting so long. They considered it too unstable to move and decided the only thing to do was blow it up right where it sat.

Only a couple of months after I started flying for the project, on a fairly nice spring day when I didn't have much to do, they had me take a couple of guys and our powder man out to the dynamite at Slemon Lake to blow it up. We landed on the lake ice, which was still quite thick, and the powder man put a long fuse on his charge. I told him, "Now when you're ready to light that thing I'll go start the aircraft first, just in case."

The powder man nodded he was ready and I ran over to the Norseman and started it up while he set a 10- or 12-minute fuse so we could get far away. We took off and circled about a mile away, waiting for the dynamite to blow up. And when it blew it was the damnedest explosion I ever saw.

Slemon Lake's north end had a very steep shoreline about 60 or 70 feet high, and the explosion cleared every tree right off the hill in back of the dynamite pile. It just flattened every one of them. We didn't know it at the time, but there were a couple of bundles of concrete reinforcing bars somewhere in the pile. They blew straight up in the air and came down with about half of the bars stuck in the ice end first for 100 yards around Ground Zero. It looked like a minefield when the smoke cleared.

All the dynamite for the hydro project's first year of construction went up in that blast and they had to haul in replacement dynamite with a DC-3. In those days most supplies had to be arranged for a full season ahead, including the dynamite, because everything was shipped out of Edmonton up to Hay River and then either barged in summer or hauled by Cat trains during the winter.

Another time I was lucky to escape with nothing more than a scare when a huge chunk of rock from a dynamite blast almost hit the Norseman. I had just landed on the river below the dam this particular day and was tying the aircraft down when I heard the warning whistle for a dynamite blast. They were building up the face of the dam with rock, called riprap, which was a product of the blasting.

Normally all the rock went north with each blast, but this time I saw one large rock shoot straight up and then slowly arc over and head right for me and the Norseman. It missed the wing and a float by not more than two feet and hit the water like a cannon shell. Caboom! And the water flew all over the place. I was running by the time it hit, but that big rock could have gone right through the old Norseman. Talk about being lucky sometimes.

One poor fellow wasn't as lucky, however. A powder man for the company building the power line from our hydro project was killed when he broke the cardinal rule of using dynamite. He went back to see why a charge hadn't gone off, and then it went off.

I was flying toward our camp with a full load when I spotted someone in a canoe making very tight circles just off shore. That was the signal in the North for trouble in camp, and if you saw it you knew somebody needed help. In the winter you spread oil or anything dark on the snow or ice in an X or, if worse came to worst, you just tramped a big X in the snow. But in the summer it was the circling canoe.

Since I had a full load and it was only 30 miles to camp, I decided to fly on and return as quickly as I could after dumping my load. When I arrived back at the site of the circling canoe and reached shore, I was met by members of the power line construction crew and they filled me in on what had happened.

Most of the poles were being set in solid rock. The crew would make three or four holes with pneumatic power drills, then drop some dynamite in each one and let the charge go. The men would dig out the shattered rock, set the pole and throw the rock back in the hole around the pole to stabilize it. The powder man apparently went back to check the charge and ended up with just a little bit of the back of his skull left.

We lined the aircraft with canvas and put the remains of the powder man on the floor of the cabin and covered him. The power line crew was badly shaken by the incident and they didn't want to stay at their camp, so they came along with me and the dead powder man to Yellowknife. Why they wanted to fly with a man who'd just been killed, I'll never know.

When I pulled up to the dock at Yellowknife, there was Leary, one of our dispatchers. Leary was a pure Irishman right through to the core, and when Leary would hear I was coming in he always ran down to the dock to greet me. Leary threw open the rear door of the Norseman in his customary manner. By this time, of course, the canvas was full of blood as well as the remains of the powder man. Leary took one look, then turned around and disappeared. I don't think I saw him till the next day.

Our other dispatcher finally came down and helped with the unloading. We also got old Burying Smith, the town undertaker, down to get the body. His wife actually did all the work but he took all the credit for it. Burying Smith would celebrate every deceased's departure with a good drunk while his poor wife did all of the embalming and everything. He got the money and got drunk. She did the work.

Life in the North Country was full of characters like Burying Smith. Every day was an adventure, and I knew the only thing I really wanted to do was fly in the North. But I had agreed with Marie that when the Snare River project was over we would go back home to St. Cloud. We had been living in a rather primitive construction camp for over a year and a half, and the isolation and darkness of winter were hard on Marie.

I was able to escape the isolation and boredom in my Norseman, but Marie remained in camp month after month until she just didn't want to stay in the North Country any longer.

Reluctantly, I made preparations to return to Minnesota in the fall of 1948. I could have flown for the Northern Canada Power Commission, even using the same old Norseman, but I had agreed to return and that was it. I found out later that within six months of our departure a pilot named Dunc Matheson and Helge Eskelson, an engineer, had flown my Norseman right into the glassy water of Back Bay one evening and broke the fronts of the floats right off. The Norseman flipped over and sank. Dunc clambered up inside the fuselage to the part that was still out of the water, kicked a hole through the fabric, and both men escaped out the back end. Marjorie Ward happened to be standing on the dock and witnessed the whole thing. My poor old Norseman!

One time I carried a 670-pound steel compressed air tank in the Norseman. It was so large it wouldn't fit in the cabin, so I took both rear doors off and flew with about 18 inches of the darn thing sticking out of each side of the aircraft. I carried all sorts of crazy stuff and never put my Norseman in the drink.

Anyhow, I made my final flight in the old Norseman-PAB on September 28, 1948, and shortly thereafter Marie and I said goodbye and returned to the farm in St. Cloud. We got home, set up housekeeping and got into the chicken business.

Of all the dumb things to do.

Chapter Six

RETREAT TO THE FARM, RETURN TO THE NORTH

"Poor Marie. Going back north was the very last thing she wanted in life. But she was willing to go along if that's what I wanted. Actually, when I thought about it, we didn't have much choice. I was out of the chicken business and I didn't know what else to do."

Marie and I arrived back in St. Cloud in time to celebrate Christmas 1948 with our relatives for the first time in years. Yes, I missed the North Country and flying, but being home for Christmas on the farm was really special. I will always love the old farm I grew up on and have since retired to because I remember even as a child it has always been the gathering place for our families, a special place full of happy memories and good times that overshadow any bad.

Mom and Dad were close to 60 years old when we moved back, but they welcomed us home and gave us a bedroom in the old farmhouse until we had a house of our own. With Dad's approval, we picked a spot on the farm that was just perfect for building a basement home into the side of the hill going down to the river, which would give us a beautiful view of the Mississippi.

We built that house, Marie and I, with a little help from Dad. Marie had no intention of living in the same house with her in-laws any longer than necessary because she felt we were imposing on my folks, so she worked shoulder-to-shoulder with me to get our basement house finished.

Actually, we moved in before it was finished not only to gain some much needed privacy but also to make room in the farmhouse for another pair of new arrivals, my brother Jim and his wife, Helen, a brown-eyed beauty from Pennsylvania. They were married while Jim was still in the Air Force, but now that he was discharged the only logical place to be was back on the family farm.

It was good having Jim home. Dad tended toward the quiet side, but Jim was always bright and cheery and never at a loss for words. He loved telling jokes and swapping stories, which we did many evenings after his return. It was during these bull sessions that Jim and I hatched the idea of getting into the chicken business.

When I left the North for the farm, I really had no idea of what I wanted to do. But with Jim's arrival on the scene, the idea of going into the broiler end of the chicken business as partners with him actually started to make sense to me. We ended up tending 8,000 broilers on the farm and did our own butchering, dispatching and cutting up several hundred chickens a week.

It was a messy business and, frankly, it didn't smell very good either, especially on hot summer days in July. But Jim and I kept at it, working hard and not having much to show for it. At least we had plenty of chicken to eat, so we were never hungry.

Now that we were settled in, Marie and I began discussing the idea of adopting a child since we had been married nearly 11 years and could not have children of our own. About a mile or so north of the farm there was a large, ugly brown brick building with a tall, dark bell tower like you would see in one of those old movies that scared you as a kid. It sat all by itself on the south edge of St. Cloud, and everybody called it The Orphanage although its real name was the St. Cloud Children's Home. A relative of my mother, a woman named Clara Hunstiger, was in charge of placements at the orphanage and she became a good and helpful friend to us.

Sooner than Marie and I ever expected, a little baby boy, eight months old, became available for adoption and the decision was made that he would be our son, Christopher. We were thrilled to have such a beautiful child, and no sooner had we gotten into the routine of caring for a baby when a few months later Clara told us that Christopher was going to have a half brother. She asked if we would be interested in adopting the baby at birth and, of course, we couldn't say no. Within weeks we had a second son, Charles.

Imagine, all we had in mind was adopting a baby and now, six months later, Marie and I were the proud parents of two boys. Life can get mighty interesting if you give it half a chance, and I guess that's what Marie and I did when we decided to contact Clara about adoption. We took a chance, and look how blessed we were by doing so.

Several years passed and the boys grew but the chicken business sure didn't. Then, in 1953, I came down with spinal meningitis and damn near died at the age of 40.

It happened during a flu epidemic and old Doc Schatz thought that's what I had, the flu. He came over to the farm and gave me some flu medicine. He was so busy at the time, of course, that he didn't realize I really had meningitis and he kept apologizing for years afterward about it. Whatever he gave me, it made me feel better so I kept working in the barn. A couple of days later I collapsed. Marie and Dad carried me to the car and took me to the hospital.

Within hours of being admitted to the hospital I slipped into a coma of sorts and I couldn't move a muscle or blink an eye for five days. Marie just sat there and waited for me to either die or come back. I don't remember much about those five days except the nurses would make me so mad. Apparently the sense of hearing is the last thing to go, because I could hear what was going on but I couldn't do anything about it.

I couldn't reach the call button pinned to my pillow, or even press it for that matter. All I can remember is hoping and praying the nurses would come in and wet my

mouth because my tongue was so dry it felt like it was
going to grow right out of my mouth. When the nurses
would finally come in all they would do is ask questions,
then turn around and walk out without giving me a drop
of water. I'd lay there, just furious, unable to indicate
what I wanted or needed.

Ever since then, I've never gone into a room of a patient
who is asleep or unconscious and said anything about
the patient because they may hear it. If it's the last thing
they do, they'll hear what you say. Anyway, I guess the
good Lord wanted me to live because I came back.

My recovery took the rest of 1953 and most of 1954. I
would lay out in the sun recuperating, watching the
coming and going of the bees in our new hive and wishing I had half their energy. A neighbor, old Mr. Emslander,
and my mother had captured our bees with a catching
hive and then transferred them to a regular hive of white
boxes stacked about four feet high in a field near the
farmhouse. I was fascinated by the little critters. My
brother Jim, meantime, had shut down our chicken
business because it was impossible for him to handle it
while I watched bees all day.

During my recovery I started to receive letters from
Max Ward asking me to come up to Yellowknife and fly
for him. I turned him down, of course, but then he
started calling. "Don, you've got to come up and fly for
me," he would say. And I would tell him right back, "Oh,
no I don't!"

Max told me he had quit the flying business in 1949
after a series of mishaps and complications that would
be hard to duplicate. He and his family moved south to
Lethbridge, Alberta, where Max started building homes
for a living. But he missed flying and returned to Yellowknife in 1951 to start another charter service. It took
him nearly two years, if you can imagine that, to get
through all the government red tape and obtain a license to operate. But by June of 1953 Max was back in

business, flying a brand new de Havilland Otter with the name "Wardair" painted on the sides.

The Otter was de Havilland's new short take-off and landing, or S.T.O.L., aircraft that would become the workhorse of the North Country. Although the Otter first flew in late 1951, production didn't begin for a year and Max ended up purchasing the number five Otter off de Havilland's assembly line in Toronto where he had bought that old Fox Moth seven years earlier.

Max told me again and again how the Otter was so superior to everything else. And he had the very first one in western Canada, with greater range, speed and carrying capacity than other S.T.O.L. aircraft in the North. Max had the whole thing by the tail. He was set to make money like crazy as long as there was a lot of flying. And there was a lot of flying then.

Business was so good, in fact, that Max bought a second aircraft in the summer of 1954, a new de Havilland Beaver with a 450-hp Pratt & Whitney Wasp Junior nine-cylinder engine. Although smaller than the Otter, it was cheaper to fly and also had excellent S.T.O.L. capabilities. The Beaver was perfect for shorter hauls, and Max's Wardair Limited continued to grow to the point where he was thinking about acquiring a third aircraft — another Otter — when he started asking me to fly for him in late 1954.

Max can be a very persistent fellow, and finally I told Marie, "You know, I really should go back to flying." I remember she made some remark about my illness and said, "You go ahead and do whatever you want for the rest of your life because you're just living on borrowed time, anyway." Poor Marie. Going back north was the very last thing she wanted in life. But she was willing to go along if that's what I wanted. Actually, when I thought about it, we didn't have much choice. I was out of the chicken business and I didn't know what else to do.

In the spring of 1955 I told Max to buy the Otter, I was coming up to fly for him — if I could get my pilot's

license back. I had developed a premature heart beat from
the spinal meningitis, although it would tend to disappear with exercise. Otherwise my health was generally
good. After some tests at a heart clinic in Winnipeg, I
checked out okay and went on to Yellowknife ready to fly
for Max and Wardair with my license approved.

In the meantime, the job of packing up everything back
on the farm in preparation for our return to Yellowknife
fell on Marie. The idea was for me to familiarize myself
with the Wardair operation for a month or so, then return
to St. Cloud in late May or early June and bring the
family north.

No sooner had I stepped off the Edmonton Mainliner
flight in Yellowknife than I bumped into Max who was
about to board the same aircraft on a flight out. Max
said he wanted me to get checked out in the Otter first
thing and that his only other pilot, Abe Dyck, had promised he would check me out in the morning before leaving Wardair. Yes, Abe was quitting. (Just as Max's other
pilot, Harry Taylor, had done the day before, I later
found out.) Max told me a few things about the Otter,
said it was good of me to come, and then he was gone.

Well, the next morning I showed up at the small
Wardair office on Back Bay and said to Abe, "I understand
you're going to check me out in the Otter." He said, "Oh,
no I'm not. I'm leaving and that's it."

"Well, you could just give me a circuit in the air for a
few minutes," I pleaded. "Nope," Abe replied as he threw
together his belongings, "my flight is due out in just a
bit and I'm not taking time to check you out. Period. End
of conversation."

Here I was, stuck with a brand new short take-off and
landing aircraft which I had no concept of at the time. I
thought, well, if this Abe fellow wasn't going to check me
out I'll just have to read the manual and try it myself,
just as I had done so many times at old Harlem Field
nearly 20 years earlier.

Max had told me during our brief encounter at the Yellowknife airport that the one thing I would notice about the Otter is that it would come off the water at a pretty flat attitude.

"Remember, don't pull the nose up like you would, normally do," Max cautioned. "As soon as you're off the water, it'll start to rise and you just keep shoving that nose down until it's down about six or seven degrees. Then you'll go up just like an elevator," he said, running to catch his plane.

Gee, I thought, that's really dumb.

I went down to the dock where Max's beautiful Wardair Otter, CF-GBY, was parked. After reading the manual I fired up the Pratt & Whitney 1340 radial and taxied out onto the bay. The wind was coming from the direction of town, so I swung the Otter around and started my take-off run heading right for Yellowknife.

When I got off the water I instinctively held the Otter at a normal attitude, expecting it to climb. Instead, that darn airplane stayed just a few feet above the water as it rapidly approached Yellowknife. It wouldn't gain speed and it wouldn't gain altitude. Damn, I finally thought, Max said to push the nose down. So I eased the nose down and up went the Otter. Up to beat hell, just like an elevator! Within seconds, and with not much room to spare, I was several hundred feet above Yellowknife in absolute amazement.

Never in all my flying had I ever experienced such lift on take-off. The Otter was designed with so much flap that it totally changed the wing configuration. Instead of the wing being in line with the fuselage, the entire back half of the wing went down in sections until you had about 60 degrees of built-in flap plus the ailerons were capable of going down 26 degrees. In other words, the whole trailing edge of the wing was like a huge controlled flap.

With so much flap and resulting drag, the trick was to put the nose down once you were airborne in order to

reduce the drag and maximize lift. And when I came in
to land on Back Bay, I found the increased flaps allowed me to bring this remarkable aircraft in soft as a
feather at about 55 miles per hour on a very short approach. After just one flight it was clear to me you
could drop the Otter into the smallest places and not
worry a bit about whether you could get off again.

If ever there was a perfect aircraft for the North, the
Otter was it. I could now appreciate why Max had cho-
sen it as the main workhorse for his growing fleet, and
I had to admire him for it.

I spent the next few weeks familiarizing myself with
the Otter, the Beaver and Max's operation while his
wife, Marjorie, was kindly arranging for housing for my
family. In late May I returned to St. Cloud for Marie
and the boys.

We had an old station wagon, a 1949 or 1950 Frazer,
and a trailer piled high with furniture and all manner
of personal belongings securely tied with a generous
length of clothesline. Mom and Dad and Jim and several of my sisters and other nearby relatives had gathered at the farm to give us a proper send-off. I remember waving goodbye and watching the farmhouse grow
smaller in the side mirror as we headed down the road,
all the time wondering if we were doing the right thing.

I must admit that setting out for a life in the North
Country at the age of 42 with two small boys and a wife
who was less than enthusiastic about the idea was not
done without some second or even third thoughts. But
I worked hard at convincing myself everything would
work out and it would be a good experience for all of us.

Our drive to Edmonton was uneventful, but the
roads north of Edmonton in late May of 1955 were in
nearly the same condition that had earlier caused me
to quit the trucking business. It had been raining and
the bottoms were going out of the roads. We got as far
as the south side of Lesser Slave Lake, not too far from

where my brother Jim had rescued me from the gumbo before, when we came upon a line of bogged-down cars and trucks about two miles long.

It was a real mess, and now we had become part of it. No one could move or even turn around to go back. We were told there were a couple of big semi-trailer trucks stuck in the middle of the road at the front of the lineup and that there was no way to get around them even if we could move. So we just sat there all afternoon and into the evening waiting for the highway department people to come along and either firm up the road or pull all of us through. When the rain would let up we'd get out and wander around in the slop visiting with folks to help pass the time.

An ice cream truck several hundred yards ahead of us was running out of fuel for its refrigeration unit by early evening so the driver started handing out ice cream. Christopher and Charles were in ice cream heaven. In fact, everybody ended up having their fill of ice cream up and down the road for as far as you could see.

That night we slept in the old Frazer. Luckily the rear seat folded down and made a perfect bed for the boys. Marie and I had to settle for cat naps on the bench seats. In the morning, with still no sign of help and all of us quite hungry, I decided to walk ahead to the town of Kinuso and buy a frying pan and some bacon and eggs and other food so we could have something to eat. Any pots and pans we brought along were in boxes buried somewhere in the trailer and I wasn't about to unpack everything in the gumbo.

A railroad track paralleled the road about a hundred yards over, so I sloshed through knee-deep water in the drainage ditch along the road and made my way over to it. The walk along the track gave me a bird's eye view of the awful mess we were in, but I also noticed how every-one seemed to be coping with it in their own way — mostly visiting, reading, sleeping or playing games. I walked about three miles to town and returned with my

packsack filled with a tin frying pan, some dishes and
food enough for a couple of days if we stretched it. The
water in the ditch looked decent enough and we figured
it would be safe to drink if we boiled it, which we did.

As we prepared our meal over a small fire, people
drifted by to visit and it became apparent some had a
little food, sandwiches and the like, but many of them
apparently didn't have anything. Of course, they didn't
make much of an effort to get anything, either. Maybe
they figured somebody would come along and rescue
them within the hour. But having driven these roads
before, I wasn't too sure when we were going to get help.

On the third day help finally arrived in the form of big
D-6 Cats. The highway department people apparently
decided they couldn't move the trucks at the head of the
line so they just left them. They towed a few cars around
the trucks but the road started to get so bad they
couldn't do that any more. The Cats didn't sink but the
cars just kind of dragged along until the Cats pulled the
front ends off several of them.

They bulldozed the side of the roadway but that didn't
last long either. After dragging 20 or 30 cars through it
was impossible to drag any others. We were one of the
last and I thought they'd pull the old Frazer in half with
that damn trailer behind it, but somehow it all held
together.

Once we got to the other side, everything was so caked
full of mud the wheels wouldn't turn, so we had to pry the
gumbo loose and clean everything off before continuing.

Our destination was Hay River on the south shore of
Great Slave Lake, about 800 miles north of Edmonton.
From there we would barge the car and trailer the remaining 120 miles across the lake to Yellowknife since,
at that time, there was no road. As we continued north
toward Hay River, the road got better because parts of it
were still frozen and the surface was firm, but I couldn't
help feel our being stuck in the mud for nearly three

days was just an early warning sign that we were not going to have the easiest time living in the North and trying to raise two small children.

At Hay River I made arrangements with Northern Transportation to take the car and trailer over to Yellowknife by barge when the ice went out on the big lake in early June. Max picked us up in the Otter and we flew into Yellowknife with a few bags of clothing and some items for the kitchen.

The Baptist church in town was between ministers, and being a good Baptist, Margie Ward had arranged for us to live temporarily in the parsonage. Fortunately it was furnished and we were able to move in immediately without staying in the hotel for a time. But it was hard settling into a strange place knowing we'd be there only a short while until the minister came in and then we'd be out. We expected our car and trailer would be sent over on the first barge in a week or 10 days, but we ended up waiting over a month for our belongings.

I should have known better. The first barge of the season was always the "beer barge," with a payload of beer and liquor to resupply Yellowknife after another long, dark winter of heavy drinking. The date of the barge's arrival was always the subject of great speculation, betting pools and wagers. The barges that followed were loaded with an assortment of bulk freight that was obviously more important than my poor old Frazer and the trailer I hoped would still be attached to it.

Marie had heard stories about the spring storms that could come out of nowhere and sweep across Great Slave Lake, sinking not only barges but the tugboats that pushed and pulled them, and she became increasingly concerned about our modest belongings with each passing week.

Many years earlier, stern-wheel paddleboats operated by the Hudson's Bay Company were used to supply Yellowknife and other outposts along the big lake. When

Northern Transportation took over, they used deeper draft tugboats to push barges with payloads much greater than the old sternwheelers could carry. When the weather turned foul the tugs would string the barges out and tow them by releasing one barge at a time from the front, then attaching them to the rear of the tug with a 75-foot hawser. Each barge would be strung out further and further so they wouldn't pile up and crash into each other when the lake was really rough.

The shallow areas of the lake were the worst. Sometimes it was so rough they'd cut all the barges loose to save the tug. The tugs were very low in the stern, especially when pulling a string of barges, and they would quickly take on water and go down unless they cut the barges loose and kept running into the wind. Even then a number of tugs were lost.

Much to Marie's relief, and mine, too, our car and trailer arrived without incident in early July. Marie could finally set up housekeeping in a proper manner, although being a good Catholic she was anxious to find a place of our own instead of using a Baptist parsonage. Our trip north and first month in Yellowknife living in temporary quarters with few personal belongings had been hard on Marie. As a matter of fact, I'm surprised she even put up with either the trip or the parsonage, let alone both.

I told her many times that first month in Yellowknife that things would get better. But I was beginning to have some doubts.

CHAPTER SEVEN

LIFE WITH MAX IN YELLOWKNIFE

*"On a still evening, down on a frozen lake in
the North Country with the temperature well
below zero, you can hear an airplane 12 or
even 15 miles away. As soon as Max heard the
Otter he threw a match on his huge woodpile.
He had doused it with fuel and the pile exploded into what surely was one of the biggest
signal fires ever seen in the North."*

For most of the month of June 1955, Max and I were
Wardair's only pilots. I guess that made me Max's chief
pilot, a position I held with Wardair until my retirement
in 1969.

The second Otter, CF-IFP, arrived that June and I flew
it for the first time on June 18. With the Wardair fleet
now at three aircraft — two Otters and a Beaver — Max
quickly hired another pilot. That brought the Wardair
staff up to six, including a helper, a bookkeeper and a
licensed aircraft maintenance engineer named Johnny
Dapp who was our mechanic.

That first summer in Yellowknife we were in the midst
of a uranium rush and most of our work was close in,
usually within 100 miles of town. We worked from sunrise to sunset, seven days a week, and that meant 14- to
16-hour days at that time of year so far north as we were.
Wardair serviced a number of mines, but two of them
provided most of our business: a uranium mine at Rayrock
that was just opening up about 100 miles out and Consolidated Discovery Gold Mines about 50 miles out.

Max had developed a close friendship with the Byrne
brothers, Jerry and Norm, who owned and operated the

Discovery Mines. They had even helped Max finance the purchase of his first Otter in 1953 and since then Wardair had done a steady business with them under contract. Max prized such contracts because they could be counted on to pay the bills and meet the payroll. Business was so good, in fact, that Max built a two-story maintenance building that summer to serve as Wardair's headquarters. With a shop and small office it was the envy of all the other flying services along the shore of Back Bay.

The work was tough and I remember we spent more time on the ground loading and unloading than we did flying. We hauled heavy equipment, 16-foot mine timbers, propane tanks, barrels of fuel oil and gasoline, fresh food and Lord knows what else. I would help get everything aboard, fly 60 or 80 miles, unload, then fly back for another load of more of the same. The pace kept up like that for most of the summer, although with plenty of daylight hours available Max was always happy to schedule a charter flight or special trip if it could be worked in without interfering with the schedule of his regular customers. It meant extra income and, for pilots like myself, a break from the monotony of the daily routine.

While I was busy loading and unloading and doing a little flying in between, Marie was determined to find a house of our own so we didn't have to stay in the Baptist parsonage any longer than necessary. About the time we received word a minister would be arriving in early fall, Marie set her sights on the next best thing to a real house — a large bunkhouse that had been moved by truck from the Negus Mine to Yellowknife. It had been used as a house by the family selling it, but it still looked like a bunkhouse. It would take a considerable amount of work to make it a real home. The house had an old pot-type oil furnace with ducts into each room and, like most housing in Yellowknife in 1955, indoor plumbing.

Providing sewer and water in the northern latitudes is no small feat. In Yellowknife they did it by laying the water pipes alongside the sewer pipe and then heating the water to about 34 degrees at the pumping station down at the lake. The water would circulate throughout town and return to the station. If it started to come back at less than 32 degrees, they turned up the heat; otherwise the whole system would freeze up because the ground under Yellowknife was frozen solid all year around, except maybe for a foot or two in summer.

The house was 24 feet by 35 feet with two 12-foot-square rooms on each end and a large common room in the middle with a washroom across the back. I took out a wall between the common room and one of the 12-foot-square rooms to make a living room and dining area. Next, I divided the washroom in half, making one side into a bathroom and the other into a very small kitchen. The three remaining 12-foot-square rooms became the bedrooms. We lived in the old converted bunkhouse during all of our years in Yellowknife and gradually added on to it and improved things until it became quite a nice home.

Our house was located in the New Town section of Yellowknife high above Back Bay on a broad expanse of rock plateau. When I flew into Yellowknife for the very first time back in 1947, New Town didn't even exist.

Yellowknife in those days was a sorry looking conglomeration of ramshackle frame buildings and houses built on the mud flats of Back Bay beneath a massive stone outcropping called The Rock, which Max described as "the spiritual centre of town," in his wonderful book, *The Max Ward Story*. It was a real mining town with a few dirt roads, telephone poles everywhere and packs of dogs on every corner. It included several cafes, government offices, the Yellowknife Hotel, a number of charter air services, the Government Dock and an assortment of shops and homes, many with rooms to rent.

This was the original Yellowknife, and it stretched out to a point that gives way to Latham Island where the town's Indian population still lives. In the summer, with all the geologists and prospectors arriving, the old Yellowknife would just about double in population to around 3,000. There were poker games around the clock, although gambling was prohibited, and the stakes were often very high. The section of Yellowknife along the mud flats became known as Old Town, and it presented quite a contrast in 1955 to the New Town development of modern rambler-style homes and office buildings quickly going up atop The Rock.

During the 1930s and '40s, the year-around population of Yellowknife was mostly prospectors and mining people drawn north by the lure of gold. And, of course, there were the bush pilots that everyone in the North depended on for transportation and supplies. The Northwest Territories along with the Yukon Territory were basically run out of Ottawa. Yellowknife elected its first mayor in 1953 and in 1967 it became the official capital of the Northwest Territories. In 1969 the federal government transferred its administrative responsibilities for the Territories to the territorial government in Yellowknife. And in 1970, Yellowknife became the first incorporated city in the Northwest Territories.

The growth of government and the mining industry more than doubled the population of Yellowknife between 1955 and 1990. The population in 1955 was around 5,000 souls with the peak summer migration of prospectors and mining people, but with New Town expanding each summer there were nearly 12,000 year-around citizens by 1990.

In the 1950s the Northwest Territories remained one of Canada's last undeveloped frontiers with a population of approximately 12,000 Inuit, 7,000 Indians and 10,000 whites. The continued development of the Territories' vast mining, oil and gas reserves helped to increase the population to about 52,000 by 1990.

The Northwest Territories is a huge region covering about a third of all Canada and containing approximately 10 percent of the world's fresh water. The Territories stretches from the northern borders of the Canadian provinces along the 60th Parallel to within 500 miles of the North Pole, and from its border with the Yukon Territory on the west all the way east to Baffin Bay near the west coast of Greenland.

The Territories is divided into three very distinct geographical regions:

The District of Mackenzie covers the western third, from its border with the Yukon Territory on the west to the rocky plateau of the Canadian Shield to the east. The district in the west includes the Mackenzie and Franklin mountain ranges and the gas- and petroleum-rich Mackenzie River Valley that runs between them for some 2,600 miles. The endless forests of the west begin to thin to the east where the district's two great lakes, Great Bear and Great Slave, are located and where the Territories' great mineral deposits are concentrated. The district is the most populated of the three, with Yellowknife, Fort Smith, Hay River, Inuvik and most of the Territories' other major settlements within it. Virtually all of the Indian and most of the white population live in the District of Mackenzie.

The District of Keewatin is known as the Barren Lands, or simply, the barrens. It lies east of the District of Mackenzie and is a mostly desolate, flat expanse of the Canadian Shield rock formation with small bushes, stunted trees and a carpeting of tundra. The district extends east to Hudson Bay and beyond to the province of Quebec and the Labrador Sea. Most of the Territories' Inuit people live in the Keewatin district, fishing and hunting out of villages around the shores of Hudson Bay, on Baffin Island and some of the southern Arctic islands.

The District of Franklin sits atop the other two districts and includes the most northern Canadian peninsulas, Boothia and Melville, and all the Canadian Arctic islands. The largest of the islands are Ellesmere, the tenth largest island in the world, and Baffin, both with spectacular mountain ranges. The United States Range on Ellesmere peaks at 8,200 feet above sea level and looms over Canada's most northern outpost of civilization, tiny Alert, only 480 miles from the North Pole. Other large islands include Victoria and Banks to the west. The entire region is known as the High Arctic and has an average July temperature of below 50 degrees. There is very little vegetation and the population consists of a few Inuit settlements to the south and several government outposts — mostly weather and radio stations — on a few of the Arctic islands.

My purpose in giving you a geography lesson at this point in my story is to help you understand and appreciate some of the adventures I experienced as a bush pilot for Wardair which I'll be talking about in the next several chapters.

I remember my first relatively long trip for Wardair. It was in the fall of 1955 when we were taking teachers back to their respective villages mostly along the rugged Mackenzie River valley as far north as Fort McPherson and Arctic Red River near the Arctic coast. I remember the trip also because it was my first experience with putting holes in the floats of my aircraft.

I left Yellowknife in the Otter with eight teachers and all of their baggage. Our first stop was at Wrigley, about 300 miles west of Yellowknife. After dropping off one of the teachers we proceeded a few miles north to Fort Norman, but by the time we arrived it was getting late and I decided we would stay overnight there. I came in against a fairly strong wind and, of course, the river was always a little awkward to land on because it ran quite fast. Once down, however, things got even trickier. With these conditions I couldn't come forward into shore, but instead had to line up out on the river, cut the engine, lower the flaps and hope the wind and current would carry the Otter backwards onto shore.

The spot we used along the river to dock the aircraft at Fort Norman was the same place used to unload river barges. It wasn't a dock or anything like that, just a place along the shoreline where they had cleared away the rocks. Unfortunately, one of the barges had dropped a sharp piece of metal just below the surface. As I came in, the Otter was bobbing up and down from the wind and we apparently went diagonally across the piece of metal. I didn't know it had put three holes in my right float at the time, of course, but I did feel the float strike something and I made a mental note to check it later.

Once the passengers were off, I fired up the Otter and started to taxi a quarter mile down river to the mouth of Bear River where I could moor the aircraft overnight in a more protected area. On the way over I found the float was taking on a great deal of water so I decided to head for a little lake about a half mile away where I could pull the tail end of the float up and check it out.

There was absolutely no way to get back and forth between the little lake and Fort Norman because it was all bog and swamp. If it had been winter they could have sent a dog sled over to fetch me or help with repairs, but this time of year I would have to handle the situation alone.

I took the cover off the float and discovered three large holes in the rear half. Well, there was no way we could continue the trip until the damage was repaired, and the holes were too darn big to fix on the spot. If they had been smaller, about the size of your finger, it might have been possible to reach under and put a bolt with a washer through the hole for a temporary fix. My only alternative was to return to Yellowknife for repairs, so I put the cover back on the float and radioed Fort Norman to let the teachers know of my decision and that I would return as soon as possible.

The idea of returning to Yellowknife obviously was based on the assumption I could get the Otter airborne despite the weight and drag of a considerable amount of water in my right float. After carefully examining the size of the holes, I felt it would be possible if I warmed up the engine right on shore with the float in only a couple of inches of water and then took off in as short a distance as possible. If the holes had been larger, take-off would have been impossible unless a couple of large inner tubes happened to be handy. They can be placed inside the float and pumped up to displace enough water for take-off.

The float dragged like crazy, but I was able to get the Otter off the water. The lights along the docks of Back Bay were a welcome sight four hours later as I brought the Otter in for landing as close to our ramp as I could manage. Quickly, I pulled the aircraft up on the ramp so it wouldn't take on any more water and possibly sink. It was bad enough bringing that beautiful aircraft back with three holes in it! We had a couple of mechanics and they started repairs first thing in the morning. I was on my way back to Fort Norman by early afternoon to pick up the teachers and continue the trip, which was now going to be a four-day charter instead of two and a half days, as scheduled. And the extra 800 miles to Yellowknife and back made it a 2,200-mile excursion, which is a long way at 105 or 110 mph.

The summer and fall of 1955 I flew both the Otter and its smaller de Havilland cousin, the Beaver, and I learned to appreciate the Otter not only for its extraordinary S.T.O.L. capabilities but also for its ability to carry unusual loads on the floats as well as inside the aircraft.

There is no question the Otter was the best airplane for carrying external loads. Many times I carried canoes or large tires for earth-moving equipment strapped onto the floats of the Beaver or even the old Norseman, but it was always a struggle. On the Otter, however, we carried everything from 26-foot freighter canoes to the entire wing of a Cessna 180. I even strapped an old, heavy upright piano atop one of the floats and flew it to Lac La Martre, about 120 miles northwest of Yellowknife. One of the teachers couldn't bear to be without her piano so we were hired to fly it in for her.

The mining operations required plenty of 20-foot sections of pipe, so I fabricated a couple of racks and bolted them to the floats of the Otter, one on each end. It worked like a charm. The Otter could easily carry two 16-foot canoes, one on each side, strapped against the float support structure. Eventually I made covers for the canoes to cut down on drag. The big freighter canoe was a different story. It was so broad that you couldn't tie it forward under the wing strut. Instead, we would tie it back a bit and brace it away from the rear strut. In order to carry the Cessna wing we made a couple of racks that fit up against the fuselage, carefully placed the wing in the racks, then tied rope around both the Otter and the wing just behind the cockpit doors. We removed one rear door and placed a well padded two-by-four inside the fuselage to support the aft part of the wing outside of the cabin. Yes, the Otter was really a wonderful aircraft for carrying outside loads. About anything you could lash on you could carry.

The competition for business was always keen between the half-dozen or so flight services operating out of Yellowknife in those days and enterprise in delivering payloads would help give Wardair an edge over the others in the years ahead.

Associated Airways and, later, Northwest Territorial Airways were the largest competitors. Associated was headquartered at Edmonton and was run by a fellow named Tommy Fox. Max had worked a short time for Associated in 1949 and it was the only outfit that ever fired him. Our other competitors included Hank Koenen's small operation; another small outfit, Ptarmigan Airways, Ltd.; and a flying service operated by the McAvoy brothers, Chuck and Jimmy.

The McAvoys' dad had flown with Max before the two boys became interested in flying. Chuck McAvoy disappeared on a flight in the Barren Lands and they never found a trace of him. And the fellow who operated Ptarmigan, Ken Stockall, eventually disappeared in the Nahanni River country, which is notorious for swallowing up people. It's very wild country about 400 miles due west of Yellowknife where the Nahanni River descends southeast through rugged mountain valleys in twisting, turbulent and very narrow channels to join up with the Liard River. The loss of Ken was really sad. He had flown for Wardair at one time and was a highly respected pilot as well as a wonderful person.

During my years with Wardair we always flew pretty much by the book, although sometimes it was a fine line between being enterprising or being just plain stupid in the competition for business. Everyone bent or even broke the rules, of course, but the trick was to get away with it. It was illegal, for example, to haul dynamite and detonation caps on the same load but often there was no way to avoid this problem when delivering prospectors out in the bush. Instead, we'd pack the caps in the center of the prospectors' sleeping bags and handle the bags very gingerly as we loaded them aboard the aircraft and removed them after reaching our destination.

Most of the illegal loading, however, was overloading. Some outfits would load their aircraft until it just barely flew, which was completely illegal. There were a couple of operators on Back Bay that you could just about count on to never make it off the water on their first run. They would run up and down the bay until they burned off enough fuel to be able to get off. I saw a fellow come in one time with such an overload that he had to taxi over to their dock without a stop of any kind or he'd sink, which is just about what he did when he reached their dock.

For the most part, however, the Yellowknife pilots were a capable bunch of guys who enjoyed nothing more than swapping stories over drinks when they weren't off on a job. It was rare for me to find time to join them and Max was even busier and a bit of a loner besides.

Normally when winter set in most of the pilots would head south for a month or more since business would slow to a trickle, but the uranium rush of 1955 continued and business was good all winter long because people were going out and doing what we called "staking moose pasture." These fellows would go out in winter and stake the fringes of the choice property that had been staked during the summer when people could see what they were doing, just in case there might be some ore. Usually there wasn't, of course.

As winter approached I continued to work seven days a week, although I was home most evenings and thankful for that. Everything seemed to be going well except for our engineer. I didn't trust his work and told Max a couple of times that he was not doing our outfit any good. I would take an aircraft out and the whole side of the exhaust would fall off. So I'd wire it back together and bring it home, which is why Max used to say I could take a damaged airplane out and bring it home like new. Max finally saw the light and we got another engineer. As I told Max, it wasn't so much the bull as it was the danger such a mechanic could be to all of us who had to fly the aircraft he supposedly worked on.

The work of a bush pilot is frequently dangerous, but the idea is to try and minimize the danger as much as possible. The first cardinal rule is to properly maintain your aircraft. I was always a stickler for that and often did my own work or insisted on checking out the work of others if it was an aircraft I was to pilot. Maybe that's why I was never injured and experienced only one really rough landing in over half a century of flying.

Max, on the other hand, had a number of close calls that he never even told me about in all the years we worked together. I had to read his book to find out about them, like the time he was teaching formation flying in the old Ansons during the war years and a student pilot flew right into Max's aircraft. He punched his right wing through Max's left rear fuselage and, of course, the wing broke off in no time and the plane fell away. The fabric covering the fuselage of Max's Anson came loose and trailed over the tailplane. Max could just barely maintain control, but somehow he managed to get down safely.

A few years later, when Max was flying his old Fox Moth
out of Yellowknife while I was up on the Snare River
project, he burned up an engine on the very same aircraft he had busted up in Kenora just a few months earlier. Apparently the valve on the bottom of the oil tank
was accidentally opened by a dock hand preparing to
push away the Fox Moth. The oil tank was bone dry by
the time Max was over Spud Arsenault Lake so he shut
down his sputtering engine and brought the aircraft in
safely on a small stretch of open water. Max found a
mining camp four miles away and spent the next week in
bitter cold walking out to work on the Fox Moth each
morning and walking back to camp in the evening. He
eventually replaced the engine on the spot and flew his
aircraft out.

Still another time Max found himself in trouble was in
1951 on a flight far north to Bathurst Inlet. It was November, which is always a terrible month for flying in the
Arctic, and Max was at the controls of a Bellanca Sky-
rocket. He was running out of daylight and gas at the
same time, and neither his compass nor gyro was working. Max and his mechanic opened the side windows and
began searching for the outline of a lake to put down on.
As he approached an unfamiliar lake, Max took off one
side of the undercarriage on a rock ledge. A couple of feet
lower and it would have been over. Once again Max managed to get down safely despite the damage. He was able
to get somebody in to help repair the Bellanca and then
he flew it out.

Then there was the time Max damn near killed himself
when he crashed the Beaver against a rock slope and I
came upon Max and the wreckage seven hours later. I
felt so guilty I could hardly even go and see him in the
hospital.

When I went to work for Max in 1955 I knew he was a
real slugger, so one of my last verbal agreements with
him concerned time off. "There's just one other thing," I
told him. "I get one day a week off and I'd like to have it

on Sunday so I can go to church and at least spend a little time with my family."

"Sure thing," he promised, and then I worked from May until November without a single day off. I'd mention it to him every once in a while, but he would talk about just getting started in the business and with only six people and three airplanes in the company we needed to keep flying.

During this time Marie and the boys were slowly getting used to living without Dad in a small town way up in the North Country with no chance of getting away from Yellowknife even on weekends because there were no roads out except to the nearby mines. I saw my family for breakfast some mornings and that was about it. Often I had breakfast so early that the boys wouldn't be up and they would be in bed by the time I got back at night.

In November, when things began to slow down a little and the days became very short, I finally decided it was time to enforce this day off business. I remember it was early on a Saturday evening and I was preparing to go home when Max told me we had a power line patrol in the Beaver scheduled first thing in the morning.

"Well, you might have one booked but I'm not going because you promised me a day off a week when I came to work for you," I said in a rather firm tone. "I haven't had a day off since I came here in May and tomorrow morning I'm going to church with my family and then I'm going to have, well, maybe part of the day with them at least." I could feel my resolve weakening ever so slightly.

Max didn't blink an eye and said he would take the power line patrol to Snare Hydro but that there was also a flight scheduled for noon in the Otter and somebody had to take that. "Okay," I said. "Half a day is better than nothing." Of course, I didn't believe that for a minute and deep down inside I was as angry with myself as I was with Max.

The Beaver had a very erratic fuel indicator, and when Max and a spotter, Frank Thorpe of Northern Power Company, took off at eight o'clock the next morning the gauge was indicating a full main tank. Max had filled the tank the night before so he didn't dip his tank before taking off just to make sure. If he had, Max would have discovered the main tank was all but empty.

We had an external belly tank on the Beaver at the time and it was connected to the main tank by what they call a non-return valve. You could fill the main tank and it wasn't supposed to drain into the belly tank, but you had to use a small electric pump if you wanted to get fuel from the belly tank up into the main tank. The non-return valve apparently had a little ice or piece of something in it because during the night practically all the fuel drained out of the main tank and into the belly tank although the fuel gauge was showing a full tank.

Max had flown about 20 miles and was following the power line at an altitude of about 50 feet when the old nine-cylinder Wasp Junior radial suddenly quit on him. Flying at such a low altitude didn't give Max much time to react, but he knew he was over a small swamp with a lake extending from it. It's instinctive for a pilot to turn to the left in this situation so you can see where you're going relative to the ground and the landing conditions awaiting you.

As Max swung the Beaver around, the left wing clipped some trees and then slammed against a ridge of solid rock. The wing snapped off, sending the body of the aircraft sliding like a toboggan down a rugged slope of rock and trees toward the frozen lake below.

Luckily Max had hit the downslope at an angle, dissipating the impact, but now the Beaver was hurtling down the slope on its left side with enough force to snap trees off and bend the engine back. The door on the left side of the cabin was torn off by the sharp rocks, exposing Max's head and left arm to the rock and stumps rushing by.

The poor old Beaver finally came to a rest at the bottom of the slope, on the edge of the lake. Max's head had taken a terrible beating and he had several broken ribs. But he somehow managed to free himself from the wreckage and then help Frank out. Frank, who was dying of cancer, had suffered a broken hip. He passed away a couple of months later from the cancer.

Somehow Max was able to get the floorboard and a couple of sleeping robes out of the aircraft so he could make Frank as comfortable as possible under the circumstances. We used three-eighths inch plywood floorboards to protect the soft honeycombed aluminum floor of the Beaver from damage when hauling heavy equipment or fuel drums. Once he had Frank stretched out on the floorboards in a sleeping robe, Max started gathering all the dead wood he could find for a rescue fire. He kept at it until he had a pile of wood about 100 yards out on the lake that was maybe eight feet high. But he didn't set it off immediately.

No, Max knew my noon flight in the Otter would take me out in the same general direction as the power line so he would wait until he heard me coming before setting the fire.

Back at Yellowknife, meantime, I had gone to church with Marie and the boys and then we enjoyed a big family breakfast together. I was happy to have at least half a day off. When I got down to the office to get ready for my noon trip, I noted the Beaver was still out and nobody seemed to know where it was. The power line patrol would normally take two and a half or maybe three hours at the most and here it was almost noon.

I called the people out at Snare Hydro on the phone line that ran alongside the power line and was told the Beaver had never arrived.

Well, I thought, he's had engine trouble and no doubt he's down somewhere cooling his heels on some frozen lake. Then I started gloating about it, figuring it prob-

ably served him right for keeping me working every day.
I never thought he could be hurt. It just never entered
my mind. I had my job to do in the Otter and, frankly, I
wasn't in any hurry to pick him up anyhow because he
had really annoyed me. Imagine, no day off for over half
a year and then he gives me barely half a day. Big deal.
Yup, I would let him sit on the ice for a few hours and
pick him up on the way back.

My run in the Otter took me to a point about 20 miles
south of Snare Hydro, and when I finished there I went
up to Snare but they still hadn't seen any sign of Max
and the Beaver. Now I was starting to worry a bit. By
this time it was almost three o'clock and in late November it starts getting dark about then. I climbed back into
the Otter and decided to follow the power line back east
to Yellowknife.

On a still evening, down on a frozen lake in the North
Country with the temperature well below zero, you can
hear an airplane 12 or even 15 miles away. As soon as
Max heard the Otter he threw a match on his huge
woodpile. He had doused it with fuel and the pile exploded into what surely was one of the biggest signal
fires ever seen in the North.

By now it was getting dark and I was only 30 miles or
so out of Yellowknife and beginning to wonder if I'd
missed Max somewhere when all of a sudden this great
big signal fire exploded in front of me 10 or 15 miles out.
What in the hell is going on here, I thought, and immediately headed for it.

I found Max all covered with blood on one side and
walking around his signal fire. How he managed to drag
so much deadwood out onto the lake with broken ribs
and a concussion, I'll never know. The fire burned hard
with great, tall flames throwing showers of sparks into the
twilight sky. I didn't even see the Beaver on the edge of the
lake partially in the trees. Thank goodness Max was able
to make a signal fire or I never would have spotted him.

Max and poor Frank were really glad to see me, but honestly, I felt so damn guilty. Here I'd let them lie from around eight-thirty in the morning until four o'clock in the afternoon. We had a nice little hospital in Yellow-knife and a wonderful old doctor, Doc Stanton, who was made for the North Country. He was the best. Doc made Max stay in the hospital for a week on account of his concussion and to see what they could do for his ribs. Within a few days, however, Max was able to start mov-ing around and he had no bad effects from his head injuries. In fact, he didn't even get the headache he so rightly deserved!

Actually, it was all I could do to visit Max or talk to him or even look at him. I was feeling so guilty, and rightly so. What a gosh darn awful thing for me to do to a friend, let alone my boss. He should have been dead, no two ways about it, hanging out the side like that with all those stumps and rocks going by. It was a miracle he wasn't killed.

During that first winter Marie and I had a chance to get acquainted with the rest of the population of Yellow-knife since parties were about the only form of enter-tainment available and there were always a number of them each weekend. Winter was the only time the basic population of Yellowknife returned to normal, just under a couple of thousand people back then. When spring came we started to speed up again and soon things were going like crazy. Max purchased a third Otter, which meant another pilot and a little more support staff. We gradually grew in this manner from year to year.

One of my favorite aircraft in those early years with Wardair was a beautiful old Supermarine-built Stranraer amphibian that we used when the ice went out. It was a big all-metal biplane with twin tailfins and a pair of 875-hp Bristol Pegasus X radials mounted on the top wing high above the cabin. The Stranraer had been around since the late 1930s but it never failed to draw a crowd whenever it pulled up to the docks of Back Bay.

Most of the year, however, I spent my time in the Otter getting better acquainted with the North Country and especially the Barren Lands those first few years with Max. You had to learn the country, to recognize its features, because maps were almost useless and all of our flying was visual. I learned to recognize certain lakes and river valleys, the lakes by their shape and the river valleys by the way the tree line would run much farther north as it followed the waterway.

The Coppermine River probably took the tree line 150 miles north of where it normally was found. If you saw trees far north of where they should have been, you were no doubt over one of the large river valleys. Then you had to learn which valley by the way the trees ran along it, and by their size and shape and type.

That's why you never went up to Yellowknife to be a bush pilot and immediately started flying to the farthest point that Wardair went. You worked your way out gradually until you knew the country in all of its seasons and moods and beauty.

CHAPTER EIGHT

ICE ROADS IN THE BARREN LANDS

"Characters like John Denison were what made the North Country such a great place despite all the hardships. Most folks in the North were just content to survive, but people like Denison and the other characters I knew actually thrived in this land. They wouldn't have it any other way."

It really used to annoy me when I would fly over the Barren Lands and people would sit in the back of the airplane and read a book while all that beautiful country was going by. I suspect it's a beauty that can only be appreciated after you've learned to cope with the country and begin to see that it's not barren at all.

Similar to the tundra landforms of Siberia and northern Europe, the barrens is basically a thick mat of peat moss and lichen resting atop the Canadian Shield and hundreds of feet of permanently frozen ground, or permafrost. The barrens covers most of central and eastern Northwest Territories, generally above the 65th Parallel which lies about 100 miles south of the Arctic Circle. It is virtually treeless.

During midsummer, however, when the sun is visible for nearly 20 hours and the top six to 10 inches of permafrost has melted, the barrens explodes into color as tiny flowers carpet the landscape as far as the eye can see. The colors run from white to various hues of purple, orange and yellow. There are no reds for some reason. As you go north the granite of the Canadian Shield becomes more exposed and the flowers grow in a million small patches. It amazes me how those little flowers can hang on and even thrive as far north as the High Arctic islands considering the brief summers and rugged terrain.

In winter the barrens is completely white and all but
featureless, except perhaps for an occasional column of
steam rising up through the snow and ice from a water-
fall or rapids on one of the rivers. On gray days you can't
tell where the lakes are or even the horizon. It makes
winter flying very interesting and keeps you on your toes
trying to find your way.

This was especially true before we had all the modern
navigation aids up in the North. The compass became
less and less reliable the farther north you flew due to the
influence of the North Magnetic Pole, and unless we were
using the astrocompass it was just a matter of trying to
navigate by visual flying. I would say almost 90 percent of
our Barren Lands flying was visual.

Fortunately, not all the barrens is flat. If you know the
country at all, you know the section you are in by the
types of hills and valleys that generally run north to the
sea. In most places as you approach the Arctic coast the
land becomes hilly and may gradually rise to a height of
800 or a thousand feet of sheer rock coastline. But in
those places where the barrens runs flat to the sea, it's
difficult in winter even to find the coastline because the
frozen straits between the mainland and the islands
looks much the same as the Barren Lands. The sea and
land blended into one white expanse without depth.
Some fellows flew off the coast and travelled a considerable distance over the sea ice before realizing what they
had done. And a few of them never made it back.

The southern barrens is known for its small evergreens
that grow in swamps, but the evergreens become even
smaller and fewer the farther north you go; likewise the
alder which grow to a height of 15 or 20 feet in the south
and were the only source of wood for the trappers and
prospectors. You find them growing along streams or in
front of a south-facing rock with water at the base of it.

The alder is really an amazing little tree because it has
adapted itself even to the harsh climate of the Arctic is-

lands where it grows flat along the ground and is a favorite food of the muskoxen.

There are so many lakes in the barrens that we never had to worry about finding a good landing spot in the summer, as long as the aircraft had floats. You were never more than a half-mile from a staking effort that there wasn't a lake. The tundra, of course, is completely saturated in summer from the melting of the permafrost and it's often difficult to walk on because there's water everywhere. Snowmobiles were the answer and the men would bring them along so they could zip across the soggy bog. Or they would have us bring in these vehicles with the big balloon tires on them so they could wander over the tundra at a more leisurely pace. And if it got to be a big operation then we would bring in what were known as tundra buggies in the early spring before the ice was going out. They were a track vehicle that was big enough to haul a fair amount of supplies across the tundra into the larger camps.

One of the most unusual but important features of the barrens landscape was created thousands of years ago when the glaciers receded, leaving ridges of sand and gravel deposits called eskers. These ridges of glacial debris can stretch for 50 miles or more, sometimes running north and south in fairly straight lines out on the main barrens. From the air these rows of eskers looked as if Paul Bunyan had drawn his fingers across the landscape. In other areas, however, the eskers were anything but straight. They would snake across the barrens in loops or arcs, frequently broken by gaps where glacial melt water flowed through at one time. These eskers probably were formed by water that flowed ahead of the glaciers when their retreat would slow or stop for a relatively short period of time, perhaps a thousand years or so.

The eskers were important to us not only for navigation, but also because with a little improvement they quite often made very good airstrips. Our airstrip out at

Tundra Mine, about 190 miles northeast of Yellowknife, was atop an esker that was 50 feet above the surrounding tundra and broad enough so there was little danger of going off one side or the other.

Despite all of its beauty and intrigue, the barrens remains in my mind one of the most inhospitable places on earth for man or beast. In the air survival was easy but on the ground you became easy pickings for good old Mother Nature at her very worst, winter or summer. In the summer the insects are so bad that animals as well as humans can be driven to such distraction that the end result is death. I often thought that if a person went down in the barrens it would be much better if it happened in the spring or fall because the winter has its harsh realities and the summer has its insects. Clouds of them.

It was unbelievable! There were days in the Barren Lands when you couldn't eat a sandwich outside the aircraft because it would get covered with the scourge of the barrens, the pesky mosquito. You had to have mosquito dope to survive. Of course you can have yourself all doped up, but you couldn't put dope on your sandwich. When you left your aircraft, you always made sure it was closed up tight so the mosquitoes wouldn't invade the only safe refuge you had from them.

Clouds of mosquitoes would begin forming even before the ice on the lakes had gone out in late spring. I'd fly in to some lake on a nice warm day and land the old Otter on the ice, taxi over towards shore and there would be a herd of mosquitoes coming out to greet us. Those spring mosquitoes were the really big ones. Later in the summer you'd get the little ones with the big bite.

The black flies were worse than the mosquitoes, however, because they took an even bigger bite out of you and you didn't even feel it until the next day. Some people were allergic to the black flies and I've seen men with their legs all puffed up like balloons. You would have to tuck your pants legs into your boots or put rubber bands around your pants legs, otherwise those darn flies would crawl right up your leg and bite you all over. They would get in your collar line and bite your neck or cover your wrists with red welts if you were foolish enough to leave them exposed. Even as few as a half-dozen fly bites would leave you feeling miserable.

The deer flies were bad, too. That's the fly that buzzes around your head and then hits you, takes out a chunk and is gone. You take a few slaps at it and usually you only hit yourself, although sometimes you get lucky.

Then there were the bulldogs. They're like the deer flies only twice as big and they would be in droves sometimes. Their main activity was always trying to figure out a way to get inside the aircraft, especially when I was sitting in it. They would hang on the windows in such numbers that it was difficult to see out. Our dope didn't work on the flies, only on the mosquitoes.

The three-inch dragonflies that populate the barrens like to eat mosquitoes and even black flies. But their very favorite meal is a bulldog, and I would sit in the aircraft and watch those dragonflies devour one bulldog after another like you never saw anything in your life. The bulldogs would be hanging on the windows trying to get in and not paying attention when, zap, the dragonflies would pick them off. Zap, and all that would be left were the wings falling off. Zap, zap, zap!

Except for the insects, and maybe because of them, you don't see much other wildlife in the open barrens with the exception of waterfowl and my favorite, the ptarmigan or Arctic grouse. The ptarmigan, like the Arctic fox and many other creatures of the North, turns completely white in the winter and then back again to the mottled brown in the summer. It's the only bird I know of that has developed this camouflage adaptation and it makes the ptarmigan very difficult if not impossible to spot on the ground. Unless the hen moves and you are able to spot her little yellow chicks following her through the tundra, the ptarmigan is able to conceal itself against a landscape that offers little in the way of thick cover.

There are basically two kinds of lakes in the barrens and the difference between them is most noticeable from the air. There are black lakes with muck bottoms where the water tends to stay a little warmer and the ice doesn't get quite as thick in the winter as the other kind of lakes which have clear bottoms.

Most of the lakes are clear bottom and contain an abundance of lake trout and jackfish, or northern pike as we call them in Minnesota, and the fish come in almost any size you want. The black lakes are home to the walleyed pike, especially lakes with rock ledges or outcroppings to fish along. The walleye could also be found in the rivers along with the beautiful Arctic grayling. Up on the Snare River when I was flying for the hydro project we used to catch walleyes up to eight pounds and then some.

With the patchwork of lakes stretching all across the barrens, winter freeze-up made motorized travel across the country possible. One of the first men to recognize this and do something about it was a former Mountie by the name of John Denison. He pioneered ice roads in the Barren Lands.

The Cat trains, moving at only four or five miles per hour top speed and considerably less when they were punching their way through the bush, were simply too slow to keep up with the demand for freight and supplies by the mines out in the barrens during the uranium and gold rushes of the 1950s. Some of the mining equipment got to be so big and heavy that Cat trains or air transport simply could not deliver when and where needed.

Denison came up with the idea of plowing ice roads across the frozen lakes and building them across the tundra and through bush portages so that a fully loaded truck could travel at a speed of 30, 40 or even 60 miles per hour with a payload of up to 30 tons. He knew that

Cat trains were not only slow and had to take one sleigh at a time across the more difficult portages, but that Cats were also unsafe. Many of the 20-ton machines rested on the bottom of North Country lakes.

When the ice on the lakes was thick enough, Denison would send out a Bombardier tracked vehicle named the "Bug," with skis in place of front wheels, to scout the portages between lakes. Next he would send in TD-14 International Harvester dozers, which are painted red but are the same size as Caterpillar's yellow D-6, and they would punch a road through the bush and across the tundra between lakes. The trick was to level the ice road as much as possible, and Denison's TD-14 dozers would move mountains of snow to fill valleys and creek beds. The snow had to be packed down to remove its air content, then left for at least 24 hours so it would "set" in much the same manner as concrete. The colder the temperature, the quicker it would set up. Once the ice roads across the portages were in place Denison had to pack down any new fallen snow so it would become a part of the ice road instead of a blanket of soft snow that would weaken the ice beneath it.

Denison's trucks were huge machines, with bigger engines and bigger everything. Most had bunkhouses behind the cabs for the crew. Denison himself traveled in a pickup truck camper. His plow truck, Number 36, had been named The African Queen and considering its size it was probably appropriate. The Queen had a two-ton plow attached to the front with wing plows on each side that gave it the appearance of the Angel of Death as it broke trail at 30 miles per hour across the surface of some frozen lake. Originally a Mack truck, the Queen had been modified and customized by Denison to get the job done. That meant opening a 16-foot wide roadway across the lakes and keeping it open after a snowfall or ground drifting.

The longest and best known ice road was the Echo Bay Road which was also known as Denison's Road. It

began about 70 miles northwest of Yellowknife and
stretched over 200 miles north to the uranium mine at
Port Radium on the east shore of Great Bear Lake.
Later Denison built ice roads each season out to the
Tundra Mine northeast of Yellowknife, which was clear
out in the Barren Lands. Once the ice roads were in
place, regular semi-trailer trucks and flatbed trucks
could usually make it to Port Radium or out to Tundra
Mine in anywhere from 24 to 36 hours. Denison would
also keep a TD-14 dozer stationed near some of the
more troublesome portages in the event a truck needed
assistance or there was fresh snow to be compacted.

Denison's interest in pioneering ice roads wasn't just
the challenge of it. He was also part owner of the Canadian trucking outfit, Byers Transport Limited, that
would put up the money for his ice roads each season.
Even so, you could always count on Denison to be ac-
tively involved in scouting the routes for the season's
ice roads into the barrens. His pickup camper was usually somewhere between the Bombardier Bug and the
TD-14s as he directed the operation each step of the
way by radio.

How Denison managed to survive the rigors of building ice roads when the temperature was 40 to 50 below
zero or worse is something I'll never understand. His
health was terrible. When Denison quit the Royal Canadian Mounted Police and went into the barge end of
the transport business out of Yellowknife in the late
1940s he developed ulcers and eventually had to be
hospitalized. His stomach was always acting up during
his years building the ice roads and his six-foot-four
frame was mostly skin and bone. In fact, Denison's
pallor was pretty much that of a cadaver most of the
time and his men would always be after him to see the
doctor. He wouldn't, of course, saying the only thing he
was going to see was that the freight got out to the
mines each season and that was all there was to it.

Characters like John Denison were what made the

North Country such a great place despite all the hardships. Most folks in the North were just content to survive, but people like Denison and the other characters I knew actually thrived in this land. They wouldn't have it any other way.

Take Pete Baker, the Arctic Arab, for example.

I first ran into Pete Baker at Norman Wells during the war years when I was flying the Northwest Staging Route along the Mackenzie River. How a Lebanese fellow ended up in the North I can't explain, but I know Pete Baker couldn't have been his real name.

Pete Baker was a gambler, a prospector, a merchant and a politician. He came north in the early 1920s and opened a small outpost store northwest of Yellowknife at Old Fort Rae. Most of his customers were Indian and over the years he became their trusted friend. When I met him at Norman Wells he had sold the store and was running a dog sled operation between the town and the Imperial Oil camp and the Canol camp, which were on opposite sides of the great river. Old Pete would deliver mail and ferry people and supplies back and forth. The river was about three miles across and Pete would be asleep most of the time in his sled as his dogs took him safely across the frozen river to the other side. Pete would wake up, deliver the mail, then go back to sleep in the sled while his team made the return trip. Then he'd stay up all night gambling, mostly poker.

Pete turned prospector after the war and spent the next 10 years or so out in the barrens gambling, fishing and staking an occasional claim. He never was one to worry much about cleanliness or grooming, so you can imagine how Pete looked and smelled after weeks or months alone out in the barrens.

One morning in the spring of 1956 I flew about 150 miles north of Yellowknife to pick up two prospectors employed by the Giant Yellowknife Mine near town. The mine usually had prospectors out in the field. Back Bay was mostly open so we had the Otter on floats, but there was only a little open water on this particular lake and it was along one side of a point while the two prospectors were on the other side.

I landed with the idea of walking across the point to get the prospectors and help them with their gear. No sooner had I stepped on shore when who do I run into out in the middle of nowhere? Old Pete Baker, whom I hadn't seen since 1944. He had a little camp nearby and since Pete was the kind of fellow who would give you the shirt off his back he insisted that I join him for breakfast.

Just one look at Pete and his camp and his old frying pan convinced me that if you were going to meet Pete Baker out in the bush it was best if it wasn't mealtime.

The frying pan was covered with old egg and potatoes or whatever, with a little place in the middle reserved for whatever he planned to cook for me. He poured a cup of coffee and handed it to me. Before I could check to see if the cup was reasonably clean I noticed all kinds of caribou hair in the coffee from Pete's clothing. As I tried to fish out some of the hair, Pete dug out a loaf of bread and slapped it up against his mostly bare chest, hair, grease and all. Holding the bread firmly against his chest, Pete sawed off a piece and gave it to me with a big smile. He was so generous, always wanting to feed you or do something for you, but it was damn near impossible to sit there and look at the bread and the frying pan and the caribou hair coffee without getting sick.

Shortly after our chance encounter, Pete went back to Fort Rae and again ran a small outpost store for a few years. Fort Rae was close enough to Yellowknife so that Pete was a frequent visitor. He would spend weekends in Yellowknife playing poker and talking politics. Almost on a whim, Pete ran for public office in the early 1960s and at the ripe old age of 80 was elected Yellowknife area representative to the Northwest Territories Council. What a character!

Caribou hair in your coffee or tea, I learned, was just something you put up with. The Inuit were very social and whenever I would fly into one of their villages along the coast they would always insist I have tea with them. Invariably in the winter the tea would have a generous amount of caribou hair floating in it. Caribou hair is brittle and sheds continuously. If you have tea with the Inuit with any frequency you become quite adept at tilting your cup enough so the hair sticks to the inside of the cup and you can flick it out.

I started wearing some of the native clothing, mostly mukluks and a caribou parka, and found that it was the first time in my life that I was ever warm in the North during winter. I flew in the RCAF for five years and every winter we froze because the aircraft had little heat or none at all. We would be flying up there for hours with the temperature 30 or 40 below zero in the cockpit. My winter in the old Norseman flying for the Snare hydro project was not much of an improvement. Only after I discovered the natural insulating properties of native wear and began using it did I feel really warm and pro-tected, not only in flight but down on the ground out in the barrens or the Arctic islands.

My feet were always getting cold and making me mis-erable until I started wearing mukluks with dry-tanned moose hide bottoms and either heavy canvas or caribou skin tops. A dry-tanned skin is an insulator while an oil-tanned skin is not, so nearly all native hides are dry tanned. Moose hide was used because it's very heavy and tough and will last a long time. I only wore the muk-luks when it was 20 below zero or colder, otherwise my feet would get too warm.

First I would put on an inner sock of cotton or light wool, then a thing called a duffle sock which was noth-ing more than Hudson's Bay duffle cloth sewn into a sock. A thick piece of felt insole was placed in the duffle sock and then you pulled the mukluks on over the whole works. My feet were never cold again, thanks to the Inuit.

My face was a different story, however. It took a severe case of frostbite in early 1957 for me to discover the added protection a beard can give you in cold weather. Up until that time I was always clean shaven.

We had reluctantly put an old prospector that we didn't know out in the barrens about 10 days before New Year's because he needed to check some property. He asked to be picked up on New Year's Day, and we agreed. We didn't know how he would handle himself in the barrens because he came in from the outside. We didn't know if he was well versed in providing for himself if something went wrong, which it did.

A terrific storm roared across the region the last day of December and blew all New Year's Day. The morning of January 2 dawned bright and clear with a slight breeze, but it was colder than heck. At least 40 below zero, maybe more.

I figured we had better get in the air as soon as possible and see if this poor fellow had made it and bring him in. We didn't know if he had enough food or knew how to keep a tent up in a storm. We didn't know anything about him. The only problem was the storm had drifted in all of our aircraft, so I enlisted our two engineers and we started to dig out the Beaver.

After a few minutes I stopped and told the boys, "Now, don't stay out here too long because there's enough of a wind chill that either of you could freeze up your face and you won't even notice it." So they both went in. Of course, I'm too bright to go in with them. "Nope," I thought, "I'll just keep digging until they come back out and then I'll go in."

I started to get warm from shoveling and shoved my parka hood back so my bare head was hanging out there in the wind. When the boys came out a few minutes later they took one look and said my jaw line was white for an inch or two on each side and that my nose and earlobes were frozen. They got a big kick out of this because I was so smart. One of our other pilots had to come down and take the flight for me while I thawed out. By the next day there were water blisters up both sides of my jaw and my nose and the tips of my ears were so sore I couldn't even touch them.

That's how I started my beard, and after about a month or six weeks it felt so good that I hated the thought of shaving it off. But that's what I had intended to do when my jaw was completely healed. I even carried my electric razor along on trips in anticipation of the day that I could use it.

A couple of months after freezing my face I was on a flight down the Mackenzie River with a government crew and we stopped overnight at the village of Fort Good Hope, which is about 500 miles northwest of Yellowknife and sits high atop a river bluff as protection against high water during spring ice jams. Most of the villages along the Mackenzie were built on high ground for this reason. I tied the Beaver down on the frozen river shoreline and the next morning walked back down the steep trail from the village to warm up the aircraft. Cold air sinks and as I descended the trail I could feel it getting colder. It was about 40 below zero up in the village, but down on the river the aircraft thermometer read 51 below.

I had intended to shave the beard off that morning. But after sitting under the engine tent with the blowpots for about two hours to get the Beaver warm enough to start, I had pretty much thought it over.

That beard felt damn good. It was going to stay, and it has ever since.

As for that old prospector out in the barrens, he wasn't in half bad shape when they found him later the day I froze my face. His tent had blown down but he had the presence of mind to stay under it in his sleeping robe. He figured we were coming and didn't make the mistake of running out all over the countryside in a panic. For a fellow from the outside, that old boy handled himself pretty darn well.

Prospectors are real loners, just like the trappers. If a property was coming open, they'd want to go out in the barrens at night and be in position to restake it at the stroke of midnight so nobody else could. They'd be out there, most of them, all by themselves for weeks or even months at a time. Like Pete Baker and John Denison, the real loners were usually unmarried. Their kind of life just didn't allow for it.

I guess there was a little loner in all of us who spent much time out in the Barren Lands or flying over it. We sort of preferred it that way and, if given a choice, would just as soon haul freight instead of passengers. This was especially true as my flights in that old single engine Otter began to take me across the barrens and out over the High Arctic where passengers were just about the last thing you needed to deal with in the event of a forced landing.

Imagine spending several days in some God-forsaken igloo or snow cave with a couple of whining passengers. No thanks!

During my 14 years with Wardair I was stuck a number of times out in the Barren Lands and also up in the High Arctic without any way of communicating, and I know that was hard on Marie and the boys. Max, of course, always had a good answer for those situations and that annoyed Marie to no end because she simply didn't believe him. He would come up with stock answers like I was probably safe at some Eskimo village or something like that, when she was certain I wasn't.

Only now do I really understand how difficult it was for Marie not knowing if I was dead or alive. Like the time that I spent three days in an igloo on DeSalis Bay, where I began my story back in Chapter One.

CHAPTER NINE

BACK IN THE IGLOO

"I climbed into the Otter and cranked the engine over. It started up. I breathed easier until I remembered my fuel supply was low when I landed. The warm-up would have to be no longer than absolutely necessary if I was going to make it across Banks Island to Sachs Harbour."

It was now the third morning of my forced landing on DeSalis Bay and the storm had finally run its course. I worked my way feet first out of the igloo to begin heating the Otter for take-off.

It was dark and the air was very still and crisp. After three days of a constant howling wind the silence was just incredible. I remember standing there, looking at my little igloo with the crazy thought that I hated to leave the darn thing behind. It was a good igloo by my standards at least, and I was quite proud of it. It had saved my life, no question about that. Inside, alone, safe from the storm, I developed a tremendous sense of peace as, in between naps, I thought about my family, my work and my faith.

I started heating the Otter up in the dark so I would get over to Sachs Harbour on the other side of the island in the daylight. The engine tent was wrapped around the nose of the aircraft. I untied it and dropped the sides to the ground, packing snow around the edges to make it tight. Normally I used two blowpots to heat the engine, but they can be very unreliable and I had one that wasn't working well at all. I sat in the tent under the engine for nearly two hours with one blowpot. With two blowpots it would have taken an hour. The blowpots are placed directly under the engine and I would open the

two bottom cowlings in the Otter and let the heat go
straight up to the big radial engine. You can actually see
the frost go out of the parts of the engine.

The Otter had a wonderful device called a dilution
hopper that eliminated the old practice of draining the oil
at night and heating it the next morning over a stove as
we did with the old Norseman. The oil in an Otter is carried in a separate tank in the engine and it is pumped
from there to the engine and back. When you shut the
Otter down at night you can dilute a small portion of
your oil with gasoline in a special hopper tank built inside the regular oil tank. The idea was to shut the engine
down for up to half an hour and then, when the oil was
starting to cool, restart the engine and hold the dilution
button for about five minutes if it was going to be 40 below in the morning or around three minutes if it was only
going to be 20 below. This would feed gasoline straight
into the hopper tank where it would dilute some of the
oil, enough to help fire the engine in the morning and get
it going until the rest of the oil softened up so it could
flow into the hopper. This required a slow warm-up and
I've seen men seize engines right up by trying to take off
without the outer oil warm enough. They'd be in a hurry
and take off with only the diluted hopper oil. You just
couldn't do that.

I climbed into the Otter and cranked the engine over. It
started up. I breathed easier until I remembered my fuel
supply was low when I landed. The warm-up would have
to be no longer than absolutely necessary if I was going to
make it across Banks Island to Sachs Harbour.

After being airborne for about half an hour my radio
came back to life thanks to a little bit of heat that got
back to it in the rear of the aircraft. I called Sachs
Harbour and told them I was very low on fuel. "If I don't
make it, send a team down to that series of lakes I'll be
coming in over. I'll be on one or the other of those lakes,"
I said. But I made it in with just a few gallons to spare.
When I climbed out of the Otter the greeting party in-

cluded an Inuit and his young son who had traveled by dog team across Banks Island during the storm to ask if I would please come and pick up this old man in their camp who was dying. They had arrived at the Sachs Harbour weather station only an hour before I landed, and their story was absolutely amazing to me.

This man and his son were from one of the last roving bands of Inuit in the Arctic and during winter they usually made camp at the north end of DeSalis Bay where the hunting and fishing were good. They had heard me fly over the bay three days earlier and figured I was going to Sachs Harbour since that was the only station within hundreds of miles. They also knew the chances were darn good that I would be stuck at Sachs Harbour for several days because of the approaching storm. So they hooked up their dog team and started out that night on an 80-mile trip across the rugged island in the storm to ask for my help.

They had no way of knowing, of course, that instead of being warm in Sachs Harbour I was spending a really miserable night on DeSalis Bay in the cabin of the old Otter only about six or eight miles from their camp.

For three days and nights, during the worst of the storm, they crossed the island. Eighty miles and rugged. How they could find their way or even see in that storm, I'll never know. Perhaps it was the dogs. If the dogs had ever crossed that island before, they would somehow find their way back across the island again. To me, it was just the most remarkable thing that this man and his son managed to reach Sachs Harbour. And just an hour ahead of me.

After hearing their story, I assured the pair that I would be ready to go well before daylight the next morning. First there were the tasks of unloading the Otter and refueling, then I would enjoy my first good meal in quite some time and a good night's sleep as well. Actually, I wasn't all that hungry. I found that you don't eat much when there's only a few hours of daylight and you're stuck in an igloo. I ate only one day's Air Force ration in three days.

The man and his son took their meal with us and also stayed overnight. There wasn't room for their dog team in the Otter, so they started back across the island the next morning just as they had come. I stopped at their camp on my return and picked up the old gentleman. One of the younger women came along to attend him and I flew them to Yellowknife. The poor old fellow never did recover. He died in the government hospital for native people in Edmonton.

The year 1957 was not only memorable for me because of my spending three days in an igloo or growing a beard, but it was also the year of the Bristol Freighter.

Max had been working on a plan to take Wardair to a new level of service and he purchased a used Bristol 170 Freighter Mk. 31 from Transair of Winnipeg for the hefty sum of $300,000 in the belief that mining and oil companies and others would pay handsomely to have heavy equipment and large payloads delivered to remote locations.

The Bristol Freighter, with the call letters CF-TFX, was just about the ugliest aircraft I had ever seen when Max and a Transair pilot brought it into Yellowknife. I thought to myself, good Lord, Max, what have you gone and done? I didn't suspect at the time that old CF-TFX and I would get to know each other really well over the next dozen years. Or that photographs of her would appear in newspapers around the world in May of 1967.

With the addition of the Bristol Freighter, Wardair now had over a dozen employees and a fleet of aircraft that was the envy of Back Bay. Max, however, was pushing harder than ever and when business was in a slump he would get so worked up about getting the aircraft in the air that you wouldn't even want to be around him. He'd keep bugging us about getting in the air even when everyone knew we weren't going anywhere because it was a slow week or the weather was bad.

Several of us decided to buy a little brass bell and mount it just outside of the office door. Whenever Max would get all worked up about doing something, our plan was to ring the bell to warn everybody that we had better start doing something or get out of sight fast. The idea backfired when it worked exactly the opposite of what we intended. As soon as Max heard the bell the first time and the staff either disappeared or had an excuse, he figured it out. From then on when he'd get going on something, Max would run out and ring the bell himself instead of one of us. Max turned our warning bell into an assembly bell. I always got a big kick out of that.

Our life in Yellowknife eventually settled into a sort of routine. I worked most of the time, both boys were in school and Marie busied herself with looking after all of us. In the winter I kept snowmobiles for the prospectors and miners to rent and I had the two boys help me so they would have something to do. Christopher helped out with the maintenance and Charles handled much of the book work and ordering parts.

I was able to buy a used Republic SeaBee amphibian back in St. Cloud in the summer of 1959 so the family could get away for at least part of a day on weekends in the summer. The Franklin 215-hp engine in the SeaBee had a terrible reputation, and I remember giving the aircraft a real workout during a test flight before buying it. I flew the darn thing all the way from St. Cloud to Sioux Falls, South Dakota, and back, nearly 400 miles round trip. Once in a great while I would get a whole Sunday off and we would fly out to some small lake with the boys and pick berries, do a little fishing and have a picnic lunch. Those were good times.

Also in 1959, Marie and I were approached by the social worker in Yellowknife about providing foster care for one of the many babies she was trying to place and we agreed to take one, maybe even two. The first one she brought over to us was a cute little guy named Joel. His

mother was Chipewyan Indian from a small village
called Snowdrift on the southeast side of Great Slave
Lake, but they didn't know who the father was other
than he was white. Joel was hard to care for at first
because he was born prematurely. He wasn't very big
and he was always crabby, but after a few weeks he got
to be a real likeable little tyke and we decided we weren't
going to give him up even if I was now 46 and old
enough to be his grandfather.

Christopher and Charles took a big interest in Joel and
let us know they, too, thought it would be really nice to
have a little brother. After three or four months we told
the social worker we wanted to adopt Joel and she said
we would have to see Judge Jack Sissons. We knew the
judge, so that was no problem, but we were unsure
about the adoption procedures and legal red tape.
Christopher was a big help in that department. Before
the proceedings began Judge Sissons asked him if he
wanted a little brother and Christopher replied, "Oh,
sure!" So it was a done affair by the time we entered the
judge's chamber for the formalities. We now had three
sons instead of two.

Marie had given some thought to going back to nursing, but now with a little one and two fairly rambunc-
tious older boys that was out of the question. She had
her hands full on the home front and I guess by now she
could see that my work was taking me away for longer
and longer periods of time. My three days in the igloo
with no communication, I am sure, made her even more
leery of my chosen line of work and caused her to worry
that something much worse might happen to me. I never
spent much time worrying about such things, however,
and back then it was hard for me to understand why
others should be worried if I wasn't. After all, I knew my
aircraft and felt I could handle most situations.

As the 1950s drew to a close Max was doing most of
the flying in the Bristol Freighter. I continued to spend
most of my air time in the old Otter, which was fine with

me, although smaller aircraft like the Otter had one peculiar problem in the northern latitudes when conditions were just right. Ice crystals would form on the aircraft in flight when it was quite cold, a very fuzzy light crystal that didn't weigh much, but it really disturbed the air flow and made the plane difficult to control at times.

If you were flying north with the sun coming up in the east, that would usually clear the ice crystals from the right side of the aircraft. You would have to use more and more rudder trim to keep the aircraft flying straight because you had one side all frosted up and the other side clear. Sometimes I would actually have to turn around and fly back for a few minutes to get the other side clear, then turn around and resume my normal course. Larger aircraft like the Bristol Freighter never experienced it because they could always fly up and out of the stuff. But the old Otter couldn't climb very high with a big load and you flew most of the time at three, four or maybe five thousand feet.

There were a couple of other peculiar things about flying in the North Country, especially out over the High Arctic. You could never rely on your radio communications or your compass.

We used what was called a high frequency radio, and it was good whenever it felt like being good. At dusk and just before dawn it would fade and maybe you would get it back during the day, maybe not. You just never knew. Sometimes it would be gone an hour and if you were up over the Canadian Arctic Islands it might be out all day. This was all due to the ionosphere and the way high frequency radio signals bounced against it or sometimes not at all. It worked when conditions were right but there were days when you couldn't contact anyone. Other times you could contact stations in England or the southern United States, but you couldn't contact Yellowknife or even the Arctic stations you were flying over at the time.

One night in the late 1960s I happened to be flying
the Bristol Freighter and we were coming down from
Isachsen on Ellef Ringnes Island to Resolute. An SAS
airliner was on a transpolar flight and I could hear on
our radio that the SAS crew was having a dickens of a
time giving their position report, which they were required to do every so often in order to keep track of the
flight. They were trying to contact the weather station in
Isachsen, which I had just left. I finally picked up the
mike and told the SAS crew, "If you want me to relay
your position, I'm in contact with Isachsen and can get
the information to them." SAS agreed and gave me their
information, which I then relayed to Isachsen. It took
quite a while because conditions were so poor.

When I was done and feeling quite good about my
deed, SAS came back on the air all of a sudden and this
fellow said, "Say, Bristol CF-TFX, where and what kind
of station are you? We can't find you anywhere on our
map." They didn't realize I was another airplane. When I
told him I was a Bristol Freighter enroute to Resolute,
there was just dead silence.

The ionosphere's effect on radio communications,
however, was nothing compared to the way the North
Magnetic Pole messed up navigating by compass. As I
mentioned earlier, you simply had no magnetic compass
at all from about 300 miles north of Yellowknife until
you were within perhaps 300 miles of the North Pole.
The North Magnetic Pole is currently at about 77 degrees north, near the north coast of Bathurst Island,
and it moves very slowly in about a 300-mile circle. Anywhere within an 800 to 1,000 mile radius of that pole
the magnetic field curves inward so much that you don't
have the field to keep your compass in alignment. Once
you were 300 miles north of Yellowknife you forgot about
your compass and, weather permitting, depended on an
astrocompass which read the angle of the sun during
the day and the stars or moon at night. We had tables
for major stars and for the positions of the sun and

moon at any given time. Once we got to within a hundred miles of Yellowknife we could usually start to pick up some of the directional radio signals to bring us the rest of the way home.

If it was a really gray day or overcast night, then we would have to rely on our directional gyro for navigation. The aircraft gyro is very similar in principle to a child's toy gyroscope wheel that spins when you wind it up. You had to have a good gyro in the aircraft all the time because you were dependent on it so often. The many times I went out into the Barren Lands or the Arctic islands in a single engine airplane I never once forgot to set my gyro. It was one of the cardinal rules. The gyro was often the only thing you had to go on and you didn't dare forget to set it. You just made damn sure you did it. If you were going to come back after each trip out, there were certain things you had to remember. And setting your directional gyro was probably the most important.

The other important thing to remember was always to trust your instruments. Second-guessing them was something you could never do. That's like not trusting your lead dog. He knows where he's going if you'll just let him take you there. It was the same idea with your instruments. I knew one old trapper who twice forced his dogs to go in the direction he wanted, and both times he became lost.

Once you think you know more than the instruments do, you're lost either way. If they're right, you're lost. And if they're wrong, you're also lost and there usually isn't much you can do about it by then. You just have to hope that you know the country well enough to recognize something eventually that will get you back home. Out in the Barren Lands on a gray winter day, it also might help to pray because there isn't much to go by.

Life in the North Country is like that, full of surprises and uncertainties, and your best bet is always to be ready for the unexpected. "Be prepared," as the Boy Scouts say. Even our family had its share of surprises, like the time we encountered a bear at a place called Fishing Lake when we were on one of our Sunday picnic outings in the SeaBee.

We had eaten our lunch and decided to walk a little ways up the river at the head of the lake. We left the remains of our lunch, never thinking about bears or anything like that. When we came back down the trail, there was a big old black bear in our lunch. I told Marie to take the three boys down along the river and out to the sandy beach where I had parked the SeaBee, and to get into the aircraft as quickly as possible. In the meantime I would try to distract the bear long enough to gather up our lunch box and coffee pot and whatever else I could salvage.

About the time Marie and the boys were out of sight, I turned and saw the old bear starting to amble up the hill toward me. There was a fair size spruce tree between the bear and me, and I was carrying a beauty of a trout that must have weighed about eight pounds. I thought, well, if I pitch the trout toward the bear on the other side of the tree and stay put behind the tree maybe he'll take the fish and go away.

Like hell he did.

That darn old bear walked right by the trout and past the tree while I took off like a shot to grab the lunch box and head for the SeaBee. When I looked back, however, the bear had walked far enough up the hill that I was able to go back and retrieve my trout. Then I came back and started to gather our picnic supplies when, sure enough, the bear started coming back down the hill toward me again. I grabbed what I could and ran for the airplane. The old bear sat right down on the beach and watched all the fuss we were making. Little Joel was screaming and if that didn't scare the bear away I thought he would take off when the engine started up. Nope, not this bear. He just sat there and watched us as we taxied out. Bears are funny like that, unpredictable. You never know what the heck they are going to do.

Another time a cow moose swam out to meet the SeaBee. With the windows only a couple of feet out of the water I was worried the old gal might try to board us and kick in the windows in the process. I taxied around her and went a half-mile down the shoreline to another sandy beach. She followed us in and came right up on shore, standing little more than 15 feet away from the SeaBee. She looked at us for a while and then wandered off into the bush, totally fearless of us.

Fishing Lake was only about 50 miles north of Yellowknife. It was a beautiful spot, with excellent lake trout and northern fishing and the most beautiful sand beaches. The spruce trees near shore grew quite large, but further inland they were the small, scruffy variety common to that area. There were strawberries every-where and we would eat them until we were almost sick. Those Sunday afternoon picnics at Fishing Lake with Marie and the boys were just about the happiest times you could ever imagine, but it couldn't last forever and it didn't.

The 1960s were tough on our family. Marie started to suffer bouts of depression and the kids had to fend for themselves as I was gone for weeks at a time on one trip after another across the Canadian High Arctic.

CHAPTER TEN

HIGH ARCTIC FLIGHTS

*"During an overnight at one of the villages
along the Arctic coast I was served seal liver.
They used to mix it with macaroni to cut the
taste a little since it was very strong, very oily
and very fishy If you were going to eat with
the Inuit, that's what you ate. I ate more of the
macaroni than the seal liver."*

Why the muskox picked the High Arctic for its homeland
is beyond me. I can't think of a worse place to live, especially if you're a vegetarian and have to spend each winter pawing the ground in search of a little alder or a bit
of swale grass beneath the snow. Yet the fact remains, if
it's muskoxen you're after then you had better head
above the Arctic Circle because that's the only place in
the world you will find them in their natural habitat.

As it turned out, one of my flights out over the Canadian High Arctic in 1960 was in pursuit of muskoxen.
Not to study or photograph them, but to shoot four of
these magnificent creatures for the Los Angeles County
Museum.

The introduction of the high-powered rifle made the
muskox easy pickings for Inuit hunters, and it was now
a protected species. The museum had received permission from the Canadian government to take four animals
off Ellesmere Island, which is about as far north as a
person or even a muskox can go on land. The hunt was
closely supervised by a government mammalogist named
John Tener, a really fine fellow. In addition to Tener our
party included two Inuit, a couple of museum scientists
and a rather obnoxious person who was one of the
museum's big benefactors. He had bankrolled the hunt
and obviously fancied himself a great hunter.

The museum's muskoxen exhibit was going to feature two cows, one with a calf, and a bull, so the hunt was scheduled for May when the weather up on Ellesmere is only around zero or 10 below and the calves are being born. We departed Yellowknife in the Otter and headed northeast nearly 1,400 air miles to Ellesmere, with refueling stops at Cambridge Bay on the southeast tip of Victoria Island and Resolute on Cornwallis Island farther north.

Cambridge Bay was one of a great number of radar stations put in place by the United States that formed the DEW (Distant Early Warning) line in the 1950s. The DEW line stretched from Alaska to Greenland, generally along the 70th Parallel, and Cambridge Bay was one of the few stations that would service civilian aircraft with fuel. Arrangements had to be made ahead of time, however, and I soon became quite unpopular with the Americans in charge of the station because I never seemed to arrange things far enough in advance to suit their protocol. The Americans had a real attitude problem and I didn't take kindly to it. In fact, I became rather obnoxious myself.

What really annoyed me the most was the fact the Americans were permitted to build these stations on Canadian soil and Canadian officers and enlisted men even helped man the sites, yet the American officer was always the top man in charge. It would make me so damn mad to have to get permission from an American to land on Canadian soil and I was not shy about expressing my feelings about it. The Americans were all for kicking me out every time I came in and I wasn't welcome anywhere on the DEW line in all the years I flew for Wardair.

Refueling at Cambridge Bay was not an option, however, when you were taking a fully loaded Otter from Yellowknife out over the Arctic. There weren't many places you could gas up, and the farther north you went the more your fuel would cost. The first leg of our flight up to Cambridge Bay was a little over 500 miles and the leg to Resolute was around 425 miles. Resolute was the second most northerly Canadian military outpost, with Alert being first. It was equipped and manned to handle civilian traffic and was actually quite busy considering its remote location.

The base for our muskoxen hunt was the tiny weather station at Eureka about halfway up on the west side of Ellesmere Island and a good 400 miles north of Resolute. My first task was to fly an 80-mile square area so John Tener could survey the muskox population. As he suspected, the area was loaded with them and he counted over 600 in just that small survey area. John explained that the government had given permission to take four muskoxen from this region because there were more animals than the area could support. Muskoxen need tremendous range in order to find enough forage in winter, about six pounds a day to sustain themselves and more if they are going to reproduce.

John said a muskox will search out low spots and paw down where there was water running during the summer months because that's where the high swale grass grows. They'll paw down and nip the swale grass off at the very bottom. The alder growing along the ground for protection is the main source of sustenance for the muskoxen. The barren-ground caribou, or island caribou as they are called up on the Arctic islands, live mostly on lichen and moss. Not muskoxen, which are in the goat family.

Muskoxen run in herds and when they are threatened they will form a circle for protection against wolves and other predators, including man. The bulls often weigh up to 600 pounds and position themselves on the outside of the circle. If there are enough bulls to go around, the cows and all the calves will be inside the circle, otherwise even some of the bigger cows will stand shoulder to shoulder with the bulls in the outside rank. The bulls will eventually charge out to challenge their foe, but only for a few lengths and then they back right into their place in the circle.

I was fascinated by the little calves born that May. Before the herd was disturbed, when the muskoxen were grazing or at rest, the calves were usually right under the cows and darn near invisible because the cows had belly hair up to 18 inches long. This helped protect the calves from the wind and cold after they were born, until their own soft hair dried out and formed a cashmere-like wool several inches thick. The wool of the adult muskoxen is quite valuable and must be gathered off the ground since the animals are both wild and protected.

Those little calves have the most beautiful blue eyes. We took one aboard the Otter during the hunt when I came in too close to a herd and the muskoxen panicked, leaving the little guy behind. John Tener said they wouldn't return for the calf and asked me to land, which I did. We took the bleating calf aboard and landed behind a hill just ahead of the herd where John let the calf off. Sure enough, when the herd came over the hill the cow came out from the herd and retrieved her calf with the blue eyes.

We made three trips out of Eureka, returning each time with a muskox and once with a calf besides. I felt sorry for the calf, that it had to die to be a museum piece. But that's one reason John Tener was along, to make sure our party took a cow and a calf that were coupled. And to make certain the other cow we took was not one that was carrying a calf.

My job was simply to fly the Otter to locate the herds, then land in a way that wouldn't panic the muskoxen, usually in a low spot or over a little rise. Then we would walk over and John would point out the animal we could take. The first time we did this the museum benefactor announced he would take the shot since he was footing the bill. This guy was so egotistical you could hardly stand him, but everyone respected his wishes and our two Inuit guides proceeded to walk around the herd so it would form its defensive circle and give this fellow a clear shot. If you come at the herd from just one side, they'll usually run.

John pointed out a big bull that was facing us from not more than 50 yards away and this great hunter aimed, fired and missed everything. It turned out he was a lousy shot besides being obnoxious. After that the Inuit wouldn't walk around behind the herd if this guy was going to shoot because he might hit them. I couldn't blame them. John resighted his rifle that night and he did a little better the next day, but the Inuit never trusted him after that.

Our party would take each muskox back to our camp at Eureka and skin them out one at a time, carefully removing the hide and photographing and labeling the bones so they would know how to wire everything back together back in Los Angeles. The meat was given to the Inuit.

Although the muskox is protected, the Inuit would take them illegally during hard times. That kept the muskoxen population fairly stable except in places like Ellesmere Island where there weren't many humans. Nobody lives on Ellesmere other than the weather station people and a small number of Inuit in two settlements, one on the east coast across from Greenland and a larger village on the southern end of the island, Grise Fiord, which is the most northerly natural Inuit village. The tiny settlement across Kennedy Channel from Greenland was farther north than Grise Fiord, but the government had posted the Inuit and a couple of Mounties there to protect Canadian interests from Greenlanders who were coming across the channel and poaching on the Canadian side, so it wasn't a natural Inuit settlement.

Inuit settlements are scattered all along the Canadian and Alaskan coasts and the lower tier of Arctic islands. Settlements are a little more prevalent in the eastern Arctic around Hudson Bay and Baffin Island because of the early whaling ships and also hunting generally is better in that region. The villages range in size from 30 to as many as 300 people. The larger settlements are right on the coast where hunting and fishing are good and where the villages can be supplied by air and by a Hudson's Bay Company freighter. The ship would supply settlements from the mouth of the Mackenzie River all the way to the eastern Arctic, and the Hudson's Bay people would attempt to do this in just one trip during the summer.

Also in the summer the Mackenzie River would become a great water highway with barge shipping running the length of the river, from Great Slave Lake all the way north to the Arctic coast. Towns along the river would pack in supplies for the long winter in the same manner as the settlements along the coast. Wardair used the river barges and coastal freighter to lay in supplies of fuel for our aircraft at many of the larger settlements along the Mackenzie and across the Canadian Arctic coast to Hudson Bay and Baffin Island. Shipping costs added tremendously to the cost of supplies and prices were quite high. I would pay perhaps two dollars for something that might cost 50 cents back in St. Cloud.

The first few years I flew for Wardair the smaller Inuit settlements would often be moved to follow the hunting. The Inuit still used dog sleds and large tents in those days, and they could pull up stakes and move the entire village very quickly.

Then came the snowmobile and government housing in the 1960s and everything changed. The Inuit didn't trust the snowmobile at first, but as the machines became more reliable the hunting expeditions were made in two or three days instead of months. The same was true of outboard motors, which made the Inuit more productive at sea.

The old way of life is pretty much gone, replaced not only by snowmobiles but also by electric generators, high-tech Arctic clothing and even VCR television for entertainment.

I can remember the time when the Anglican or Catholic mission church in a settlement was not only a center for worship, but also for community. Some of the missionaries built very nice churches, usually all by themselves, with their own living quarters and a community room. It was a great meeting place for the native people. They really enjoyed getting together in a warm room.

The Inuit are very self-reliant people, and their winter tents served them well before all the modern conveniences arrived on the scene. They would start out with a plain, ordinary tent that could sleep six or eight and then build an ice wall all the way around it. The wall would extend eight to ten feet in front of the tent so the sleds, harnesses and other gear could be thrown over the top, out of the reach of the dogs. The dogs would eat or chew just about anything within jumping reach, but the front wall was always quite high. The inside of the tent was lined with skins, and this would be their home for the winter, or until it was time to move again.

In those days the Inuits still did quite a bit of cooking over seal oil lamps made from a large piece of soapstone, roughly two feet long by two feet in width and about 12 to 14 inches high. The stone is soft and would be hollowed out, then filled with seal oil made from chunks of seal blubber that had been rendered during the summer in a large container of some sort. It stinks to high heaven, but a good supply of oil in the fall was important because the lamp is kept going continuously and it always had to be kept filled. When the oil ran low they would just keep adding chunks of blubber because the heat from the bowl of the lamp would render it quickly. Caribou moss was used as a sort of wick, and it was rolled into the shape of a pencil much like you would roll a cigarette. The lamp didn't throw out all that much heat, which wasn't a problem since the Inuit ate much of their food raw.

During an overnight at one of the villages along the Arctic coast I was served seal liver. They used to mix it with macaroni to cut the taste a little since it was very strong, very oily and very fishy. If you were going to eat with the Inuit, that's what you ate. I ate more of the macaroni than the seal liver. The ptarmigan was a real delicacy, and they would drink the blood and eat some of the bird raw until they got a chance at night to cook it a bit.

Soapstone is found all along the Arctic coast although rarely in large chunks. In the western Arctic the stone is dark gray but as you get into the eastern Arctic the stone is a beautiful green to light brown color. The Inuit are skilled at carving soapstone of any size into beautiful figures of whales, seals, polar bears and other animals, or into intricate designs for display or for jewelry. Pieces that I would buy for $12 to $15 from the native people themselves in the late 1950s would now cost $50 or $60 at their co-ops and well over $100 on the outside.

The Inuit winter clothing when I was up there was practically all caribou. They wore a pair of pants with the hair in and an outer pair with the hair out. The same with their shirts. Essentially, it was two layers, the inner with the hair in and the outer with the hair out. No underwear to speak of. They would take the outer skins off when they came into the tent and they would sleep in the inner ones. I guess that made the inner ones their underclothing when you think about it. The clothing was never washed. They would hang them out in the wind and beat them, like you would a rug.

Given the hostile environment, the diet and the problems with alcohol, the native people had a lifespan that was quite short in those days. We would take doctors around to all the larger villages in the western Arctic at least once a year and, if necessary, transport the sick to the government hospital in Edmonton that handled most of the native people, both Indian and Inuit.

The Inuit who managed to survive until old age, which was younger than what we consider "old age" today, would sometimes stay behind when the others moved from one hunting spot to another. Tradition held that there was no point in surviving any more when you're not helping and you get tired of living. The old people actually preferred to leave life in this manner. When you consider they spent their entire life out in the cold trying to survive, it was understandable that you reach a point when you simply stop and let nature take over.

Some of the Inuit traditions, however, ran counter to Canadian law and one young fellow in the late 1950s found himself charged with murder for assisting his father in leaving this world in the traditional Inuit manner. Normally he would have been hauled to Yellowknife for trial, as was the practice for all native people accused of a crime. But in 1955 the first Justice of the new Territorial Court of the Northwest Territories was appointed and this remarkable man decided that justice should be taken to the native people rather than having them brought in and tried in Yellowknife where they were completely out of their element.

His name was Jack Sissons, the judge who presided over the adoption proceedings for Joel.

Jack Sissons was a tough old judge, a man of conviction who paid little attention to the controversy he always seemed to stir up. He was retirement age when appointed Territorial Court Justice and in no mood to put up with American protocol at DEW line sites or political criticism from his countrymen for favoring Inuit and Indian rights over white man's law. Sissons was struck down by polio as a child and his leg brace was a constant reminder that a little adversity in a man's life only made him tougher. Despite his disability, Jack Sissons would always be on time for our flights together around the Arctic as he took the court to the native people in the late 1950s and early 1960s.

In fact, if Mr. Justice Sissons said we needed to take off at nine o'clock in the morning, I had better be ready to do exactly that because you could count on Sissons to be there a couple of minutes early with little patience for delay. I'd sometimes be with him for three weeks at a time as we flew all around the Canadian Arctic, holding court in one village or DEW line station after another and sometimes even in the old Otter itself if it was just a naturalization or something like that.

We carried a court reporter and a public defender, so court could be set up anywhere. He naturalized a Father Henry, one of the Order of Mary Immaculate priests, at a little place called Belly Bay in the Territories. It was the damnedest place to get the Otter into shore, so the good Father came out to the aircraft and we did it right there. Most of the court proceedings were conducted in the villages, however, and they included a number of murder trials where I'd often be sent out to pick up witnesses either at outcamps or at different villages so that the Territorial Court proceedings could be held where the crime was committed or at least very close to it.

A full tour of the Arctic with Jack Sissons was usually done twice a year, depending on the case load. We would leave Yellowknife and fly across the barrens to Hudson Bay, stopping at villages such as Baker Lake and Rankin Inlet before heading northeast to Coral Harbour on Southampton Island and across the top of the big bay to Baffin Island.

Our journey would wind its way up the east side of Baffin, from Frobisher (now called Iqaluit) to Broughton Island and up to the village of Pond Inlet on the north end of Baffin. There were villages on the west side of Baffin, too, and if it was necessary we would take the old Otter across the island over mountains rising up to 4,000 feet high so the judge could hold court.

One time we even went up to the south end of Ellesmere Island for a trial at Grise Fiord, then headed east over

Boothia Peninsula to Cambridge Bay on Victoria Island.
Our final leg would take us across Coronation Gulf to
Coppermine and then west along the coast to Paulatuk
before heading down the Mackenzie River valley with
stops as needed along the villages above the river before
heading back to Yellowknife.

It was a tremendous route, several thousand miles in
length, and all because Jack Sissons insisted that justice
should be taken to the native people. He frequently let
people go free for acts that would normally send a Canadian to jail for life, but he couldn't see that native peoples
and Canadians should be subject to a common standard
or law. He respected native laws and traditions, as well as
Canadian, and tried to seek a balance.

The Inuit would gather at the church or community
center a day or two before Judge Sissons would arrive.
They revered the man and looked forward to his visits.
Usually they got together only at holidays, so a visit by
Jack Sissons was not unlike a holiday in that it was another reason for getting together as a group of people.
Our overnight arrangements varied greatly; sometimes
the local Catholic or Anglican priest would put us up or it
might be the Mounties, wherever there happened to be
room. At Rankin Inlet we would be housed and fed at a
mining camp where they could accommodate the whole
bunch of us since they were boarding 50 to 60 people.

Once in a while we'd have to bring someone back to
Yellowknife who had been convicted of an offense and a
Mountie would accompany the prisoner for the remainder
of the tour. Usually it wasn't a problem, however, because
the Inuit are so docile that most of the time the Mounties
didn't even bother with handcuffs.

The government also dispensed health care as well as
justice to the native populations, and again Wardair was
usually hired to make the medical tours of the Arctic.

The main tour was conducted in the spring when there
was plenty of daylight but the ice was still good, and

sometimes a second tour would be done in the fall, but not always. We would load up the Otter with a chest x-ray crew and their equipment and a doctor from the government hospital in Edmonton, which in those days was the closest major hospital for the natives. Our route was similar to Judge Sisson's tour, covering both the Inuit and Indian populations across the Canadian Arctic.

We would stop at small villages out in the barrens and then head east along the coast from Coppermine to Bathurst Inlet, Gjoa Haven, Spence Bay and Repulse Bay on the south end of Melville Peninsula, sometimes going as far east as Pond Inlet. Then we'd come back west to Cambridge Bay and several villages on Victoria Island before crossing Amundsen Gulf to DeSalis Bay on Banks Island where I spent those three days in an igloo. The Thresher family and some other Inuit would often spend most of the winter camped on DeSalis Bay, but if they had returned to their village at Sachs Harbour on the other side of the island we would fly there instead. Then we would fly south to Paulatuk on the coast and also to Aklavik and other villages along the Mackenzie River — Fort McPherson, Arctic Red River, Fort Good Hope, Fort Norman, Wrigley, Fort Simpson, Fort Providence — before heading home to Yellowknife. The tour usually took about two weeks, sometimes a little less and sometimes a little longer. You never knew what to expect.

On one tour, for example, when we got to Paulatuk we found only one or two Inuit and the village's two priests. They told us the villagers had moved to a winter camp about halfway up the east side of Parry Peninsula where there was a beached whale. Apparently they decided that it would be easier to move everyone to the whale to eat for a few months rather than get the whale down to Paulatuk, but no one had heard from the villagers for quite some time. We decided to investigate.

It was fortunate it was one of those spring days when the light was good because from the air there was virtually no sign of a camp or human activity in the area of the beached whale except for a few telltale chimneys poking through the deeply drifted snow of early spring.

The villagers had set up their winter tents in a spot where the snow kept covering and drifting in to the point where there was nothing visible. We landed and found the villagers suffering from all sorts of illnesses, mostly due to a lack of adequate food during the winter. Two of the young children had died and others looked close to death. We filled the Otter with the sickest people and the bodies of the two children and flew to Aklavik several hundred miles to the west where there was a small infirmary. To make room we left the x-ray group behind and I could tell they were not at all pleased to see the only aircraft in the area flying off and leaving them on an Arctic beach.

We took the deceased along simply because there was no way to bury them at Paulatuk at that time of year, so we asked the hospital at Aklavik to hold the bodies until they could be returned to Paulatuk for burial when the ground thawed.

The people at Aklavik gave us some food supplies which we quickly loaded into the Otter and brought back to the camp so the villagers could have some nourishment. We asked the villagers if any wanted to return to Paulatuk where living conditions were much better although food was not in great supply there, either. I can't recall how many went back but I know we took quite a few.

The rest of our tours were pretty much routine, except for one night in late spring that I will never forget.

It was not at all unusual for massive icebergs to find their way into the straits and bays of the Canadian Arctic islands then get hung up on the bottom as they approached the shore. We were on one of our tours and I had anchored the Otter on the water near the village of Pond Inlet after dropping everyone off on shore. The actual inlet for which the village was named was narrow enough so it made for quite a strong tiderace. Normally where there were high tides we would sleep in the aircraft at night to protect it from anything that might happen.

A large iceberg was grounded only a quarter of a mile from shore, and it had been there long enough so the bottom portion of it had worn away from the constant action of the tides. It resembled a huge bird with outstretched wings. I never thought too much about it as I prepared to bed down inside the Otter, but the people of the village who usually relied on such icebergs for their water supply would not go near this particular one because they considered it too dangerous.

During the night I was abruptly awakened by the sound of an explosion or clap of thunder the likes of which I hope to never hear again. It shook me and the aircraft and as I struggled to my feet my first instinct was to look for the iceberg. It was gone. The iceberg had broken in half, with the wings of the heavy top section hitting the water with the force and sound of a bomb.

No sooner had I figured out what had happened when the first waves hit the Otter. The aircraft pitched up and down so violently I was afraid of capsizing. In a few moments the waves were gone and the surface of Pond Inlet was calm as if nothing had happened. I reset the anchor and, try as I might, couldn't get back to sleep for quite some time until my pulse returned to normal.

Wardair was also called on frequently for medical emergency flights. We weren't the only flying service available for emergency runs, but we did more than all the other Yellowknife outfits put together. We had the newest, best equipment available while the others were flying some junky old aircraft that you wouldn't want to take out during the day much less at night. But with the good old Pratt & Whitney engines, the Beaver and the Otter could get in and out safely even in the black of night in the middle of nowhere.

Men would get hurt in blasting accidents out in the
mines or we'd have burn victims from the Inuit villages.
The Inuit were using those damn gasoline stoves and
every so often someone would get burned lighting one,
usually a little kid. We'd get a call in the middle of the
night and some brave nurse from the Yellowknife Hospital
would come along with us and away we'd go.

Night emergency runs could be tricky because sometimes they were made on very black nights to unknown
strips. In the winter, if worse came to worst, the only
thing the Inuit would have to put out for landing lights at
remote camps were what they called pyramid lights. The
natives would cut three triangular slabs of snow and fit
them together in the shape of a pyramid about 14 inches
high and then put one of their fat little candles inside.
They would leave just enough of a hole at the top so the
candle would burn, but not too big so the wind could
blow the candle out. Amazingly, you could see those pyramid lights from quite a way out.

They'd put two lights at the near end of the strip and
one at the far end, just three lights in all. I would get my
height from that and come in, hoping to hell they had
picked a spot that wouldn't wreck the airplane.

Later when the Inuit had snowmobiles they would place
two machines at the head of the runway with the beams
facing inward about 45 degrees so it would throw some
light across the near end of the strip. A third machine
would be sitting at the end of the runway, often sideways,
so if I couldn't stop the aircraft he could get the hell out
of the way. Again, just three lights were used.

When the ice was off the lakes and our aircraft were
back on floats, black night landings could be downright
hair raising because usually there would be only a light
or two on shore and that wouldn't give you an up and
down reference. I'd set the aircraft up in landing configuration about 200 or 300 feet off the water and then just
sit there and wait for the floats to touch.

I always thought I was going to run out of lake before finally touching down. Always. But eventually you'd touch down, and as long as you touched down between 300 and 500 feet a minute it wasn't a bad landing. When you hit at more than 500 feet a minute it was quite a jar but okay as long as you had the nose up.

There were many, many night landings in pitch dark on lakes and I remember most of them because they tend to be the kind of landings you never forget.

In the 1960s the fastest airplane we had for air ambulance runs was a twin-engine Piper Apache that I had purchased and leased to Wardair. The Apache is a small twin with 160-hp flat engines on it that give it a cruising speed of around 150 mph. I bought it primarily for family and vacation trips back to St. Cloud and would simply pull it off lease under the arrangement I had with Max. I remember making an emergency night flight in the Apache all the way up to Coppermine on the coast to pick up a 12-year-old girl who had been severely burned by a gasoline stove. They laid out a little strip for me in the snow with a small Cat and used some snowmobiles to light my way. I was able to get in and out without much problem.

In 1961 Max decided to expand Wardair's operations even further by getting into the international charter business. That meant moving the head office to Edmonton, shopping around for a large passenger airliner and renaming the company Wardair Canada Ltd. He ended up leasing a Douglas DC-6 with four big engines, a 300-mph cruising speed and enough room to take 91 passengers to just about any vacation, meeting or convention spot on the planet.

With Max in Edmonton, that left Wardair's Northern Division in my hands, assisted by George Bell, our chief engineer, and a staff totaling about a dozen people. We were responsible for seven aircraft: four single engine Otters, two Beavers and, of course, the Bristol Freighter.

One of my first decisions was to take over for Max as the primary pilot for the Bristol Freighter aircraft that I would eventually take to the North Pole.

Chapter Eleven

THE BRISTOL FREIGHTER

*"I would always be first in with the Bristol
until I got the landing strip established, then
the other boys would take over. Picking the
landing sites, checking them out and bringing
in the Bristol for the first time were all part
of my job. The chief pilot part."*

The British-made Bristol 170 Freighter was a big twin-engine taildragger that looked as if it had been designed by someone who didn't know the first thing about aerodynamics. It always amazed me how fast the darn thing went for how it looked, as if it should have cruised maybe 130 mph. But it would actually do 155 mph, the same as a DC-3.

It wasn't so much that the Bristol was just plain ugly, which it definitely was, but it also appeared ungainly and perhaps not even capable of flight. Whatever it lacked in glamour, however, the old Bristol more than made up for with the performance and ability to carry big payloads. The cockpit sat atop a huge nose with double doors for easy loading of heavy freight, and Max Ward recognized the tremendous potential such an aircraft would have in serving the more remote mining and oil camps in the North.

The original Bristol prototype was designed in the late stages of World War II as a military freighter for the Royal Air Force, but it never left the ground until the war was over in late 1945. A passenger version called the Wayfarer was introduced in 1946, but the 170 Freighter was much more popular and it was modified several times in the late 1940s and the 1950s with stronger wings and more horsepower. The Bristol 170 proved to be a real workhorse and could carry six tons of freight or up to 44 passengers or even some of both. Its most popular use was as a car air ferry across the English Channel.

With those wide double nose doors open, you could drive three automobiles or a D-4 Caterpillar tractor or even a fire engine truck into the belly of the aircraft. I mention a fire engine because that's one of the more unusual loads our Bristol handled. We ferried the entire rig across Great Slave Lake from Hay River to Yellowknife before the Mackenzie Highway was built around the west end of the lake.

Old CF-TFX, our Bristol 170, was an Mk. 31 model powered by two big Hercules sleeve-valve engines that were rated at 1,980 hp each and weighed about a ton apiece. The engines were a whole different technology because of the sleeve-valves and they required considerable pampering. Fortunately, Max was able to hire an engineer who knew the Bristols like the back of his hand. His name was George Bell and, in my opinion, he was the first chief engineer at Wardair who was any good at all. George had been nursing Bristol engines almost from the day the aircraft was introduced and Wardair was fortunate to employ him. Originally from Northern Ireland, George could drink with the best of them, which he often did. He would get out of bed half looped and come down to work, but he was good. George always did the right thing.

His wife, Barbara, is a real card, one of the funniest people I have ever known. She's a full-fledged English gal with a cockney sort of accent and a talent for telling stories that are so funny they almost kill you.

One of her favorites was about the time she and George went over to England so George could represent Wardair in mediating a labor dispute involving the company's growing international charter business. Imagine that, an Irishman involved in mediating an English labor dispute! Barbara stayed at the airport terminal knitting while

George went about his business. She had knitted almost an entire sweater when she noticed George wasn't back from his negotiations. As Barbara tells it, George had learned that Wardair was having trouble getting a flight off the ground in Amsterdam due to the same strike.

Without thinking about Barbara, George hopped on a plane over to Amsterdam. When he arrived there he realized, "Oh, geez, Barbara is over in England at the terminal," and he called a friend who lived in England not too far from the terminal and the friend ran over to tell Barbara not to worry. George, believe it or not, would do things like that.

Another of Barbara's favorite stories is about the time she was mopping the central hallway in their Yellowknife home when a neighbor lady called because the Bell's little daughter, Fanola, had cut her head while playing in the neighbor's yard. In a panic, Barbara threw the mop in the sink and blocked off the drain while she ran over to check on Fanola. Barbara said she stayed and "nattered" with the neighbor for a time after learning Fanola's injuries weren't all that bad. When she returned to her house, the entire central hallway was flooded with soap and water.

Barbara went roaring into her house and, of course, her feet went out from under her and she landed so hard on her back that she couldn't get up. George had been out about 30 hours straight changing an engine and came walking in the door shortly after Barbara hit the floor. He looked down at her, according to Barbara, and said, "What the hell are you doing laying in that water?" Barbara looked straight up at him and said, "Because I can't move!"

George took her to the hospital to see if she had a broken hip or worse, but she was just badly bruised. When you hear Barbara tell these stories in all their lively detail and with that cockney accent, you laugh so hard your sides hurt. She is a wonderful lady with a personality that just sparkles.

George Bell was a pilot's engineer and I could always
trust his work and judgment despite the often harsh
conditions we operated under at Yellowknife. Max eventually asked George to join the Wardair southern operation at Edmonton to be second in command of maintenance for a growing fleet of passenger aircraft. The DC-6
on lease had been replaced in 1963 by a Douglas DC-6B
which Max purchased from KLM Airlines, and it was
joined in 1966 by a Boeing 727 jet airliner as Wardair's
international charter business prospered and grew. I told
George that he had spent his share of time in the North
and that he should accept Max's offer. "Take it while it's
there," I told him. And he did.

As I was saying, however, the Bristol Hercules engines
were very good if you treated them right and that meant
they had to be maintained often and very carefully.
George and the other Wardair engineers didn't have the
luxury of a hangar for all their maintenance work until
one day Max came up with the idea of a big nose hangar
to protect them from the elements. The hangar stood
about 35 feet tall and was mounted on truck wheels for
mobility. It was large enough to cover an entire Bristol
engine and those working on it, with a strong enough
main reel to hoist the engine up and out with a block
and tackle. There were also several times when George
changed out a Bristol engine at a remote site with nothing more than a big tripod he would rig up and perhaps
some canvas tenting for protection against the wind.

Since we didn't have a real hangar for the Bristol, or
for any of Wardair's aircraft at Yellowknife, the old Bristol
sat right out in the open all year around just like the rest
of the fleet. We would have to heat the engines each
morning with what was known as a Herman Nelson
heater, which was a box about 20 inches wide and maybe
three feet long that burned fuel oil or gasoline. It had a
blower motor on the back which blew air over the com-
bustion chamber and out flexible ducts on the other end.
The Herman Nelson could be dangerous, especially with
gasoline as fuel, and if the motor quit for some reason

there was a trip door held shut by air pressure that would fall open and shut the fuel off. But it was a crude contraption and you never could trust it. The Herman Nelson had to be watched all the time. I burned the nose cowling right off my Piper Apache one time when I left the Herman Nelson unattended.

The fire engine wasn't the only unusual load we were able to haul in the Bristol. One time we went out and picked up a damaged Otter over on the Thelon River near Baker Lake, a good 500 miles east of Yellowknife.

It was early spring, as I remember, and there was good light again. The Otter had gone in the summer before, wrecked on take-off. It belonged to the Lamb brothers of Lamb Airways out of Churchill, along the west shore of Hudson Bay in northern Manitoba. They hired us to go in and bring it out, which we did. The Thelon River was a fairly swift river and it froze too rough for an aircraft to land, especially a wheel-equipped aircraft like the Bristol. I decided to land on a frozen backwater, or snye, a couple of miles from where the Otter had gone in. We built a big sleigh much like an Inuit sled, with everything lashed together with rope so the runners would give a bit. But we built it big enough to haul the Otter fuselage with engine intact.

When you look at an Otter and see how big it is you wouldn't figure it would fit inside a Bristol, but it did, in pieces of course. It took two trips by sleigh, with the fuselage one trip all by itself. This was another one of those jobs where we flew over in the early morning and spent most of the day loading and tried to get off before dark. The Lamb brothers had a couple of snowmobiles on the scene and we hitched them to the sleigh with the fuselage on it and had a heck of a time covering the two miles to the Bristol. Every time we'd stop it was almost impossible to get moving again, but finally we made it over to the Bristol and managed to slide the fuselage inside. The second load consisted of the tailplane and a wing, which were in good condition, and the remains of the other

wing. It was a lighter load and we covered the two miles
to the Bristol much faster. We slipped the wings into the
Bristol alongside the fuselage and the tailplane went in
last before we closed the big nose doors and prepared
for take-off.

The Lamb brothers must have had a camp at the site
because one of the snowmobiles went down to mark the
end of the snye since it was getting quite dark. The snye
curved just a little and it wasn't a perfectly straight take-
off. Somebody on that snowmobile was good enough to
give me a light for direction and I figured whoever it was
must have been planning on staying the night or he
would have come with us.

While hauling the Otter out was a challenge, I'd have
to say our toughest load was the time we took two big D-8
Cats into a remote mining camp in the mountains just
west of Watson Lake in the southern Yukon. The Cats
had to be dismantled because they each weighed over
20 tons and the Bristol could only handle six tons on a
short haul. We had to haul the engines, tracks and
siderails separately. The C-frames, the large part that
held the bulldozer to the Cat, were so broad that the
only way we could load them into the Bristol was at a
45-degree angle. They were very heavy, of course, so
we used a truck with a boom to suspend them and
then chained the frames so they were at the proper
angle. Then it was a matter of carefully sliding them
into the belly of the Bristol and more or less reversing
the process at the mine. I had the corners timbered
because I was afraid the frames would go right through
the fuselage of the Bristol if they shifted even a little.
It all worked out and we delivered the big Cats without
a problem, thanks to the Bristol.

During the spring and fall when the Mackenzie Highway was impassable and the ice on the big lake was
either going out or hadn't formed yet, we'd haul cars
between Yellowknife and Hay River. We would put three
full-size cars in the Bristol and still have room for nine

passengers in the back. In fact, we often stuffed building materials and other supplies in among the cars and passengers until the old Bristol was so full you couldn't get from one end to the other. The idea of leaving the very last bag of insulation behind was unthinkable, so we would have the boys push and shove the bag in through the hatch and then push and shove the hatch until it was secured. That's just how things were done.

The Bristol really paid off for Wardair during the oil exploration boom in the Canadian Arctic islands in the mid-1960s. We did hundreds of hours of flying for the oil companies for several years, landing the Bristol on beaches, river deltas or the ice itself, anywhere we could find a smooth enough place close to 3,000 feet long, which is what we needed for the Bristol. Actually, we could get by with a little less, but we always preferred 3,000 feet just in case.

I remember one time we were flying into an oil company strip at the foot of the Nahanni Mountains southeast of Fort Simpson. They had cleared a strip that was somewhat less than 3,000 feet, with a river at one end and a foothill mountain at the other end. The foothill was covered with trees, but they had cleared out some of the trees and brush at the base in the event anyone overshot the runway. The only way in, of course, was over the river, landing toward the mountain, unloading, then turning around and taking off toward the river.

Once the old Bristol was empty, I suppose we could have made it taking off toward the mountain. But it would have meant pulling off and making a really steep turn right off the end of the strip. I never cared much for that kind of thing.

Anyhow, I had asked them to put up a windsock. Normally the wind cooperated and we would come into it on landing and then take off with a slight downwind without much problem. This particular day, however, I could see the wind was from the river toward the mountain and I had to decide whether or not to attempt a downwind landing. I hated like hell to go back and thought, well, maybe I can make it — it's going to be tight but I'll try it.

I didn't quite make it.

I dropped the Bristol right at the river's edge but still ran the full length of the strip and off the end into the muck at the base of the foothill. They had a small Caterpillar tractor in the camp and we tried to pull the Bristol out with chains hitched to the main wheels, but it wouldn't budge. We dug the wheels out and shoved planks under them before the Cat was able to get the aircraft out of the mud and back on the strip. It took over half the day, and the Bristol hadn't even run all that far off the end. The tail wheel was still on the runway. The whole episode convinced me that 3,000 feet of runway was what the Bristol needed, even if it could sometimes get by with less. This obviously wasn't one of those times.

Finding natural landing strips for the Bristol up in the Arctic islands was a task best done in the reliable old Otter. The oil companies would pinpoint on the map where they wanted their camp, on Melville Island, for example, and it would be my job to fly out in the Otter and locate a strip as close to that point as possible. I would be out for a day or two and the single-engine Otter was perfect for the job. It had adequate range and it allowed me to fiddle a lot more with take-offs and landings without using so much fuel. On good days I might find two landing strips, but sometimes I'd search for a whole day and not find any.

Ice was usually my last choice as a landing strip for the Bristol because it's so unpredictable, always changing from one day to the next, especially during the spring warm-up. The river deltas found along the coasts of most Arctic islands sometimes made good landing sites. A number of them have grown quite large over the centuries, with level, smooth and hard sand surfaces extending well out into the sea. Finding one that just happened to be located near a drilling site was rare, however. More a happy coincidence than anything else. No, the best and most common sites for landing the Bristol were the remarkable Arctic island beaches.

The Canadian Arctic islands have been rising out of the sea for thousands of years, and the beaches with them. Many of the beaches around the islands rise 80 or even 100 feet above the sea and slope gently toward the water in a huge expanse of hard-packed sand. They made good and often excellent landing strips for the Bristol, almost like an actual airstrip. In winter the snow was usually hardpacked or even blown away by the wind off the sea, and the beaches remained the best place to land a Bristol.

Alone in the Otter, I would fly low along a beach and look for a stretch at least 3,000 feet long that might make a good landing strip. Then I would set the Otter down and walk every foot of the beach, checking for erosion ditches or large rocks and probing the snow in winter for these same hazards. The cabin of the Otter was full of 45-gallon fuel drums for refueling myself during these extended scouting trips. I used the empty drums as markers where I thought the landing strip should start when I brought in the Bristol.

I would always be first in with the Bristol until I got the landing strip established, then the other boys could take over. Picking the landing sites, checking them out and bringing in the Bristol for the first time were all part of my job. The chief pilot part.

Wardair flew a lot of freight between the islands in the mid-1960s, using Resolute as a base. The old Bristol was the only aircraft we flew that required a crew of two, and I remember one time being stuck out on a lake on Melville Island with only one good engine and a copilot who was fairly green and not much use for anything.

We had a cracked sleeve in one engine and, of course, the sleeve does the same thing that valves do in a standard engine. The sleeve provides the intake and the ex-

haust timing. When it cracks, it will usually crack
through one port. This one had cracked through the intake port when we delivered a load out on Melville Island,
about 250 miles west of Resolute, early one spring. My
first thought was to get another engine in and change it
out on the spot, but then I started thinking about the
logistics of that and decided it would have been impossible. The job was too big and it was just too cold to work
without proper protection.

The boys at the oil camp were good enough to put us
up for a couple of days while I tried to figure out a solu-
tion to our predicament. Meantime, Joe McGilvray, another Wardair pilot who had been copilot to Max and
myself in the Bristol many times, flew in with the Otter in
the likely event my young copilot would need transportation out. When Joe arrived I told him that maybe I could
get the Bristol airborne and back to Resolute with the
one good engine and whatever power I could get from the
one with the cracked sleeve. I explained that as long as
we kept the bad engine below the pressure that was developed by a normally aspirated engine, it would suck in
only enough fuel to run without blowing fuel in with the
supercharger, which would back gases up and explode
into the rest of the intake. If that happened, the engine
would shudder a couple of times and quit. Joe thought it
over and agreed it should work.

We set about getting everything ready for take-off and
I asked Joe and my copilot to place one of our empty 45-
gallon fuel drums down along the landing strip at the
point where we either needed to be in the air or quit trying. When they came back to the Bristol after placing the
barrel, the copilot looked rather pale and said he would
just as soon stay behind if I didn't mind. Before I could
answer Joe said he would take the seat next to me and
he asked the young fellow to take the Otter back for him,
which he did.

I told Joe, "Holler at me or even whack me a good one
if we come to the barrel and we're still on the ground

because we're not going to have enough lake left to get out of here." Joe and I finally got started and sure enough, I overboosted the bad engine and lost it. We had barely started rolling. On the second try, Joe marked the spot on the throttle for the bad engine that I couldn't exceed and he actually put his hand around the throttle to make sure I wouldn't get past the mark on that side. The whole idea was to get the big old Bristol rolling so I could develop enough horsepower in the good engine, because after that I wouldn't really need the other engine.

The Bristol got off to a pretty good start the second time. I hadn't intended to watch for the barrel because that was Joe's assignment, but I could see it coming out of the corner of my eye. By the time the barrel went by, both Joe and I knew we were going to make it. We didn't say a word. We just knew it. The lake was down in a kind of hole, which meant we had to climb out of it. As soon as we did, I shut down the bad engine and we flew back to Resolute on the good one.

Resolute had a big nose hangar and we were able to keep partly warm when we changed out the engine. It wasn't the first time old CF-TFX needed a new engine, either. I had to have engines replaced two other times, both at DEW line sites, and Max blew an engine over at Wrigley by the Mackenzie River.

Another time, in the fall of the same year, we were flying off Melville again and this time I lost an engine about halfway between the island and Resolute. It was over Viscount Melville Sound, as we were approaching Bathurst Island, and it was mostly open water. Because it was fall, it was just stormy enough so there was a really bad chop. When the engine quit I didn't know why at first. Again, I had a perfectly green copilot who had probably made no more than three trips. He didn't know the airplane and he was absolutely no help at all.

When you have an engine failure in the Bristol you have to go into automatic rich in order to get the horsepower you need to maintain altitude. But when I tried to

transfer fuel from the three tanks in the wing of the dead
engine over into the wing with the good engine, nothing
happened. As I fiddled with the transfer controls it slowly
seeped into my mind that the problem might be ice in the
system. Well, I thought, it's only a matter of time before
my tanks go dry and I lose the other engine! Fortunately,
I didn't. Although we found the problem side was solid
with ice when we took the filters off, we also noticed a
couple of small tracks in the ice where a little fuel apparently was flowing through. But I knew there wasn't
enough fuel to make it to Resolute on auto rich, which is
the power you would normally need.

We were at 6,000 feet, and I thought even if I settle all
the way I might make it into Resolute in lean. So I cut
back to the highest power I could get in lean with the
carburetor dropped back to auto lean, which is normally
not supposed to be enough to maintain flight. At 2,800
feet, however, we started to hold altitude if I was very
careful to maintain minimum single-engine speed,
which was about 95 to 100 mph. A stall in the Bristol
is 83 mph.

I held altitude but then thought we might as well lose
a little to gain a bit more speed when I saw the coastline
of Cornwallis Island and knew we only had another 15 or
20 miles to go. My confidence increased, of course, once
we were over land and had left that black, dirty water
behind us. I actually started to think we might make it
into Resolute instead of going down.

My green copilot didn't know what was going on, and
while he wasn't exactly panicky, he wasn't much help
either because he lacked experience. Copilots were supposed to know all the aircraft systems. But when you
read it in a book it's entirely different than the real thing.
I always knew the aircraft from helping work on them. If
there was a problem, I was usually out there trying to
help find out what it was.

As we flew over the coast there wasn't much gas showing on the instruments, but I knew we had 15 gallons.

There is a header tank under the main tanks in the Bristol, and you always knew you had 15 gallons that wouldn't show at all on the gauges. It also occurred to me that the runway at Resolute ran east-west, and that if I landed straightaway there was no way I could turn onto the taxiway with the one engine out. If I came in straight, I thought, I'm going to leave this big brute sitting right in the middle of the runway with no real way to get it off unless they get a truck out that could tow me into the taxiway.

Knowing I had those 15 gallons in the header tank, I decided to take a chance and go around the runway holding my height so if the engine did quit on the way around I was still high enough to glide in. I came around quite high, but dropped the old Bristol on the far end of the runway so I could use my good engine to turn onto the taxiway and park the aircraft out of the way. The first person to greet me when I stepped out of the aircraft was a good friend and fellow pilot, Bert Burry. He had his own charter service and flew the Canadian Arctic islands more than I did, but usually with smaller aircraft.

"I knew it! I knew it!" Bert said. "There would be only one guy in the whole Territories who would come in on one engine with no gas and make a circle in the air so he could get in on the ramp!" Bert had been listening to my radio communications as I was coming in, but you only identify your aircraft and never yourself so he could only guess it might be me.

We figured the icing problem was due to water in an above-ground fuel tank at Cambridge Bay, where I had refueled the Bristol on the way up to Resolute. They had a big tank and apparently didn't bleed the water off very often. During the day the tank would heat up from the last of the sunshine in the fall and condense some moisture inside, some of which ended up in our tanks. Quite often we couldn't check our fuel drains because they would be frozen, and you couldn't very well take a blow torch to heat up the fuel drain to check if there was water in the system. Nope, after it was cold we just assumed that any water would stay in the storage tanks or settle down and freeze in the header tank. The header tanks would take quite a bit of water before the water sumps got full and the ice eventually worked its way into the filters. In this case enough water somehow got into the system and then it froze.

As the oil companies settled in and established themselves on many of the Canadian Arctic islands, they also put in big airstrips. Within a few years they were using bigger, faster and more efficient aircraft than the old Bristol. The Bristol, however, continued to earn its keep servicing the mining and oil industries closer to home. There was also polar scientific survey work going on up in the islands which required air transportation and support, and Wardair was hired for some of it. Although we were becoming underdogs in the competition for servicing oil camps in the Arctic islands, clearly the Bristol remained the best aircraft for difficult jobs.

One such job took us over a thousand miles to the southeast when we helped put in a small oil rig with the Bristol at the bottom of Hudson Bay. I had found an old beach to land on, but it was fairly soft and I found I couldn't even turn the Bristol around without burying the wheels unless I was very careful. The drill foreman had one of those little four-wheel drive rigs that was sort of a cross between a dune buggy and a Jeep, and like a lot of the equipment at the drill site it didn't have much of a muffler on it. I told him I'd like to drive down the beach a mile or two in the buggy and see if we could find a better section of beach for the Bristol because we still had more deliveries to make. We scouted the beach for a better landing site but didn't find one and continued to use the original section of beach.

On the way back, however, we ran into an old cow polar bear that was quite capable of overtaking us if she decided that's what she wanted to do. The idiot driving the buggy decided to chase the polar bear along the beach despite my protests and warnings that the bear could outrun us if she had a mind to. The driver didn't pay any attention to me and now that I think about it, he probably knew the buggy was making so much noise the bear would never turn on us. Still, the bear kept looking over her shoulder at us and I figured any time now she'll change her mind, get mad and then come after us. As it turned out, we chased her all the way down the airstrip. But the experience scared the hell out of me because you never know what a polar bear might do. Or any bear, for that matter.

I'll never forget the story about old Tom Forrest who maintained the landing strip year around at the Tundra Mine about 150 miles northeast of Yellowknife out in the barrens. He had an encounter with a bear that was too close for comfort.

Old Tom was a little guy, but a tough one, and a real loner. He could have lived at the mining camp three miles from the landing strip, but he preferred instead to live on the edge of the airstrip in a tent that was fortified with plywood with a bit of insulation between the plywood and canvas. The roof was floppy like a tent, but there were two sash windows in the sidewalls, one by a small kitchen area and another over by Tom's bed, right above his head. Tom more or less built the airstrip, which was located atop an esker. He had an old off-brand bulldozer with a small blade that he used to grade and maintain the strip hour after hour, day after day, so we never had a problem bringing in the Bristol. Tundra was a gold mine with about 60 men in a camp that had permanent buildings and a nice dining hall. Why Tom wouldn't eat and sleep in camp with the rest of the men, I'll never know. He had a family back at Yellowknife but he was one of those who couldn't stay sober in town, so he'd stay out. We'd bring him a bottle maybe at Christmas, but that was about it.

Tom wasn't too careful about garbage and a big old Barren Lands grizzly that had been chased off the main camp garbage finally found his. The barrens grizzly isn't all that big as grizzly go, about the size of a big black bear, but it's like a polar bear in temperament in that it has no fear of a human being at all. Tom knew this grizzly was around because he had heard it sniffing outside the tent at night, so he took to sleeping with a loaded rifle by his cot.

One night Tom heard the bear rummaging around just outside his tent window and as he sat up in his cot the bear reared up and put his paw right through the window, showering glass all over Tom. Tom had just gotten a new watch, quite an expensive one to hear him tell it, and as he reached around for his rifle he smashed the watch against the stock of the gun.

By this time the bear had gotten his head in the window and was about to tear the window and sidewall apart when Tom whirled around with the rifle and fired it before he could line it up on the bear. The gunshot scared the bear off without even coming close to hitting him. The next day Tom got another window from the mining camp and replaced the damaged one in his tent. As for the grizzly, the bear never came back.

When I saw Tom and heard his story I asked him how big he thought the bear was. He said, "Hell, at that range, they're all big!" I can just see that bear with his head in the window, face to face with Tom.

While the old Bristol taildragger was our big workhorse aircraft, de Havilland came out with the Twin Otter in the early 1960s. Like the single-engine Otter, the Twin was a high-wing aircraft that was Pratt & Whitney powered and had excellent S.T.O.L. capability. Only instead of a single radial engine it had a pair of new Pratt & Whitney 500-hp PT-6 turboprop engines mounted on the wings, and it could haul up to 21 passengers or a ton and a half of freight faster and farther than its smaller namesake.

George Curley, a really sharp businessman who was an accountant for Max's backers, the Bryne brothers, before Max hired George to help run the business end of Wardair's Northern Division, became as convinced as I was that we needed to buy a Twin Otter. Little did we know that even before the first Twin came off the production line Max had long before made a commitment to Russ Bannock, sales manager for de Havilland at the time and later its president, for two of the aircraft when they were only in the preliminary design stage. It was another example of Max thinking ahead of the rest of us, although George eventually went on to become the president of Wardair in 1985.

We took delivery of our first Twin in 1963 and gradually added others as some of the Otters and Beavers were phased out. On one of my early flights in the new Twin I lost oil pressure in one of the engines and was forced to land on a small mountain airstrip about 150 miles southwest of Fort Simpson.

I just happened to be working in that area when an oil seal blew and, of course, the PT-6 engines were completely new to us but I managed to shut the engine down and feather the prop. Although it wasn't my destination, I knew about this particular Imperial Oil Company airstrip and that I was close to it. It was one of those little temporary strips the oil companies would put on the side of a mountain while they were drilling in the area so food and supplies could be flown in. My only thought was to get the aircraft down because I didn't know if it was something I had done wrong and perhaps the other engine might fail. I had gone to de Havilland's Toronto headquarters to study the aircraft, so I thought I knew what I was doing. But I had no idea why the engine lost oil pressure or even that the engine had lost its oil since I never saw any sign of it going. Evidently it went through the burner section of the engine and burned along with the fuel, I learned later.

The landing strip wasn't the best, sort of rough and ugly since it had been hacked out of the timber, but I managed to land the Twin safely. I radioed the nearby oil

camp and they radioed Yellowknife that I was down on
their strip and that I would like the Apache sent over
with an engineer who might have some idea of what had
happened to my engine. One of our pilots brought in Art
Lockwood, who was second in command of the Northern
Division and a fine mechanic.

When Art arrived he sort of scratched his head and
said, "I just don't know."

What he meant was that the PT-6 engine at the time
was so new that de Havilland didn't have any in stock.
They had to be ordered, which would normally mean a
wait of a couple of weeks, but Pratt & Whitney was on
strike. In fact, it seemed every time something like this
happened, either de Havilland or Pratt & Whitney was
on strike. We couldn't even get anyone from Pratt &
Whitney to come out and see what had happened to the
engine.

I said, "Well, Art, what would you think if we hand-
feather the prop and try flying this thing home on one
engine?" Art and I both knew that a prop feathered in
flight from the cockpit will still turn slowly. "I don't want
that engine turning the least bit if I try to take it home
on one," I told him.

Art suggested I check with Max.

I was able to make contact with Max and ask him
what he thought about it since his neck would be on the
line probably more than mine. He said, "Well, do you
think you can do it?" I said, "Sure I think I can do it." He
was always like that to me; if you think you can do it,
then just do it!

That evening we hand-feathered the prop and tied it in
place with some rope. The next morning I checked the
wind and found there wasn't any to speak of, which
wasn't much of a problem since the landing strip ran
downhill. If there had been even a little breeze coming
up the mountain, it would have been better, but at least
there wasn't any wind coming down the mountain. I

thought we had better get off before the wind does come up because you never know if it's going to blow up or down the mountain.

Normally it's hard to get started rolling with only one engine because your aircraft always wants to turn away from the live engine. The Twin Otter has nose steering, however, and that is a big help along with the fact its props are fairly close in and not way out on the wing. I was able to get rolling and when we were halfway down the strip Art and I knew we were going to make it very nicely. We lifted off with room to spare and flew the 400 miles back to Yellowknife at about 120 mph. The Apache, of course, made it home much faster than we did but our speed on one engine was quite good, in my opinion.

The flight back on one engine with the other tied down was against the rules, and we all knew it. Especially Max. But we needed to get that airplane back in business as soon as possible, so we took a chance on me losing my license and Max maybe losing his business if the authorities found out about it. I didn't think much about it on the way back, however. What worried me most was wondering if the other engine might blow a seal and quit, too.

As it turned out, the labyrinth seal failure was an isolated case. I've never heard of another labyrinth seal failing in a Twin Otter either before or since. The PT-6 turbine engine had a high idle speed and wasn't particularly efficient, but it beat anything we had flown up to that point. Time on the engine was determined as much by the number of starts as by total running time because the starts ran up so hot that they caused as much deterioration in the engine as long running. You were much better off on longer hauls with the Twin. At first the engines had to be opened up every 500 hours, but eventually it was improved in the later models to 1,500 and even 1,600 hours. In terms of power, performance and reliability, however, the PT-6 was a big improvement over pistons.

The sleek Twin Otter and its turbines represented the future of aviation as much as the Bristol Freighter with its fixed landing gear and sleeve-valve engines would become a relic of the past in a few years. Still, it was a Bristol Freighter, old CF-TFX, that took the honor of being the first wheeled aircraft to land at the North Pole.

CHAPTER TWELVE

THE NORTH POLE LANDING, 1967

*"As I brought the Bristol around for a third
approach and landing attempt, I asked the
good Lord to bring us in safely and silently
thanked Him for giving us such a clear day
and very good weather all around."*

The oil exploration boom in the Canadian Arctic islands
helped to keep the Bristol in the air in the 1960s. The
boom was stimulated in part by the Polar Continental
Shelf Project, a long-term scientific research effort spon-
sored mostly by the Canadian government.

The project was set up to study the islands and the
straits surrounding them, all of which sit atop the continental shelf that stretches from the top of Greenland
southwest to the Mackenzie River Delta region. Eventually
the project moved beyond the shelf to study the Arctic
Ocean and its depths, up to and including the North Pole.

Every summer for at least a dozen years a team of 20
or 30 scientists would be put on the Arctic islands or
even the Arctic ice to analyze everything from minerals to
marine life. They measured ocean currents and depths,
mapped the ocean floor and tracked the movement of the
polar ice pack. When the first satellites were placed into
polar orbit, the project measured the degree of deflection
in the orbit as the satellite would pass over the North
Magnetic Pole area. By 1967 the project leaders had set
their sights on the North Pole and were organizing an international expedition for May of that year.

Wardair did a considerable amount of work in support
of the project over the years, hauling in teams and their
supplies and moving their equipment around. Flying for
the project in the late 1950s, in fact, was actually the

first time I flew for any length of time in the Arctic islands. That experience paid off when a few years later the oil companies got interested in the islands and hired us to support their camps with the Bristol.

We would cache fuel, housing material and staple supplies at prospective campsites on the islands in early spring in advance of the oil crews and the Polar Continental Shelf people. There were years when we had caches of fuel and supplies scattered all across the Arctic, which was somewhat reassuring to me and the others who flew with me in the Bristol across this desolate area. We would put in our own caches of fuel, too. Most of them were on the mainland but we also put our own caches in at some of the remote weather stations up on the islands. For the caches out in the open, of course, the trick was to locate them in a place where the snow depth wouldn't be so great that you could find them again. We always carried along some bamboo fishing poles with flags on them and we would stick one of them between the fuel drums so that in the event the cache was buried there would be something sticking up in the air. Sometimes the flag would be gone. But that old fishing pole would still be there, which was a good thing because often our destinations were too far away to make it round trip without refueling.

Housing provisions for both the oil crews and the Polar Continental Shelf teams seemed to become more sophisticated each year. We would haul in semi-permanent buildings made up of four-by-eight insulated panels that bolted together or a contraption we called orange peel buildings that were made of fiberglass. The orange peel buildings looked like a Quonset hut, except the ends were round and composed of curved, overlapping sections that reminded me of an orange. You could bolt one of these buildings together in minutes and make it 20 or 30 or even 40 feet long, depending on how many side panels you used. They had an insulated plywood floor and were quite impervious to wind.

The scientific teams would usually set up their camp on the shore of whichever island they were studying.

They routinely sent out small parties to the interior of the island or out onto the sea ice, but never for more than a few nights at a time since all they had to sleep in during these excursions were plain old double tents. By the mid-1960s, the scientists were venturing far out on the Arctic Ocean ice to conduct seismic tests. I put one camp out on the ice about 200 miles west of Mould Bay, which is a weather station on Prince Patrick Island. The scientists would drop a depth charge and fire it near the surface if they were measuring depth or they'd let it sink to the bottom before setting it off if they were mapping the ocean floor. Two big helicopters were used to move the camp back toward Prince Patrick Island in stages as the team conducted a series of seismic tests along a 200-mile line.

In early May 1967 six of us were up in the northern Arctic islands with the Bristol doing some camp moves for the project and we were also scheduled to fly some helicopter fuel from Alert on the tip of Ellesmere Island and cache it over on Greenland. When we arrived at Alert, Dr. Fred Roots, the man in charge of the Polar Continental Shelf Project, greeted us and said his expedition team for the trip that he had been talking to Wardair about for several years was ready to go.

"You mean the trip to the North Pole?" I asked, knowing full well that's exactly what he meant. He nodded, and I said, "Yeah, I suppose we are. We've sure talked about it often enough." So, without returning to home base, we prepared the Bristol to go to the pole. Our job would be to take the team and the bulk of their equipment and supplies to the pole while smaller, ski-equipped aircraft from another outfit would fly support for the entire mission. We would make at least two flights to the pole because of the amount of fuel we needed to bring in for the other support aircraft as well as the Bristol.

Dr. Roots had asked Wardair several years earlier if we would be interested in taking a team to the pole in the Bristol. Max, who had to approve a flight of this nature because he was the man in charge of everything, gave it thumbs up. With the flight pre-approved, Dr. Roots and his team made their preparations at Alert and waited for us to finish our other work and show up at Alert with the Bristol so he could tell me, "Well, now, we'd like to make that North Pole flight if it's okay with you." Talk about short notice.

As luck would have it, I was fortunate to have with me at the time five of the best crewmen you could ever hope to find. Since the first trip to the pole was going to be a bit shaky, I decided to take a minimum crew which, for this kind of flight, would be three. I would be in the pilot's seat, of course, but we flipped coins for the other two spots. Copilot Jeff Braithwaite and engineer Harry Kreider won the honors. Copilot Wes Barron, a young engineer named Art Morrow and loader Del Hamilton would remain behind at Alert and perhaps have a chance to make the pole on a second flight in a day or two.

The team leader for the North Pole excursion, which had been dubbed "Operation SUGAR," was Dr. J.R. Hans Webber of the Canadian Dominion Observatory, one of Canada's top Arctic experts. It was a seven-man international team, and the other six members were: Neil Anderson, Axel Geiger, R.M. Ivy Iverson, Robert L. Lillestrand, Olaf Lungaard and Michael D. Pearlman. There were several military personnel assigned to Operation SUGAR, but according to Sgt. R.C. Dennett, RCCS, the military members were not allowed to go to the pole because the scientific team intended to visit one of several Russian camps that were already on the ice in the vicinity of the pole. Sgt. Dennett, a licensed amateur or "ham" radio operator, remained at Alert and was in communication with his amateur radio contacts in Ottawa (Walt Wooding) and St. Paul, Minnesota (Jack Fisher), during the expedition.

Dr. Webber told me that two single-engine Otters from another flying service were expected at any moment. Although Alert, at 82.30 degrees north, is the closest jumping-off point to the pole, 525 miles to the north, the round-trip distance is well beyond the range of the Otter and the idea was for the two aircraft to carry extra fuel and leapfrog their way to the pole and scout a safe landing site for the Bristol. This was good news because the big old gal I was flying weighed 22 tons loaded and although I had a lot of sea ice experience under my belt I had no intention of bringing her in to a landing spot at the pole that had not been thoroughly checked out.

It's difficult enough simply to fly off and try to land a ski-equipped Otter on a patch of sea ice sight unseen. But it would be just plain stupid to attempt the same thing at the North Pole with a 22-ton aircraft on wheels. As a matter of fact, no one had ever landed a wheel-equipped aircraft at the pole before or had even been dumb enough to try. I would be the first one, if we made it.

The two Otters had been working over on the western Arctic islands, but the weather was poor and they failed to show up at Alert. After waiting for three days, Dr. Webber and the team were getting impatient and I was becoming concerned because the time span for doing anything at the pole is limited to a few weeks in May. Dr. Webber approached me and said, "Look, we're just sitting here wasting time. What would you think of flying to the pole and we'll just take a look and maybe find a landing site? What do you think our chances would be?"

Dr. Webber and I had quite a discussion. I told him straight out our chances were maybe one in 50 with a little luck. And it would probably be a lot worse than that. "I don't mind flying up and back, but you need to understand that our chances of landing a big aircraft on wheels are very slim. I've never landed the Bristol on sea ice without previously landing with an Otter to check it out and no one to my knowledge has ever landed a wheel-equipped aircraft of any kind at the pole," I said. He said he understood and we agreed to leave in a few hours, which happened to be very early on May 6, 1967, since it was virtually daylight around the clock.

It was a beautiful, clear day when we took off from Alert shortly after midnight for the three-and-a-half hour flight to the pole. Jeff was a good pilot and we saw to it that we did everything as carefully as we could from the time we took off. We came right back over the runway and made sure we were on the heading we were supposed to be on, checking our astrocompass steadily and also the drift site we installed in the old Bristol in the event we had a cross-wind pushing us one way or the other. We didn't have the instrumentation back then that they do now, no earth induction compasses or anything like that. And a magnetic compass was no good at all, even though the North Magnetic Pole is a good 1,200 miles south of the North Pole. No, we had to rely primarily on our astrocompass to give us readings from the angle of the sun or any of the stars we knew or could pick out of the manual we carried, provided we knew the time of day and also our latitude.

Although I didn't know it at the time, two of us out of the total of 10 men aboard the Bristol were from St. Cloud. The other, Bob Lillestrand, was born and raised in a house on 11th Street South and was now a rising executive with Control Data Corporation in Minneapolis. He was one of the top earth navigators in the world. You could put Bob down anywhere and within a couple of hours he could tell you within a mile or two where he was on the earth's surface with only the sun to go by. On my later trip to the pole the team navigator had a light-gathering instrument called a theodolite that could shoot the stars during daylight, which made it possible to identify our location within a dozen yards in only an hour or two. But neither Bob Lillestrand nor his equipment were of much help in keeping the old Bristol on line to the pole. Besides the astrocompass and the drift site, we used time and distance calculations to figure our progress north.

When we reached the point where we reckoned the North Pole ought to be, the condition of the ice pack below was anything but encouraging.

The Arctic ice pack is an ever-changing landscape, always on the move because of the ocean currents beneath it. There are open leads no matter what time of year and great chunks of ice carved from glaciers a thousand miles distant. The ice moves in a counterclockwise direction, faster in summer than in winter, but always moving and grinding edge against edge. The constant grinding creates huge pressure ridges that can stretch for miles and then disappear into open leads where two ice sheets separate. It's a tremendous, constant force, which makes it a perilous place to try to land an airplane.

There are two kinds of ice up in the Arctic, old and new. The only kind of ice you can land an aircraft on is new ice from the previous winter. The old ice is too rough, eroded by the melting and freezing of the seasons. It's a jumble of pot holes and snowdrifts and pressure ridges. And it was old ice in all directions as far as the eye could see that greeted us as we flew over the pole in search of a landing site.

Dr. Webber had prearranged for us to turn 45 degrees left at the pole in the event of bad ice and maintain that heading for up to 10 minutes since a camp established anywhere along this line would likely drift back over the pole within a few days. About three minutes after making the turn I spotted a place that looked pretty good and began thinking, by golly, maybe I can land this old gal at the North Pole without looking first, although I knew it still wasn't the best idea in the world.

On my first approach I could see that I had made a mistake. It wasn't a frozen lead of smooth new ice at all. It was a stretch of rough old ice with a hummocky surface that had fooled me from a distance. As I was pulling up with the idea of turning around and going home, I spotted a promising landing site and decided to check it out.

It clearly was a frozen lead of new ice, a spot about 600 to 800 feet wide and about 3,500 feet long that had opened up and then refrozen over the winter. You can get some idea of the ice depth by its color and the amount of snow that has accumulated on it, but it's not always accurate. I've had friends put aircraft through the ice doing this although I had gotten away with it a couple of times.

I know this manner of flying sounds kind of devil-may-care, but up there you flew and landed on what you'd call calculated risks. Otherwise you just wouldn't get your work done, that was all there was to it. If you calculated the risk was worth taking, you went ahead and usually it worked out. One of the things I did, for example, was fly the length of the frozen lead both ways at 120 mph and time it with a stop watch. This not only gave me a fairly accurate measure of the length of the strip, but it also gave me an idea of wind direction. The slowest time was naturally going to be the direction of our landing approach. And since there had been very little drift north and south on our drift site on the trip up to the pole, I figured we wouldn't have much of a crosswind to worry about. Besides, the old Bristol didn't mind crosswinds too much. Even with that great big fuselage you could bring her in on a 30-mph crosswind without much problem.

The next step was to calculate whether the surface of the lead was smooth enough to land on, and this particular stretch of ice looked good except for a room-size hummock of ice sitting on the edge of the strip about halfway down its length. The hummock itself wasn't the problem. It was the two-foot high snowdrift downwind from it that bothered me. The drift crossed the landing area and there was a good chance it had been there for months, probably rock hard by now. Strange as it may seem, there isn't much snowfall at the top of the world and much of what is on the ground becomes wind-packed hard over time.

I asked Dr. Webber to climb up into the cockpit to discuss the situation and then told him there was a very real possibility the drift would be so hard that we could damage the aircraft. The Bristol, I explained, was quite an ingenious old aircraft in that it was designed for off-airport or otherwise very rough landings. The problem, however, was that the undercarriage wouldn't break away without demolishing the structure of the aircraft and even the engine mounts. While the drift was only a couple of feet high, it would be too high for the Bristol to jump over if it wouldn't break through on impact.

"Do you want to take that chance?" I asked. Dr. Webber said, "Well, really, it's up to you if you want to take it." I told him the way the Bristol is built, the worst we could do would be to tear an undercarriage leg loose. "In that case, we'd have to abandon any plans to stay here and instead return immediately to Alert with a seriously damaged aircraft," I said. Dr. Webber nodded, replying, "Let's give it a try. Why don't you hit it as slow as you can go."

Actually, that's what I had in mind all along, but I wanted to hear it from him. I quickly surveyed the other frozen leads in the area, but none looked safe. There are so many things that can be a little fishy looking about a lead, so I brought the Bristol around and began my first approach to the lead with the snowdrift across it. There was no way for me to get the old gal down before the drift or after it. We simply had to go through it.

I brought the Bristol in at just about stalling speed, trying to keep the wheels within a foot of the ice. I really didn't care if it was rolling on the ice or not, just so I didn't put the full weight of the aircraft on the ice and had flying speed when we hit the drift. I wanted to make certain we weren't on the ground because the old Bristol might not be able to take off again in the event it was damaged.

We hit the drift and broke through almost clear down to the surface of the ice. Big chunks of snow flew forward and also back over the wings like an explosion, but the drift was not particularly hard and there wasn't much of a jar when we hit it. Jeff and I agreed it felt okay and the drift shouldn't be a problem. We decided to make a second run down the length of the lead, only this time we kept the wheels on the ice. After pulling up we circled the lead and checked to see if any water had been drawn to the surface by the pressure of our wheels. None appeared, so I decided to take a chance on actually landing.

Our first order of business on landing would be to check the ice depth. The plan was for me to stay in the cockpit with the engines running while someone checked the ice with a power auger. "As soon as we're solidly down, get the auger cranked up and then get out the back door the moment we stop and check the ice," I shouted to the men over the engine noise. "But remember one thing," I cautioned, "Jeff and I are going to be sitting up here watching for any sign that we're drawing water around the wheels. If you hear me rev up either engine, just drop that damn auger and get the hell back in here because I'm moving out immediately."

We needed about three and a half feet of sea ice to support the Bristol and I figured we had at least that by the color of the ice. If I was off by a couple of feet, of course, the aircraft would go right through the ice as soon as we stopped. The more likely danger was "minimal" ice, which would slowly stretch and give way beneath us. That's the reason Jeff and I planned to keep a sharp eye on the wheels for signs of drawing water.

Sea ice is more rubbery than lake ice because of the salt. It takes more sea ice to support aircraft, especially heavier aircraft like the Bristol. If we had been landing on a frozen lake in the barrens, for example, we probably could have gotten by with only 24 to 30 inches of ice. Sea ice gives you more warning before you go through it, but you can go through thicker ice than you would with lake ice. The Russians have done a great deal of research on all of this. They've published studies of marching troops on different thicknesses of ice, including different numbers of men both in cadence and out of cadence. They have studies on trucks following each other on the ice at all different speeds. One interesting study dealt with whether you could race a heavy truck across minimal ice to avoid sinking. As the truck travels across the ice, it's generating a wave in the ice ahead of the vehicle because the ice is sagging under you all of the time. If you go at the right speed, you're fine. But if you go too fast, the wave gets bigger and bigger until the ice fractures and breaks in front of the vehicle and down you go. And if you go too slow, you gradually sink out of sight. The

Russians had facts and figures on just how much it took
for a six-ton truck to make it across at various speeds
and thicknesses of ice. They also had dead weight studies and almost anything else you wanted to know about
ice. It was interesting reading, but very slow.

That's where we got most of our information about sea
ice, from the Russians. I always wondered how many
people and equipment they put through the ice to get all
their information.

As I brought the Bristol around for a third approach
and landing attempt, I asked the good Lord to bring us
in safely and silently thanked Him for giving us such a
clear day and very good weather all around. We touched
down at approximately 4 a.m., on May 6, 1967, at 89.40
degrees north and 120.30 degrees east.

Someone fired up the power auger near the end of the
landing roll and when the Bristol came to rest the men
with the auger were on the ice in seconds while Jeff and
I watched the wheels. In no time at all the auger was
down well past three feet and finally punched through
the bottom at six feet of ice.

We had done it, something I never seriously considered possible when we departed Alert several hours earlier. We had landed the first wheel-equipped aircraft at
the North Pole. And without a ski-equipped Otter going
in before us! Within two hours Bob Lillestrand's calculations via radio link with one of his company's computers
in Boston proved us to be 18 miles down the other side
of the pole, the Russian side. So, we were very close and
in all likelihood the camp and the ice platform it sat on
would pass over or very near the North Pole, itself, if the
ocean current beneath us cooperated. While Bob was
doing his calculations, the rest of the party helped us
off-load the Bristol. There was a suggestion that we
should check the ice depth up and down the lead, but I
told the men the thickness is fairly uniform. The depth
may be a bit greater out toward the edges, but out in the
middle it's always dead uniform the length of the lead.

A little over two hours after making history by landing
Bristol CF-TFX near the pole, we returned to Alert, having dumped off the seven-man research team, their basic
camp supplies, a small radio and a big ball with mirrors
on it. Dr. Webber's "crystal ball," we called it. Our job
over the next day or two would be to make at least one
more run, plus lay in fuel supplies for the Otters that
were scheduled to service the camp in the weeks ahead.
Since they were the same Otters that were supposed to
scout a landing strip for the Bristol but never showed up, I
had serious doubts about the welfare of Dr. Webber's expedition.

Back at Alert I could tell that Wes, Art and Del were
disappointed about remaining behind, but they tried to
hide it. I decided that on our second trip up we would go
one fuel drum light and take a couple of people in its
place. So that's what we did. Harry volunteered to stay
behind and Art took his place as our engineer on the second flight, May 9, 1967. Wes and Del were more than
happy to substitute for a barrel of fuel, and it was in this
manner that all of our men would be able to say they
were at the North Pole.

We put in a gas cache halfway between Alert and the
pole with a small radio beacon good for 30 miles out so
the Otters could find it, and Dr. Webber also placed a radio beacon at the North Pole encampment for the Otters
to home in on. All the Otters had to do was turn their radios on, tune to the frequencies we set and fly in that direction. I thought it should have been a relatively simple
matter for the Otters to get to the pole and back considering all the equipment we put in for them. You could
even see Dr. Webber's crystal ball reflecting sunlight from
10 or 15 miles out. And Alert had a good directional beacon that you could pick up about halfway in on the return.

Even with beacons, the two jokers flying the Otters
couldn't figure out how to navigate around the North
Pole. You've got to use your head. For example, most everyone knows all the longitudinal lines run south from

the pole. So, instead of using north as a reference, I would use south with the astrocompass. It's the same thing, only reversed 180 degrees. As long as you know where the sun is from Greenwich Mean Time, it works fine. Depending on the time of day you're starting from, you set your gyros on whatever longitude you want and then go in that direction, whichever longitude you want to go down, just like we did everywhere in the barrens.

One very lucky thing we had going for us were the Russian stations out on the ice, and we would get a pretty good idea of where they were on the way in and then on the way out we could use them as back bearings. You used everything you could, everything that was up there. In fact, I had asked the Canadian government to contact the Soviet authorities and let them know we would be in the area in the event we needed to make an emergency landing or required their help. No problem, they said, indicating the Russians already knew of our plans and had fuel on hand for a Bristol Freighter.

After two or three days the Otter pilots had themselves so damned confused they didn't want to stay with the North Pole encampment. Somehow they convinced the entire seven-man scientific team to abandon their camp on the third day with very little research accomplished. They just pulled the personnel out and left everything to float away simply because they had no idea of what they had gotten themselves into. That's why a second expedition was conducted in 1969, because most of the work in the 1967 effort was never accomplished. All because of a couple of guys that should never have been up there in the first place. The only time they could do a job right was on a bright, sunny day. If it was the least bit windy or overcast, they were lost before they got off the ground.

In the meantime, we had other work to do with the Bristol and figured the North Pole expedition was all set. Back at Alert, I climbed aboard an old Sikorski S-5 helicopter and we flew over to Greenland in order to check a lake out before I went in with the Bristol to establish a

fuel cache. The lake was shown on the map, but we had
no idea if it was accessible with the Bristol. As it turned
out, the lake was suitable as a landing site for the
Bristol because all of the lakes had plenty of ice on them
in early May in the Arctic.

Art Morrow was my flight engineer on the trip from Alert
to the lake on Greenland, and I'll let him tell the story of
that flight:

> Flying helicopter fuel from Alert into the
> rugged mountains of Greenland was an expe-
> rience I will never forget. May of 1967 brought
> strong winds and relatively warm tempera-
> tures of up to 10 above at Alert. The midnight
> sun and 24 hours of daylight causes the Arc-
> tic tundra to radiate heat, and I recall big
> chunks of ice smashing and grinding as they
> fell into the Arctic Ocean. We would rush out
> of our bunkhouse to witness the birth of mas-
> sive icebergs, falling chunks of ice crashing to
> their fate.

> The wind was blowing steadily at 55 mph
> with gusts to 60 as we struggled to load 45-
> gallon barrels of fuel for caches in Greenland.
> We loaded the drums through the rear door of
> the Bristol because the front clam-shell doors
> would have been ripped off by the wind if we
> had opened them.

> Captain Don Braun and copilot Jeff Braith-
> waite handled the take-off well, but 45 minutes
> out of Alert it began to get bumpy as we ap-
> proached the coast of Greenland. No one had
> to be warned to secure their seat belts as the
> air became increasingly turbulent. I was be-
> coming airsick, which had never happened
> before, yet I told Don over my head set that I
> was going down the stair-ladder from the
> cockpit into the cargo bay to check the chains
> that secured the fuel drums. Not once did I let

go of the handhold as I eased my way down into the cargo bay. Several chains had loosened and I quickly tightened them as I was thrown against the drums while hanging on for dear life.

As I approached the ladder back up to the cockpit, I felt a drowsy sensation and all I wanted to do was lay down and pass out. Just then the aircraft heaved violently and I grabbed the ladder with both hands, slid down to my knees, closed my eyes and tried to compose myself. After a few minutes the turbulence had eased a bit and I scooted up the ladder to my seat. I noticed Jeff also looked white and that made me feel better, knowing I wasn't the only crew member suffering. Even Don looked quite worried about the situation.

I heard Don and Jeff talking about making a 180-degree turn and heading back to Alert, and I grabbed my mike and pleaded to Don to turn back because I'd had about all the punishment I could stand. Don answered that he was going to try making it a few more miles and see what the Greenland coast offered in the way of turbulence. He never smiled when he glanced back at me, and this concerned me to no end. Any time I had ever felt uneasy about something, Don would always tease me a bit. But not this time.

No sooner had we reached the coast of Greenland when a sudden burst of turbulence put the Bristol up on its wing tip. The big freighter lay on its side, drawing me tightly into my seat and I couldn't move a muscle for several seconds. Don lunged for the controls and brought the aircraft back to its normal position. Thank God for that one, I thought to myself; now Don will surely head for home.

He didn't, of course, so I gazed out the cockpit window at the white-faced mountains with solid granite peaks that were mostly clouded in. The Bristol lurched up and down as Don put it into a medium bank and then told us over our headsets: "Prepare for landing. We're going to take a try at it."

Jeff, an exceptionally good young pilot, was also looking worried and ready to ask for an immediate turnback. Instead, he made his usual check of the cockpit and kept his eyes open for any danger. As usual, I sat there and prayed for help as I watched our descent through the rugged peaks and held onto my seat tighter than ever. Rugged mountains appeared to be closing in on us as the Bristol descended down into a canyon.

Finally I could see what Don was aiming for: a beautiful, windswept lake with only enough snow on it for traction. Down we came, only six feet off the ice and we were still bouncing from the wind. A fast flare out, one thud, and the great Arctic Fox, Don Braun, had done it again.

After landing and turning the airplane into the wind for shutdown, we struggled to open the side door against the wind. With two of us heaving against it, we managed to secure it open and then took up our duties for off-loading the fuel drums with Don loosening the chains and Jeff and myself rolling the drums down the cargo floor and out the door. Without the load the airplane was lightened enough for the raging wind to become its master. Don let out a yell and, as I turned around, I saw the whole blasted tail end of the airplane

Top left — For the record, here's what I looked like when I graduated from Cathedral High School in St. Cloud in 1931. *Top right* — My mom and dad, Alphonse and Theresa Braun, were salt of the earth and deeply religious. If ever parents had a lasting impression on their children for the good, these two did...on all eight of us! *Below* — My Standard Mead glider attracted all the neighboring kids when I built it in 1932. I don't recall the name of the lad in this photo but it's a wonderful picture of the glider in the farmyard.

Top left—Here I am at the helm of a wagon, giving my sister Marge (the cute little one with the bow in her hair) a ride along with two neighbor kids. *Top right*—I fashioned a windscreen on this old 1928 Indian motorcycle and rode it from St. Cloud to Colorado Springs in 1934 where I completed a one-year aircraft maintenance apprenticeship. *Left*—I developed a real knack for welding and welded wing spar fittings for Stinson Aircraft in Detroit after my year in Colorado. *Below*—As a teenager I delivered milk for the family dairy business and in winter it was not unusual to become stuck in snow and freeze your ears off trying to dig out.

Above — A Braun family portrait on the St. Cloud farm in the early 1950s. Back row, left to right: Jim, Mary, Bob, Lou, Marge and me; front row: Fran, Dad and Mom, and baby sister, Helen. *Right* — Marie Nolen took me for her husband, for better or for worse, on June 4, 1934. I don't know why she settled for me because with her charm and good looks she could have done a lot better.

Plate Four

Top — An aerial view of Harlem Airport with B&F Service on the left and my American Eaglet parked in front. *Above left* — B&F's Waco 9. *Above* — Opal Anderson's tricky little Laird Speedwing. *Below* — My Eaglet with the nose cowling, spinner and wheel covers that I fabricated for it. *Left* — Younger brother Bob also worked at Harlem Airport.

My ski-equipped American Eaglet was the only airplane flying in the Chicago area after a spring snowstorm closed down everything on April 3, 1938. This photo, one of my favorites, was taken on April 6.

Plate Six

Above left — Royal Canadian Air Force Pilot Officer Donald Conrad Braun, a commissioned officer after only four months training! *Above right* — In early 1943 Marie was finally able to join me in Edmonton, ending our separation during my first two years in the RCAF. *Below* — The line of twin-engine Avro Ansons at Rivers, Manitoba.

Above — My Anson, No. 6499, was named for Marie. The Anson was like a greenhouse with wings — many windows, fabric-covered body, wood veneer on wings and tailplane, metal engine cowlings and nose. *Below* — Our ground and flight crews at the RCAF base at Rivers, Manitoba, with one of the Avro Ansons we used for astronavigation training. I'm front and center.

A North American Harvard advanced fighter trainer with 600-hp Pratt &
Whitney radial engine, known as the AT-6 (U.S. Army) or SNJ-4 (U.S. Navy).

Fairey Battle, 1200-hp Rolls Royce
Merlin engine.

The Avro Oxford, a twin-engine
trainer used by the RCAF.

A Stearman N2S-5 (U.S. Navy) or
PT-17 (U.S. Army) trainer.

The deadly Fleet Fort made by
Canadian Car and Foundry.

These are a sampling of the aircraft I flew as a test pilot at the RCAF
Number Ten Repair Depot at Calgary, Alberta.

The Fleet Fort was a deadly aircraft. We lost many students in crashes like this. Take-off speed was 90 mph and it cruised at 110 — a 20-mph margin for error.

The Lockheed 10 I flew along the Northwest Staging Route from Edmonton to Alaska my last two RCAF years. It was a thing of beauty — all-metal body, pair of Pratt & Whitney 420-hp engines, top speed of over 200 mph.

My first bush flying was in this RCAF Noorduyn Norseman Mark VI, No. 2489, on wheels here instead of floats. The Norseman was the first true "bush" aircraft in the North.

RCAF Norseman No. 2489 on floats during one of our flights into a staging camp along the Mackenzie River.

In my modified Ford Model T race car in Alberta during the war years.

Above left — Lloyd Toutant and I started a trucking business after the war hauling goods from Edmonton to the Peace River country for a year until we went broke. *Above right* — Nothing like a good pipe and some RCAF forms to complete at the end of the day.

An aerial view from my Norseman of the completed Snare River Hydro project 95 miles northwest of Yellowknife. My job during construction in 1947-48 was to fly supplies, mail and personnel to the project site.

The Norseman I flew for the Snare River project was CF-PAB, an old Mark IV that had been completely rebuilt. Here I am delivering a 670-lb. compressed air tank to the construction site. It was so large it stuck out of both sides of the aircraft.

Plate Twelve

Above — One of the joys of living along the Snare River during my time with the hydro project was the great fishing. *Below* — Marie joined me at the Snare River hydro project construction camp and we enjoyed frequent picnics in the woods, away from the primitive quarters of camp.

Above — Our living quarters at the Snare River construction camp consisted of a single room in the staff house on the right while the 80-man crew slept in a two-story bunkhouse. *Below* — Marie and two puppies on the steps of the staff house.

Above — Young Max Ward and his new de Havilland Fox Moth in 1947, doing business out of Yellowknife as the Polaris Charter Co. Ltd. He was frequently hired to fly supplies into the Snare River hydro project. *Left* — Every so often Max would bring his lovely wife, Marjorie, out to the construction camp for a visit and we became good friends. Max was tireless, a real hard-driving fellow and you just knew he would amount to something. (Photo by Bun Russell)

The Snare River hydro project was a real engineering challenge. The project site was only 225 miles south of the Arctic Circle and the construction crews worked through the winter months in temperatures of 50 below zero. Above are a couple of typical construction photos.

Cat trains first began crossing frozen Great Slave Lake in the late 1930s, hauling tons of supplies to Yellowknife and the mines. Moving 24 hours a day at three to five mph, the 140-mile journey across the ice was full of danger. Many Cat trains broke through and went to the bottom. Those shown here took their 80-ton payloads an additional 60 miles to the Snare River hydro construction site.

The Norseman Mark IV, CF-PAB, that I flew during my two-year stint with the Snare River hydro project was a beautiful old machine with a rebuilt 550-hp Pratt & Whitney Wasp 9-cylinder radial engine. That's our mechanic standing to my left.

Warming up the Norseman in the morning in the dead of winter at 30 or 40 below zero was always a pain in the neck. We would drain the oil out at the end of the day and heat it up in pails over a stove in the morning. Our maintenance facility, as you can see, was very primitive.

Above — Marie and I built this "basement" house into the side of a hill overlooking the Mississippi River on the family farm in St. Cloud in 1949 after I returned home from my stint as a bush pilot for the Snare River hydro project. *Right* — Mug shot of a not-so-successful broiler chicken farmer in the early 1950s. *Below* — Our three sons up in Yellow-knife; from left, Christopher, Joel and Charles.

Above — I love this '53 photo of young Max Ward with his new de Havilland Otter, CF-GBY. It was Wardair's first aircraft and the first Otter to operate in Western Canada. (Photo by Twyman Studio) *Below* — Our Yellowknife home was a converted bunkhouse hauled from the Negus Mine. With some additions it was the only house we lived in during our 17 years in Yellowknife. That's the old 1949 (or 1950?) Fraser station wagon we brought from St. Cloud.

Above — The Wardair crew in front of two Otters on frozen Back Bay in Yellowknife in 1956; from left: Max Ward, me, Hank Fulgrabe, John Langdon, Dick Huisson, an unidentified man and Janet Lamb who later married George Curley. (Photo by de Havilland) *Below* — N.W.T. Court Justice Jack Sissons, left, used Wardair to bring his court to Inuit villages across the North. *Life* photographer Carl Iwasaki took this photo of us in a Wardair Otter on one of our trips. (Reproduction with permission of *Life* magazine)

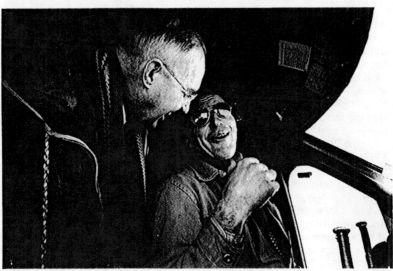

Above — These muskoxen may look alive, but they are actually mounted specimens in a display at the Los Angeles County Museum. I was the pilot for a 1960 expedition to remote Ellesmere Island in the Canadian High Arctic where these beautiful animals were taken with high-powered rifles.

Above — We could always count on the Catholic or Episcopal missions in the North for a hot meal and warm bed. Father Maurice Beauregard was my friend and frequent host at Norman Wells, N.W.T. *Right* — Father John Kemer of Our Lady of the Arctic mission at Cambridge Bay, N.W.T., included this photo of his little outpost in one of his Christmas cards to our family in Yellowknife.

Right and below —
Wardair's third Otter, CF-ITF, went through the ice on Reliance Channel of Great Slave Lake in the spring of 1958. I don't recall who was at the controls, but we all helped hoist it out with a pulley system and jacks.

Right — I put a Wardair Beaver through badly candled spring ice one time — the only time I ever pulled such a stunt. Here's the very same Beaver through the ice near Fort Rae in December 1957. Again, I don't know who was at the controls. But it wasn't me this time.

Plate Twenty-Two

Top — This lovely old Supermarine Stranraer, CF-BXO, was my pride and joy during the first few summers I flew for Wardair in the 1950s. The ice couldn't go out soon enough for me to get her back on the water and in the air again. *Middle* — Just about everything in my life involved flying. Even in my spare time I would build and fly model airplanes during my early years with Wardair. *Bottom* — Here I am with the little Republic SeaBee amphibian I bought back in Minnesota so our family could escape from Yellowknife for picnics and weekend camping trips. It's Franklin 215-hp engine had a bad reputation but it never gave me much trouble.

Right — I'm not sure when this photo was taken or what the story was behind it, except that it was shortly after I began wearing a beard and the oil splotches in the snow beneath the Otter's engine certainly have my attention. *Below* — One of my favorite aircraft was this PBY Canso shown here at the Wardair float base on Back Bay in Yellowknife sometime in the mid-1960s.

Wardair's first Bristol 170 Freighter, an Mk. 31 model powered by a pair of 1,980-hp Hercules sleeve-valve engines, ferried cars, trucks and supplies to Yellowknife during the spring and fall when the Mackenzie Highway was impassable. Old CF-TFX shown here became famous when it was the first wheeled aircraft to land at the North Pole in 1967.

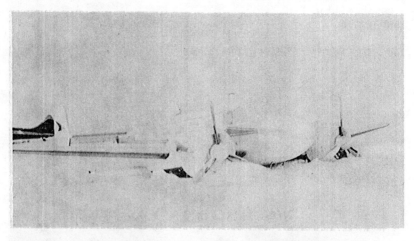

I landed this Beech 185, CF-PCL, wheels up on Pellat Lake after losing an engine in December 1966. My passenger, an Inuit man heading home with a new snowmobile, thanked me for the safe landing and took off across the lake. A Wardair crew of engineers landed shortly after and salvaged the old Beech, among them Art Morrow, Guenther Moellenbeck, Peter Cockton and John Mulholland. (Photo by Art Morrow)

Right — I always
believed that a
good pilot in the
North had to be a
good mechanic,
too, even if it
meant fixing a light
indicator. (Photo by
Ted Grant, Na-
tional Film Board
of Canada) *Be-
low* — We cached a
supply of helicop-
ter fuel in one of
the most forbid-
ding places on
earth, the north
coast of Greenland,
just prior to our
flight to the North
Pole in 1967.
That's me with the
scarf, leaning into
the wind.

Above — Here we are loading fuel aboard the Bristol in preparation for our flight to the North Pole. *Left* — A polar bear poked around our garbage dump at Alert looking for his next dinner, but left after a few minutes with nothing more than a few appetizers. *Below* — Copilot Jeff Braithwaite and me in the cockpit of Bristol Freighter CF-TFX as we prepared for our historic flight to the North Pole. (Top and bottom photos by Ted Grant, National Film Board of Canada)

Above — We made history by landing the first wheeled aircraft at the
North Pole on May 6, 1967. We had a great crew that included, left to
right: Wes Barron, copilot; Art Morrow, engineer; Del Hamilton, loader;
Jeff Braithwaite, copilot; and me on the far right. A sixth crew member,
engineer Harry Kreider, had returned to Alert when Art Morrow took this
photo by timer on May 9. *Below* — Bristol Freighter CF-TFX at our 1967
base camp, which was actually 18 miles from the pole when we landed.
We hoped the ocean current would cause our floating camp to drift
directly over the pole but it never did. (Photos by Art Morrow)

Left — It's no secret I'm fond of Scotch and it was only natural that a bottle of the stuff was included in our provisions at the North Pole in May of 1967. *Below* — We used this Wardair Twin Otter at the pole in 1969 to scout a landing site for the much heavier Bristol Freighter and to ferry scientific teams around the pole so they could make readings and conduct experiments.

Old CF-TFX, the Bristol 170 Freighter that made the first wheeled-aircraft landing at the North Pole in May 1967, was retired and made into a monument honoring Canadian bush pilots. The old taildragger sits proudly on a concrete pedestal near the Yellowknife Airport, thanks to Max Ward.

Above — Marie christens Wardair's first de Havilland Dash 7 the *Don Braun* in Toronto in 1978. It was the first aircraft in Wardair's northern fleet to be named. *Below* — The *Don Braun* made several landings at the North Pole in 1979 in support of yet another scientific expedition. (Both photos by Terry Wildman, with permission of de Havilland Aircraft of Canada, Ltd.)

Max Ward (left) and Wardair President, George Curley (right), with Marie and me in France in 1987 to receive the first three Wardair A-310 Airbuses. Within two years Marie had passed away and Max sold Wardair.

The marriage of Joel and Jackie in 1991. Left to right: Christopher and Lynda, the old Arctic Fox, Joel and Jackie, granddaughter Tanya, Marilyn and Charles. Fifteen years earlier I never dreamed such a portrait would have been possible.

I discovered ultralights in the 1970s and, despite old age and deteriorating eyesight, got into the business of selling the machines and giving instructions on how to fly them. The young men I've trained in ultralights remind me of me back in the early days. They love to fly.

Don Braun
1913 – 1993

coming at me and I leaped out of the way just
in time. The wind had picked up the tail of
the freighter and swung it around to face in
the opposite direction. Lucky for us — and for
the airplane — that we had rolled our fuel
cache well clear of the tail.

Don Braun's harshest words, "Gull darn it!"
with an added, "This is no place for us," had
us running for the Bristol. We climbed in and
proceeded with a quick take-off. As we
climbed out of the valley I looked back for a
last glimpse of Greenland. It was the first
time I had set foot on the largest island in the
world and I wondered if I would ever return.

Because of the still present turbulence in
the air, I couldn't go below to carry out my
normal routine. After dumping our cargo and
taking off, I usually headed down the ladder
to tidy up the hull of the freighter. Hanging
up the chains on their racks and sweeping
the cargo floor added that personal touch to
our aircraft. I would then check our log book
and prepare myself for mechanical snags that
may have been recorded by the pilots or
noted on my own daily inspection routines.
As I sat in the cockpit waiting for the turbulence to cease, I began to relax and started
thinking how lucky I had been to have flown
with the North's best pilots the past several
years, especially Don Braun.

Don was also an excellent aircraft welder,
mechanic and machinist; obviously a special
breed of bush pilot, having all of these qualifi-
cations on top of being an outstanding pilot.
It was often said that Don could probably
crash and then build another airplane out of
a tree and fly it home. When Don retired he
left behind a very small handful of the true

bush pilots. The only man I could ever place a close second to Don is Weldy Phipps of Resolute Bay. Weldy owns Atlas Aviation and is a legend in his time.

Don was never content unless he had something apart mechanically. It might be an airplane or a washing machine. He was always eager to teach and I gave Don a lot of credit for helping me complete my apprenticeship as an aircraft mechanic. It was a pleasure to work with and learn from him. Don was in his early 50s when I first met him and he was a tough man against the Arctic elements. No two men could outwork him for endurance. He wore a beard, gray in color, and while it wasn't groomed in Hollywood style, he always kept it clean and neatly trimmed.

Airplanes came first in Don's life and people who didn't know him well sometimes expressed the notion that he must be a very hard man to work for. I know. I had thought so several times during our initial association. All he ever asked, however, was for a mechanic to keep his airplane well maintained in airworthy condition, clean it after each flight and neatly stow everything in its proper place. I always tried to please Don because he was absolutely right. His copilots received the same treatment, and the aircraft was flown to his excellent standards.

The reader should know that while I appreciate Art's nice words about me, I was more interested in using only the part about our flight. But Art said if we were going to include his piece, then we had to use the whole thing and I reluctantly agreed. Art is one-of-a-kind, very special, and the stories I could tell you about some of our escapades would fill another book. Maybe Art will take that on someday since I know he likes to write and is good at it. Besides, he's younger than I am and has a lot more tread than I do.

Our historic landing of the first wheel-equipped aircraft at the North Pole made quite a splash in the news. The story of our landing was carried around the world on the news wires and it appeared in hundreds of newspapers and broadcast reports. I honestly never imagined there would be such interest. It was just remarkable.

Bristol CF-TFX was retired from service in 1968 and Max Ward donated the aircraft to the city of Yellowknife to be used as a permanent bush pilot monument. The old gal sits proudly on a pedestal in a park near the Yellowknife Airport looking like she's going to fly right over your head. A plaque commemorating our flight reads:

> *On May 6, 1967, a Wardair Bristol Freighter, with Captain Don Braun in command, became the first wheel-equipped aircraft to land at the North Pole. The same Bristol Freighter was retired from service in 1968 and in 1970 was officially dedicated by Max Ward to Bristol Park in Yellowknife, where it stands today, a monument to its historic past and a tribute to the role of bush aircraft in opening up the Canadian Arctic.*

CHAPTER THIRTEEN

RETURN TO THE POLE, 1969

*"I remember at the end of a particularly cold
day near the pole we all climbed aboard the
Otter for the return to base camp some 25 or
30 miles away and one of the engines wouldn't
start. You've never seen such a worried bunch
of guys, judging by the looks on their faces,
although I'm sure the look on my face wasn't
much better."*

If Operation SUGAR in 1967 was a failure, at least
it impressed upon Dr. Webber and others the importance
of choosing your air support more carefully if you intended to spend any time at all at the North Pole. Dr.
Webber called on Wardair to provide the complete air support for his 1969 expedition to the pole, and I like to think
his choice was based on our performance two years earlier. Partly to make up for the aborted 1967 mission and
what they failed to accomplish, Dr. Webber's team planned
an ambitious schedule of experiments at the pole during
April of 1969.

My job would be flying the lead plane, a ski-equipped
Twin Otter, to scout a landing site on the ice for the
Bristol that would be close to the pole and serve as the
expedition's base camp. I would then stay with the team
at the pole during the expedition, daily flying groups of
scientists to various sites around the pole so they could
conduct their experiments over a two-week period.

The expedition was officially underway when I lifted off
from Alert on April 7 with Dr. Webber and a cabin full of
fuel. I couldn't help but think how different — and better —
things were now than in 1967 when I had little warning
or time to prepare for a mission to the North Pole. Unfortunately, the weather wasn't as nice as the first time

when I was trying to find a place to land the Bristol. But our navigation was better.

We had one of the new Omega systems on board. It was a triangulation navigational system like the old Console that feeds everything into the flying aircraft, only back in 1969 it took up the space of two passenger seats in the Otter. It wasn't displayed, so we had an operator along who had to figure everything out. Today, of course, everything is miniaturized and computerized, with information constantly being fed into the system and your exact location continuously displayed right in front of you. The Omega system we had was so new, in fact, that we agreed to check its accuracy. We used it to find fuel caches we had placed out on the sea ice and could fly within sight of them every time. Before Omega, you could fly within a mile of a cache and never spot the old bamboo fishing pole. Once the cache gets a little frost on it, you've got to be right on top of it to see it.

As luck would have it, once again the Russians were a big help to us and they didn't even know it. They had a large station on an ice island right straight across the pole from Alert. I knew they had several beacon stations around the Arctic, so I fished around on the radio and just happened to pick up the one that would lead us right across the North Pole.

When we arrived in the vicinity of the pole our immediate task was to find and mark a landing site for the Bristol as quickly as possible, then radio Alert for the Bristol to head north with the rest of the team and join us. The turbine engines in the Twin Otter were real fuel guzzlers, however, and you only had to make a few landings and take-offs to burn up over an hour's worth of fuel. Every landing and take-off is like flying 100 miles and the Twin Otter only has a range of about 600 miles. Even with our load of extra fuel we wouldn't have much chance of returning to Alert unless we found a landing site on the first or second try.

My first choice for a landing site was a smooth frozen lead that turned out to be only 24 inches thick, enough to support the Twin Otter but the Bristol would have gone right through. I guess I didn't know as much about sea ice as I thought. Two feet of sea ice is much darker in color than four or five feet of ice, but this particular stretch had a real heavy cover of frost. It looked nice and white and it fooled me completely.

We used the stop to pump most of our fuel supply into the aircraft's tanks and then flew off to check out a second site which, as it turned out, wasn't any good, either. Now we had to make a decision. We still could make it back to Alert after this second landing, but if we attempted a third there wouldn't be enough fuel for the return. It was probably kind of stupid, but we decided to continue looking. Once the decision was made and there was no turning back, we started to slow down and take our time about finding a place for the Bristol to land and bring us fuel as well as the rest of the expedition.

In the early morning hours of April 8, on the fifth try, I finally settled on a frozen lead that seemed safe enough for the Bristol. It turned out to be only 22 miles from the North Pole.

The Bristol headed north to find us and I was able to tell them that åll they had to do was home in on the Russian radio signal, get the time and distance right, and we'd be within sight. When the Bristol was only 30 or 40 miles away I could hear it, and I told them, "You've got to come over this way, guys, we're over here!" We also had some flags along and we flagged out the runway for the Bristol.

The Bristol made a total of six trips in because the expedition was larger and had a more ambitious schedule than the one in 1967. They brought in quite a bit more scientific equipment and four of those orange peel buildings, including one big enough to sleep a dozen men. The first Bristol in brought enough turbine fuel to fly the Otter for about a week, which made me feel a whole lot better, but I used most of it to make two runs to Alert in the next few days to help bring in the supplies and equipment. The base camp went up in about four days and finally we were ready to begin the scientific work. The camp would slowly drift counterclockwise around the North Pole during our two-week stay, but we would always be just a short hop to the pole itself, which would be our navigation reference as we moved about.

We started each day by flying out from the base camp to try to find a landing site as close to geographic north as we could to take readings. Then, depending on where they wanted to go, the scientists would give me the fixes and we'd fly out from the pole to some particular spot on the ice where they would conduct experiments. Sometimes I would have only a couple of scientists along and at other times as many as five or six. The toughest part of my job was trying to find frozen leads to land on that were safe and yet in the area the scientists wanted to visit. Usually everything worked out and we'd land and the scientists would do their work and then we'd move somewhere else. Sometimes we made as many as four or five landings in one of our daily outings. And if I couldn't find a good landing spot, all we had to do was wait for the ice to move and return to the same area a day or two later. There would be an entirely new landscape before us, usually with a landing spot for the Otter.

The ice cap near the pole looked much the same as it did from the air in 1967, an endless sea of white occasionally broken by small, thin leads of open water. Although the ice is moving slowly, there is no sensation of movement when you're standing on the surface and you can't detect it from the air. By contrast, the outer edges of the polar ice cap move more quickly, like the outer rim of a wheel. You can actually see it move past the shore ice of the Canadian Arctic Islands or Greenland, grinding along and breaking up; large islands of ice that crush against each other and form huge pressure ridges. In April, however, the ice at the pole has few open leads, and you can imagine my surprise when I came across a lead of open water near the pole that was

at least 80 miles long and anywhere from one-quarter of
a mile to two miles across. It was typical of a lead you
might encounter much further south, not up here; one
of those that if a surface expedition would have come
upon it, that would have been it. There would be no
choice but to turn and go back. Fortunately for us, however, it led right to the North Pole so it served as a handy
visual navigation guide during our daily flights.

The scientists not only had more sophisticated equipment with them than in 1967, but more of it. They even
brought along an Inuit native to build igloos to protect
the instruments out on the ice. The teams I hauled
about would blast holes in the ice to measure currents
and water depth at various locations. They studied all
the different types of sea life, including an amazing and
relatively unknown world of tiny creatures that live on
the underside of the Arctic ice. The dip of satellites in
polar orbit as they passed high above the North Magnetic Pole was measured again. And the scientists also
had an experiment to determine just how much of a
wobble there might be in the earth's polar axis spin.

The only way they could measure the wobble was to
take a piece of hose about 300 feet long and fill it with
antifreeze, then stretch it out lengthwise across the ice.
A graded tube was inserted into each end of the hose
and the Inuit fellow built an igloo over each end so the
weather wouldn't interfere. The scientists figured the
antifreeze would be higher in one tube for about 12
hours, or half the earth's daily spin, and then higher in
the other tube the next 12 hours. Then they could measure the wobble. The poles are the only place this experiment could be done, I was told, but I never did ask
the men how it came out.

We never stayed long at any one spot. I helped the
teams by drilling holes in the ice and doing other odd
jobs, but I never got much involved in the scientific side
of it. The Twin Otter was my only responsibility and our
only means of travel back to a hot meal and the relative

warmth of an orange peel hut at the end of a long day out on the ice.

I remember at the end of a particularly cold day near the pole we all climbed aboard the Otter for the return to base camp some 25 or 30 miles away and one of the engines wouldn't start. You've never seen such a worried bunch of guys, judging by the looks on their faces, although I'm sure the look on my face wasn't much better.

Because of the cold, I had stayed with the Otter most of the day and tried to keep the cabin warm for the men with the propane heater. Those heaters, of course, cause a lot of frost to build up in the cabin and after a few hours I had to quit using it. Sometimes they would even quit on their own after a time if it was cold enough. The propane would start to solidify in the tank and the burner would just quit. Since it was April, however, it wasn't all that cold. The temperature was only about 20 below, but there was a stiff wind and it was miserable out on the ice. A couple of the men would be out working while a couple others would warm up in the Otter, then they would change places until the fellows outside couldn't stand it any longer. After our third landing that day the team was ready to call it quits and return to base.

I would always start the right engine first, when the battery was at its best. The left engine is closer and you're able to watch it better in the event a problem develops, so I would fire it up second. Well, the right engine started up fine. I hit the starter for the left engine. Nothing happened. There was just nothing there. I couldn't hear what was happening so I shut the right engine down, which I hated like hell to do because you've only got a couple of starts at 20 or 30 below. As a matter of fact, most Twin Otters today are started with a power unit. Max Ward, for example, won't start his personal Twin with batteries. He's got to have a power unit to start it at both ends. And here I was, up at the North Pole, starting on batteries all day long!

When the right engine wound down and everything was quiet, I hit the starter for the left side. I could hear the solenoid clicking, which meant power was getting out as far as the starter. But the starter wasn't turning the engine.

The Twin Otter has a really big starter generator unit because it needs to get the turbine engine turning at 11,000 rpm in order to get the burning fuel going the right way. Otherwise it could stall the engine and burn it up. I always watched the temperature when I started the turbines, and if the temperature didn't peak and come back down then I either had to shut the fuel back off or get more rpm one way or another. But the problem at the moment was that the starter wasn't even turning.

I knew these starters had brushes that were prone to wearing down very fast in cold weather, and with all the multiple starts and stops we had been doing I was convinced the damn brushes were the problem. It was the only thing I could think of because I was getting the solenoid click but nothing else. Not even a hum.

My flight engineer was another young kid, a real good kid but very green as engineers go. I told him we had to take off an inspection plate above the starter so we could take a look inside. It was what they call a stressed plate, about six by 10 inches with screws every inch or two all around. It took us about 20 minutes to get the plate off without losing any of the screws. Our fingers would go numb in minutes, forcing us to take turns with the screwdriver.

After looking inside, I told the young fellow to get a three- or four-ounce hammer out of his tool box. "Then I want you to come up here and hit the starter right around this ring," I said and then waited for him to climb up and join me. We looked down through the small opening and I pointed to the ring. "That's where the brushes are. But don't hit the soft part that covers the brushes; hit either behind or forward of the cover that's over the brushes." Then I returned to the cockpit.

With my green engineer out over the starter, I hit the starter in the cockpit and he gave it a rap with the hammer. And I'll be darned, it started to turn. I yelled out to him that I was going to fire up the engine and then feather it so we didn't have to sit there in the prop blast trying to put that cover back on. The engine fired up and I got it feathered so the prop was barely rotating although the engine was turning just fine. We left it running and took turns putting the screws back in since our fingers were about ready to fall off for good. By the time we had the plate back on the battery was charged up enough to restart the right engine, and it fired up without a hitch.

I guess it was just lucky that it went through my head about the brushes. It would have taken days to get another aircraft up there and it would have been too dangerous to walk back to the base camp. Also, I wasn't about to try another one of those one engine take-offs and leave people behind. We had four scientists along that day, plus my engineer, and I have to admit that when the starter took hold I was just as relieved as anybody else in that aircraft. The North Pole is about the last place on earth where you'd want starter trouble.

After a few days at the pole the continuous daylight really started to foul me up. You lose all sense of when you're supposed to be awake and when you're supposed to be asleep and when you're supposed to eat. Your clock goes haywire. It didn't make any difference when you went to bed or got up because it was light anyway. The camp was run on a fairly loose schedule and we found ourselves working and sleeping in six-hour shifts. After six hours out on the ice you'd be ready to go back to bed again, although sometimes we would be out for 10 to 12 hours at a stretch and just about ready to collapse when we returned to camp.

The Inuit fellow we had along to build the igloos was complaining all the time about being up at the pole. He couldn't believe there was a place where the sun never went down at all but just kept traveling around the horizon in one great big circle. I honestly think he felt we were trespassing in some special place and that it was only a matter of time before we all came to a bad end.

Our clothing during the stay at the pole wasn't much different from what I would wear on the mainland in the middle of winter, except for our footwear. We couldn't wear the warm moose hide mukluks because they were designed for dry conditions. The salt in the sea ice keeps the surface wet and mukluks would soak up the water in no time. We used a regular Air Force boot with an insulated rubber sole. They weren't as warm as the mukluks but at least they kept our feet dry.

I wore a heavy t-shirt and a pair of old dress pants over my net longjohns, anything that fit sloppy loose. Then I would put on a pair of big, loose-fitting Arctic pants and a light shirt of some kind with a heavy wool shirt over that. I would wear a pair of light wool socks and then pull on a pair of heavy wool socks that came all the way up to my knees. Next I would put on a heavy coverall and finally a plain old canvas parka over the whole thing. Not a native-made parka; they weren't sturdy enough and would get torn when I was working around the airplane. I usually wore an extra long parka with an imitation sheepskin lining from one of those department stores like Penney's or Woodward's or Eaton's, wherever you could find them in Canada where they were priced half decent and came with a big hood. As far as hoods went, the bigger the better. We'd have wolverine sewn around the edge of the hood because it's the only fur that sheds frost.

To keep our hands warm we wore big brown dog sled driver mitts over a regular pair of choppers or sometimes gloves. I liked gloves but they were not the best for keeping your fingers warm. The driver's mitts were on a cord so when you took them off you could sling them back over your shoulders out of the way of whatever you were doing. You didn't want to get far away from the mitts because in 20 minutes or less you had to get your hands back in them again.

I also wore my six-foot wool muffler that Marie knitted for me and I would wind it around my neck, cross it over my back, bring it around and tuck it into my waist. My beard also helped keep my face warm so I didn't have to wear any protective devices like a mask. Frost would build up on it quite a bit, however, and I would have to get it de-iced every once in a while.

After flying around the pole a few days doing experiments we decided to take a day off and check out the new Omega navigation system I mentioned earlier. I was given a number of navigation points or fixes that we would locate using Omega. It would require me to return to Alert for a third time, then continue south to the north coast of Baffin Island before returning north to the pole across the top of Ellesmere Island and the northern tip of Greenland. As it turned out, the fixes happened to be the readings recorded by the two men who each claimed to be the first to reach the North Pole shortly after the turn of the century.

Admiral Robert E. Peary claimed he reached the pole in April of 1909, but another American explorer, Frederick A. Cook, insisted he reached the pole a full year earlier. After a lengthy investigation by the government, Peary's navigation records were thought to be more accurate and he was given credit for being first to the pole. The controversy still lingered, however, and the idea was for us to see if we could confirm which explorer had the more accurate readings by checking their fixes with the latest and best navigation system available, Omega.

The system performed beautifully, always right on the money and we were able to locate and confirm all the fixes from Baffin north to several points along the north coast of Greenland and a tiny island just off the Greenland coast called Kaffeklubben Island, which is Dutch for coffee club. It's said the island was named by some Dutch explorers who accidentally broke their coffee cups when they were having coffee during a stop on the island many years ago. Kaffeklubben is also the closest piece of land to the North Pole, about 430 miles distant (unless, of course, you count the ocean floor only two and a half miles or so beneath the polar ice cap), and we returned to our base camp at the pole from there after checking all the points. Our fellows, by the way, concluded that Peary's readings were more accurate than Cook's.

On April 15, after being up at the pole about 7 days, I took time out to write a letter to Marie and the kids. Five days later I wrote a letter to Dad back on the farm in St. Cloud. Mom had passed away and Dad was living alone in the old farmhouse. I knew he would like to hear about life at the North Pole and I'd like to share the letter with you:

> 20 April 1969
> North Pole Camp

> Dear Dad,

> I've been out of touch for a couple weeks so will send this home hoping it catches up to you soon. With the exception of three trips to Alert I have been living at the Canadian North Pole base camp since April 7. Alert is a weather station and Army experimental station on Ellesmere Island, 525 miles from the North Pole, and is used as a jumping-off point for our polar flights.

> On the morning of April 8 we found the present camp site which is on a suitable piece of ice for the Bristol. The Bristol brought in six loads of fuel, food, scientific gear, tents and temporary buildings and by April 12 or 13 we were all set up and ready to work. I've been flying the Twin Otter in an area of about 200 miles in all directions so that gravity measurements and water depth can be checked. Incidentally, our piece of ice was situated over 13,800 feet of water yesterday.

It is 7:20 in the evening now but I just got up an hour ago. We will have something to eat in the next hour or so and then get the Otter ready and be away from camp for about 10 hours. There is no difference between day and night here as the sun is always the same distance above the horizon (about nine degrees now). It is just about impossible to keep track of time because your watch doesn't tell you if it's morning or evening and if it weren't for the fact that we have to have the right time and day for navigating purposes I'm sure we would lose all concept of time.

One of the experiments here involves measurement of ocean currents and quite a large hole was dynamited in the ice and then covered with a tent to shelter the current meters and recorders. Yesterday morning the young fellow in charge of the experiment came running to the kitchen and reported that a seal had surfaced at the hole in the tent. I don't think anyone here had any idea that there were seal this far from land areas anywhere and particularly not this far north. Maybe the lonely little guy was just lost.

The Russians maintain two or three ice stations on a continuous basis all across the polar area and one of their stations is only 90 miles from our camp. In the last two days, five or six of their aircraft have flown over our camp and circled at low altitude. They are still flying some single-engined biplanes that look out of place in this day and age. We have some work to do in the direction of their camp soon, so we may stop in and visit them.

Dad the envelope this letter comes in will have historical value so please save it. There

are so many interesting things going on here I
could write for hours, but I guess I'd better
get to work.

Love,

Don

Three days after we returned from the Omega check
Dr. Webber announced that we were going to fly over
and visit the Russian ice station 90 miles away, the one
with the powerful radio beacon I had been using continuously. It was the beacon I had used to fly to the pole
from Alert and it would lead me to within five miles of
our camp every time. We had a little beacon that was
good for 20 or 30 miles out, but that was about it.

I learned that the Russian station was on an ice island,
not a frozen lead, and that most if not all of their stations were on islands of old ice about 40 to 50 feet deep
because they didn't want to take a chance on leads.
They would actually bulldoze permanent runways for
their bigger aircraft. The Americans had an ice island
station that lasted for several years called T3, but I don't
know what the Russians called theirs.

The Russians had been visiting us regularly, flying
over our camp. But they would never land. Since they
were flying some very interesting aircraft, I had suggested several times to Dr. Webber that we visit their
station. First, however, we would make our usually daily
flight to the pole 18 or 20 miles away and see if we could
find a spot to land and conduct a few experiments before heading over to visit the Russians. Our camp never
strayed more than 30 miles from the pole during our
stay, but each day the ice at the pole changed and you
never knew if there would be a frozen lead for landing
the Twin Otter. It was sort of hit and miss.

As we circled over the pole I couldn't see any ice that
looked good and I told Dr. Webber that I didn't think we

could attempt a landing. Then, just as we were pulling away and heading for the Russian camp, I spotted a little lead and figured maybe I could get the Otter into it. I took a closer look and saw the lead was surrounded by jumbled ice, but it was a good couple of thousand feet long and you could get the Otter in, using reverse, in about 1,200 feet, even on skis. I made the approach and came in.

The nose gear on the Twin Otter isn't very strong, and on skis you have to be particularly careful because you can actually twist the nose leg right off if you happen to hit any little obstruction during a tight, fast turn. The minute we touched the ice with the main skis I would hold the nose ski up as long as I could to keep it off the surface at high speed, so that when it came down it would be at a slower speed and not hit as hard.

Just as the nose started down I saw this little blue ice hummock sticking out of the snow and I thought, oh, geez! — and we hit it. I could feel it. We hit it on the side of the ski. I had Dr. Webber and three or four other scientists along, and they didn't even know anything had happened. But I knew I had damaged the nose, no question about it.

I told the men we had suffered some damage and that I didn't know how bad it was. We got out of the Otter and I could see right away that I had hit the hummock with the side of the ski, just enough so the ski was shoved sideways and the aircraft didn't go with it. It tore the main strut right out of the bottom of the first bulkhead about four inches. The bulkhead was thin-skinned with little reinforcement, yet it was supposed to support a tremendous amount of weight. I learned later that a lot of guys damaged the front gear, even on wheels.

So, here we were, atop the North Pole in a damaged airplane, about 22 miles from our camp and 525 miles from Alert where we had any chance of safely landing. Our aircraft had barely enough range to make it from the pole to Alert. If we made even one landing in the Twin

Otter on the way to Alert, we would be very low on fuel by
the time we got there. And here I had gone 22 miles in
the opposite direction, landed and damaged the aircraft.
Just great.

I tried to radio Alert, but it was a bad day for radio and I
couldn't make contact. Since there was no way I would
attempt a landing at the base camp, my only alternative
was to come up with some kind of temporary fix so we
could get off the ice and back to Alert. Fortunately, the
Twin Otter has a couple of really solid front steps for getting
up into the cockpit and I was able to use them as an anchor for tying the nose gear back into place with some of
our nylon tie-down rope. The gear wasn't completely back
in its socket and it always wanted to work out just a bit,
but it was solid enough that I figured we could get away
with it. The only thing was I had no nose steering and one
of the main rudder pulleys had snapped off.

The two rudder return pulleys are attached to the first
bulkhead, right up against the struts. When the strut
gave, it snapped one of the rudder return pulleys in half.
The only thing I could think of doing was to take the
cables out of both pulleys and tie them back so they'd
have a lot of slack. That way I could use the trim tabs
once I was airborne. But I wouldn't have any rudder on
the pedals at all and would have to try to control the aircraft with nothing but differential engine power on take-
off and landing since the hydraulics that steered the nose
were also out.

Turbines spool up. In other words, turbine power
comes up slowly compared to a piston engine, and you
have to anticipate its lag. If you think the aircraft is going to
start swinging right, you have to bring up the power on
the right engine beforehand because it takes that long for
the power to actually develop and help you steer. There
wasn't much room for a long take-off run and I had to get
those two engines coming up absolutely even all the way
from idle power to full power and do it fairly quickly. Believe me, that gets to be real tricky.

My take-off run started out okay, but one engine got a little ahead of the other and sure enough, I lost it. I asked everyone to get out of the aircraft and help swing it around so I could go back and try again.

On the second run I was a hell of a lot more careful and we got into the air. I found the Otter flew very nicely with the trim for rudder and we started our climb in the direction of Alert since I was convinced that's where we had to go. Despite the Twin Otter's 600-mile range and the fact we already had used two take-offs plus the aborted one, I thought we had a good chance of making it to Alert if there wasn't much headwind and everything else went well. If we lost an engine, of course, or even half of the power in an engine, there was no way we would make it without the rudder. But that was a chance we would have to take.

I told Dr. Webber and his party what our chances were and they agreed Alert was our best hope. For all practical purposes this meant the end of the expedition after 10 working days at the pole, which was far better than the 1967 fiasco but several days short of what Dr. Webber had scheduled. I knew Dr. Webber and his men were disappointed. No one said much on the flight back and no one felt worse about the situation than me.

We climbed right up to 12,000 feet, which was about as high as we could go without oxygen and the best we could do on fuel consumption, and then discovered we had a headwind and the heater wasn't working. A microswitch sensor located up front that controlled the heater valve had also been damaged. I couldn't get the valve to open and we sat there like icicles, freezing to death for a couple of hours until I was finally able to reach Alert by radio. The HF (high frequency) radio wasn't any good that day, but when we came within VHF (very high frequency) range of Alert, I was able to make contact about halfway in. VHF is a shorter range than HF and you have to be up higher to use it.

Alert advised me that we were bucking 50-mph headwinds and I thought to myself, if we hit Alert we'll be damn lucky. My best bet, Alert said, would be to drop down to about 4,000 feet. So we came down and found the going both faster and warmer.

When I saw Alert there were still a couple of gallons of gas left, not much more, and I came straight into the north-south runway and landed without any trouble at all. That old gal just sat on the runway and went straight down the strip as nice as could be. With no steering or anything. When the nose came down it wandered off to the side a bit, but I was able to hold it with the engines. Alert had all of its emergency equipment out, of course, but everything went just fine.

I went right by them and signaled we were okay.

It wasn't long before some of the Wardair boys from Yellowknife arrived in the Apache and we repaired the damaged nose gear right at Alert. I slowly worked my way back to Yellowknife in the Twin Otter, doing a few odd jobs here and there on the way down, and I remember thinking on the return that in two trips to the North Pole I had been very lucky to land the Bristol in 1967 and to escape a couple of close calls in the trip just ending. How much longer would my luck hold out? And, of course, there was Marie. How much more of this could she take?

It was then that I really began to think seriously about calling it quits in the North.

CHAPTER FOURTEEN

THE ARCTIC FOX

*"Art told me much later that he and the boys
never knew if they could call me the Arctic
Fox because they thought I was someone you
should always approach from the right side on
a good day."*

It must have been Melville Island because we did a lot of
work up there, but I couldn't swear by it. We were bringing in a D-4 Cat with the Bristol so they could clear a
larger strip for the C-130 aircraft. It was the trip where
they pinned that Arctic Fox name on me.

I can see so clearly in my mind the strip that we were
going to land on. The snow was quite heavy, I remember,
but we got in all right. We carried heavy wooden planks
in the Bristol to make a ramp so we could get the D-4
unloaded through the nose door. The idea was to lash
one end of the planks tight against the sill of the nose
door opening and then set some fuel drums under the
planks to help bear the weight of the Cat. The nose door
sill was only about four feet off the ground and the
planks were 12 feet long, so it was a fairly decent slope.
Not too steep, but enough of a grade that you had to be
sure you didn't have any snow on the planks or the Cat
would skid off and you would be out of luck. It helped to
use planks with a rough surface. The tops of the drums
were round, of course, and it all made for a kind of
shaky affair.

You hoped you had everything just right because
when the Cat moved out the door and tipped forward
onto the planks, it had to hit both planks dead center or
that was the end of it. It was such a delicate operation
that I wouldn't let anyone but myself drive the Cat out.

At home, back in Yellowknife where we had decent
ramps, I would let the younger fellows drive them out.
But out in the bush I had to do it myself.

After I had the Cat warmed up I slowly eased it out of
the front of the Bristol. When I brought the Cat down on
the planks, one plank shifted on top of the drum and
made the Cat a little bit cockeyed. The two boys I had
along with me on this particular trip included Art Morrow, and he tells me I just sat there very quietly for a few
seconds with both brakes on and thought things over. I
gently maneuvered the Cat until it was straightened out
and then slowly rolled it down the planks with the barrel
underneath still a bit wiggly.

Art said to the other crewman, copilot Bill Silvester,
"Boy, look at the Silver Fox up there. Look at what he's
done again." I paid no attention and kept on working. But
then I heard Silvester say, "Well, Silver Fox, that just isn't
right. Better be the Arctic Fox for this and all the other
things he's done." Art told me much later that he and the
boys never knew if they could call me the Arctic Fox because they thought I was someone you should always
approach from the right side on a good day.

They eventually did try it out on me, figuring that if I
didn't react too badly then they'd use discretion from
there on. So, that's how the Arctic Fox name was pinned
on me. It was nothing special; just that they happened to
think of it at the time.

We couldn't haul the D-4 and all its attachments in one
load, so we made a second flight in with the winch and
plow. It was still snowing hard and the landing, like the
first one, was quite rough although the second time I
knew where I was going to set down and I also had a set
of tracks to follow in the snow.

Taking off in the heavy snow was interesting, too, because I would always shut the Bristol's auto-feathering
off and hope we could feather an engine fast enough
manually if we needed to. With auto-feathering on, an

engine that lost 20 percent or more power would auto-matically feather without help from the cockpit. If an engine was going to die, you wanted it feathered so you had just the one good engine. The auto-feathering unit relied on a pair of air speed tubes, one out on the wing tip and the other behind the propeller. If a difference in air speed developed between the two, and it became great enough, the engine would simply shut down and the prop would feather. Taking off in heavy snow ran the risk of plugging one of the tubes with a chunk of snow and triggering the auto-feathering device. So, un-der really bad conditions when the snow was piling up, I'd shut off the auto-feathering. Just a couple of switches and you were on your own.

I guess there must have been a little bit of fox in me to do things like that and still make it to 80 years old.

CHAPTER FIFTEEN

FIRE-BOMBING AND OTHER CRAZY STUNTS

"Our fuel situation was getting desperate so I began talking about landing on a nearby ridge if we didn't make it in on the second approach. Art heard me over his headset and told me later he thought to himself, how in the hell do you find a ridge in the dark during a heavy snowstorm?"

I started fire-bombing in 1958. My log books record every flight I made from my first solo at Harlem Airport and I can tell from the entries when I was fire-bombing because there will be an hour or two of work right in the same area.

There always seemed to be a few brush fires to the north of Yellowknife every summer. They would usually start on a hot day when cool air would come off of Great Slave Lake and move north across the land on a slight southern breeze. Then, about 20 to 30 miles inland, the air would begin to warm and rise into a line of thunderstorms. The lightning would start the fire, and if it happened to be where the timber was any good then the order would come for us to help put the fire out.

In the early years we used the Otter and bolted a 100-gallon aluminum tank onto each float. The tanks had a bearing on each end and would rotate by pulling a lever in the cockpit, dumping 200 gallons of water in about five seconds. Since the tanks were spring loaded, they returned to the upright position after they were emptied. Usually there was a lake nearby and we could drop 200 gallons every minute and a half.

If we were lucky and had a lake on both sides of the fire, we could scoop up water in one lake and drop it over the fire and then scoop up water in the second lake and be back over the fire in about 50 seconds, dumping 400 gallons in less than a minute. During this time, of course, you were so darned busy because you were flaps down onto the lake to pick up your water and then flaps up to be back in the air again, forever turning and coming in low over the fire and running parallel to it, and then back up and over to the lake again.

The water tanks were filled through snorkel tubes that ran down under the Otter's floats so you didn't have to drop the aircraft into the water very deep at all. We would stay right on top of the water with enough power to pull up and away nice and clean as soon as we saw the tanks were about full. If you let the tanks overfill, then you had the snorkels in the water and all that extra water spilling over the floats and that made it much more difficult to get the Otter out of the water.

We would try to fire-bomb in the early morning before there was much wind or the fire had gotten a good start. Once we had everything dampened down, the ground crews could move in to make sure everything was out. The only time I felt it was really dangerous was late in the day when the fire was getting bigger and hotter because of the wind, and you were continuously flying through air that had a shower of burning stuff in it. The idea was to fire-bomb from a low altitude, otherwise the water would evaporate on the way down. It was the only time that we wore a full shoulder and seat harness because the air was so rough above the fires that it threw the old Otter around like a toy airplane. But if you could hit a fire early in the morning you could do a lot of damage to it with all that water. Then the ground crews could take over and stay with the fire during the day. Meantime, we'd be ready to bomb the very first thing in the morning again.

Somehow we managed to survive more fire-bombing runs than I can remember, but I will never forget the exhaustion I felt after about an hour of flaps up, flaps down, coming in over the fire at 150 or 200 feet and hitting its leading edge with as many as 50 or more loads of water. We were paid hourly, of course, just like all the other work. And we helped put out a lot of fires over the years.

Another crazy thing I did just goes to show what can happen when you combine a high-tech aircraft with a low-tech mind. The Twin Otter was a real fuel guzzler and I was always looking for ways to improve on its fuel economy. I got myself into the damnedest trouble, however, with one particular stunt.

When Wardair bought its second Twin Otter, a pilot named Daryle Brown was flying it most of the time and he was almost as egotistical as I was about flying. I was always preaching fuel economy and that led to a bit of friendly competition between the two of us to see who could burn the least amount. We both knew that taking the Twin Otter up to 20,000 feet on the return to Yellowknife after dumping a payload could conserve fuel. The Twin Otters carried emergency oxygen to help us through the several hours spent flying at such altitudes. It wasn't long, however, before I had a really great idea for gaining even more economy and getting a leg up on Daryle.

I simply put the Twin Otter into a slow idle and feathered the props at 20,000 feet when I was about 40 or 50 miles from home, then went to beat hell as the aircraft came down at 4,000 feet in a minute or more. It was brilliant, giving me maximum speed without burning any fuel. Apparently Daryle hadn't caught on to this latest trick of mine because he was still burning more fuel than I was after a few weeks. On the other hand, his health was just fine and mine was getting so bad I could hardly get out of bed in the morning. I couldn't figure out what was wrong with me. If I took just one drink of Scotch I would be so sick that I couldn't see, I couldn't stand, I couldn't do anything.

About this same time, Max, George Bell and a few others were my passengers on a short trip to Max's fishing camp north of Yellowknife. George and I always enjoyed a drink or two together, and after one Scotch at the camp I was so deathly sick and ashamed of myself that I was wishing there was some place to hide. All I wanted was to go away and die. I couldn't even fly the airplane the next morning. Max had to fly it.

Max had heard about my quick descents and figured there was something wrong with me that had nothing to do with drinking because he knew how I normally flew and drank and flew the next morning. He started to question me and then he took out some books on high altitude flight with emergency oxygen. We knew right away what I was doing wrong.

The deep descents were actually causing the reverse bends, the opposite of decompression. I was compressing myself after being up so high on nothing more than emergency oxygen. After a couple hours at more than 20,000 feet your body adjusts to the thin air and you have to take it very slow coming down. I should have known darn good and well that you shouldn't go higher than about 14,000 feet and then let down at such speeds. You save fuel, sure. But I damn near busted my neck doing it.

Speaking of busting my neck, the one time I came closest to doing exactly that was in the Twin Otter on a landing attempt with skis near Contwoyto Lake about 250 miles northeast of Yellowknife.

An Inuit family, including a new baby, a snowmobile, fuel and other supplies, asked for a lift to a village on the far end of Contwoyto Lake and I agreed to take them. It was one of those gray days late in the season when it was very difficult to see where the frozen surface of the lake begins or ends, or the condition of the snow cover on the lake. As I approached Contwoyto, the Inuit man said he didn't want to land at the village and asked if, instead, I would fly them to his cabin on a small lake some three or four miles distant. I agreed, thinking that if the landing conditions at his cabin were not good he could use his snowmobile to get his family and supplies from Contwoyto to the cabin.

The man's small lake looked big enough to land on, but it was hard to tell how much snow was on the surface. There were some rocks sticking up through the snow on the shoreline for reference, and since it was a small lake I knew I would have to come in over the rocks and land as close to the shoreline as possible. But first I would go in, touch down briefly to check the snow conditions on the surface, and then get right back in the air again. I wasn't too careful about coming in right on the shoreline and I touched down about one-third of the way onto the lake. Everything seemed fine.

When I opened up the throttles the aircraft started to pull to one side and I thought I must have run into some deep snow after all. If I had been looking at the gauges in the cockpit I would have seen that the right engine hadn't come up. By the time I figured this out and closed the left engine to get the Otter straightened out, I was too close to the opposite shoreline to stop. I ran out of lake and the aircraft rolled into the bush a couple of hundred feet and dropped into a little stream where it came to a rest. The legs were broken and the flaps and both props were bent, but I was okay and so were my passengers.

This incident happened late in my career with Wardair in the North and I remember thinking at the time that if I had been really sharp I would have glanced at my gauges and found out the right engine was gone. In that case I never would have poured on the other engine. Why didn't I just ground loop the damn thing since I knew the snow wasn't very deep by that time? I might have taken the gear off sideways but the overall damage probably would have been much less.

I also remembered we had been having a little trouble with the right engine and the boys had been working on it continuously. Sometimes on acceleration it wouldn't come off of idle smoothly. When I opened the throttle, of course, the left engine took off fine but the right one didn't. I shouldn't have been taken by surprise.

In a matter of hours the Wardair engineers arrived on the scene with legs and a couple of props which they changed out without a problem. The flaps were the biggest challenge and they straightened them out as best they could. We flew the aircraft home that way and did the flaps properly in Yellowknife.

I had a few other close calls and embarrassing moments during my career with Wardair, like the time I put a Beaver through the spring ice on a lake near Yellowknife. Max always had to fly ski-equipped until the last possible moment before the ice went totally bad. I finally got so I was like that and then I put one through the ice.

The ice seemed pretty good for late spring, but I didn't want to do a lot of taxiing on the lake. After dropping off a load at a camp two fellows asked if I would take them out, back to Yellowknife. They climbed in and I decided to turn around and taxi farther down the lake. I didn't want to chance a short take-off into the trees with the extra weight of the men and their gear. As I was turning back into the wind after my taxi, the Beaver went through the ice. Talk about disgusting!

I was fooled because the ice was badly candled from the bottom while the surface looked solid enough. Ice normally candles from the top in late spring due to the warm sunlight, but with muck bottom lakes the sun's rays go through the ice and the heat from the muck causes greater candling on the bottom of the ice than on the top. You've got nothing but a shell holding you on top. When an aircraft went through the ice we usually erected a timber A-frame affair on the ice over the plane in order to raise it up. Not this time. The ice was so bad that we had to cut long timber poles and drive them into the muck bottom 12 feet under the ice. The poles would normally be driven in a foot or two to support airbags we would inflate to raise the aircraft. The first couple of poles we drove went through the muck about four feet

and then disappeared below the surface. It was a really
bad bottom. We finally ended up using 20-foot poles to
get above the water and eventually we got the Beaver
out. Just another typical day flying in the North.

We also had an old Beech 18S twin-engine aircraft
that lost one of its 450-hp Pratt & Whitney radial engines in December of 1966 when I was flying an Inuit
and his new snowmobile back to his village. I was able
to land the darn thing with the gear up on Pellatt Lake,
which connects with the south end of the larger
Contwoyto Lake. The damage was minimal and Wardair
engineers Guenther Moellenbeck and Art Morrow were
able to make repairs on the spot so we could fly it home.
The Inuit fellow was the only one who seemed happy
about the situation. With the aircraft flat on its belly, he
didn't have to drop his new snowmobile very far to the
ground when he unloaded it.

I never thought much of the Beech 18S, especially one
on floats. You just couldn't keep the load far enough
forward. We would haul silver down from a mine at Echo
Bay and pile silver bags in the nose. Otherwise you were
flying the Beech all the time out of the rear. It was miserable.

My friend Art Morrow likes to tell the story about the
time in March of 1966 when we were supposed to deliver
5,000 pounds of dynamite at a drilling site on Mackenzie
King Island, one of the most northern of the Canadian
Arctic Islands. We were in the Bristol Freighter and the
weather turned bad as we neared our destination. It
would be impossible to land so I decided to return to
Resolute. I had calculated our load to fuel configuration
with reserve fuel for a return to Resolute, but the severe
wind made for such a slow ground speed that our fuel
supply all of a sudden didn't look that promising.

Art says he knew we were in trouble because the
smoke from my pipe was coming out in rings.

It was dark as we approached Resolute and the heavy,

blowing snow made visibility near zero. We couldn't see the strobe lights on our first approach. I pulled up and decided to go around. Our fuel situation was getting desperate so I began talking about landing on a nearby ridge if we didn't make it in on the second approach. Art heard me over his headset and told me later he thought to himself, how in the hell do you find a ridge in the dark during a heavy snowstorm?

On the second approach I caught a flicker of the strobe lights and brought the old Bristol down on the runway with the fuel tanks all but empty. Another close call, one of many over more than a half-century of flying. Art and the others call me the Arctic Fox because of these incidents. I call me damn lucky.

By 1969, especially after the incident in the Twin Otter at Contwoyto Lake, I was having second thoughts about just how long my luck would hold on. I was getting on in years, Marie's bouts of depression were worse than ever, and I found myself resenting all the attention and money that Max was devoting to Wardair's highly successful international charter business despite the fact the needs and requirements in the North were always of interest and concern to Max. With the exception of the Bristols and one single-engine Otter, the entire Northern fleet was purchased new — six Twin Otters, five single-engine Otters and two four-engine Dash 7s. We were by far the most modern fleet of aircraft of any bush operation in Canada. Still, maybe it was time to quit before my luck ran out and the Arctic Fox became one more name on a long list of bush pilots in the North who took one too many chances.

CHAPTER SIXTEEN

MANY SEARCHES, FEW RESCUES

*"The Nahanni River country is intriguing
because a number of people — mostly bush
pilots, prospectors and trappers—had disappeared into the Nahanni and never turned up
again. The territory was full of canyons with
dead ends that could prove deadly to a tired
or preoccupied or inexperienced pilot."*

When an aircraft was lost in the North, all the operators
that could afford it would start to search immediately
along the pilot's intended route. The first day or two we
would be on our own, searching along the route to see if
we could find the aircraft without having to call in the
RCAF. If the aircraft wasn't found, then the RCAF would
come in and organize the official search. We were all
given areas or lines to cover in an effort that would
gradually spread out away from the route until every
feasible area had been searched. Sometimes it would take
three weeks or more.

The bigger charter operations would always contribute
one of their aircraft to a search. Wardair was really good
about that. I always admired Max for his willingness to
donate an aircraft, even if it meant paying for gas and the
pilot's wages for 100 hours or more. It was a lot of
money, but Max would just say, "Well, let's go look for
them and stick with it." How long we stuck with a particular search often depended on how well we knew the
pilot.

We typically flew the Otter all day long with five or six
spotters in it. The trick to spotting is to be able to recognize something odd, something that shouldn't be there. I
was never very good at it, but some people have a knack

for spotting something out of place. Marie was like that. She was always picking out wild game when we drove along the northern roads, everything from bears to birds and an occasional moose. The only thing I ever saw was a moose, but it was standing alongside the road so I couldn't help but see it.

The searches would almost always start along the route and then work east first because the prevailing winds were from the west and northwest. Anybody flying in bad weather in the North usually ends up east of their track. The more experienced bush pilots were never more than five or six miles off, but some guys who had no business flying in the North could be a hundred miles or more off track.

Survival, however, depended as much or more on the downed pilot's temperament as it did on his location. I've known guys who went down right outside of Yellowknife and by the time they were picked up a day or two later they were practically out of their minds. One went down only 30 miles out of Yellowknife and when he came out of the woods three days later he was so shook up he could barely talk. Yet other, more experienced pilots, would walk 30 miles to a mining camp or outpost to report in, then walk back to their aircraft and make repairs and fly it out. A routine thing for them. But if you were panicky and couldn't stand being alone, you generally got into trouble.

There was the story about a couple of pilots with a small flying service out of Inuvik who were taking some passengers to Yellowknife when they were forced down on a frozen lake about 130 miles north of Yellowknife. I don't know if they were lost or just ran out of gas, but they apparently landed well off their track and were unable to make contact with anyone by radio. It was dead calm outside and they could hear the trucks and aircraft and equipment at the Rayrock Mine located 30 miles away. One of the pilots, a good bush man, was the type who never panicked. After a couple of days he figured the search planes wouldn't find them so he decided to walk over to the mine. He walked 30 miles in three days after making good provision for the passengers and the other pilot. Their instructions were to stay with the aircraft, which they did, until he returned with help, which he did.

And then there was the drunken Frenchman who sat in his aircraft out on a frozen lake for 56 days and lost most of his toes. He was an alcoholic and never did know quite where in the hell he was going. On this particular trip he was flying a Beaver with some government fish and wildlife folks aboard. He took them down the Mackenzie River to the coast, then east to Coppermine and finally to Cambridge Bay with maybe a few stops in between along the coast.

The government people were getting a little sick and tired of starting late each day and having the Frenchman spend the first few hours in the air each morning sobering up. They knew their way around the North and caught a DC-3 back to Yellowknife rather than make the long trek back in the Beaver with the Frenchman. Fortunately for the Frenchman they left some of their sleeping robes behind plus a bag of frozen fish.

The next day the Frenchman started south alone and it wasn't long before he was lost. He set the Beaver down on a lake 60 miles west of his track but within range of a navigation beacon station at Contwoyto Lake. The station isn't active today, but during the 1950s and 1960s it was operated by Pacific Western Airlines because they made a scheduled run between Yellowknife and Cambridge Bay. The station was manned by three men who operated the diesel generator and the non-directional beacon. The Frenchman had no idea where he was, so when he made radio contact with the station all he could tell them was that he was all right and that he would take off again in the morning.

The RCAF was alerted by the station and had several planes in the air the next morning with instructions to the Frenchman not to take off because they were on their way to help him. But what did that clown do? He took off and began flying farther west of his track. He apparently flew west instead of south because he saw some trees and thought he was getting down to the tree line when, in fact, he was seeing some of the trees that straggle down from the coast along the Coppermine River. The Frenchman didn't have much gas, but he managed to get at least 180 miles west of his track before his fuel tanks went dry and he went down in the Dismal Lakes area. For some reason or another, the RCAF couldn't pick him up on radio and they assumed he was down far to the east of his actual location. The whole thing was absolutely asinine.

To make matters worse, the Frenchman set the Beaver down out in the middle of a big lake. Bear in mind that we're talking early February when it was about as cold as it gets up in the North, yet this joker didn't have enough sense to bring the Beaver in along the shoreline where there was plenty of firewood. His excuse was that he was afraid there might be wolves! Well, if there had been wolves they wouldn't have bothered him because there has never been a recorded incident of a wolf going after a person unless the animal was rabid.

There he sat, so far out on the lake that he was afraid to walk to shore for firewood. And since he had no idea where he was he had no way of telling the RCAF or anyone else his location. In a day or two it didn't make any difference, of course, because his batteries froze up and that was the end of his radio. He tried to keep warm by draining hydraulic fluid from the aircraft and burning it inside the cabin, but he got the cabin all black and smoky and damn near killed himself choking on the fumes. He finally decided the best thing to do was crawl into the sleeping robes and stay as warm as he could, thawing a fish out in the robe every couple of days and eating it raw. In this manner he managed to survive a total of 56 days in the cabin of the Beaver before he was spotted by pure chance.

The first turbo Beaver in the north was owned by Consolidated Mining and Smelting, and it was making a run along the Coppermine-Yellowknife route in late April when the spring sun was high in the sky. There had been some engine trouble, so the turbo Beaver had taken off late and it just happened to be passing within six or eight miles of the Frenchman when the sun was at its highest. The engineer saw a glint of sunlight on a lake way to the west and both he and the pilot remembered that the Frenchman was still out there somewhere. They decided to investigate, but only after first dropping off their load and then returning to the area empty.

Sure enough, they found the Beaver with the old Frenchman still alive in it. The sun had thawed the frost off of his windshield and its reflection caught the eye of the engineer aboard the turbo Beaver. The Frenchman was lucky that he only lost his toes and not his life. It's hard for me to understand why a guy would sit in that freezing cold Beaver and eat raw fish and try to make a fire out of hydraulic fluid when shelter and firewood were so close, less than a mile away.

The story of the missing Frenchman is only a story to me because I didn't participate in the search. Of the searches I was personally involved in, the two that come to mind involved Ken Stockall and Chuck McAvoy. They were fellow Yellowknife bush pilots and their luck, unlike that of the Frenchman, ran out.

You'll remember I mentioned earlier that Chuck McAvoy and his brother, Jimmy, operated a little service that their father had started just up the bay from us in Yellowknife. Their dad had pioneered in the North Country and they fell right into his footsteps as prospectors as well as pilots. And, of course, if you were a prospector and a pilot you always had a heck of a time getting charter business from other prospectors because they assumed you were going to hook onto their property. So the McAvoy brothers eventually decided to quit prospecting and concentrate on the flying business. Following in their father's footsteps, they always tended to overload their aircraft. That was just normal procedure for the McAvoys.

Between the two brothers they had a Cessna 180 and 185, and an old Fairchild 71, which was a five- or six-place fabric-covered aircraft powered by a Pratt & Whitney radial. I remember the Fairchild had a windshield that stood well up and out of the fuselage and then was tapered back with a hatch on top that you had to go through to get into the cockpit when the cabin was loaded with freight. The old Beechcraft 18 twin had a similar hatch above the windshield. Chuck McAvoy took the Fairchild up into the Barren Lands to move two prospectors and all of their gear. He and the prospectors and the Fairchild disappeared from the face of the earth and were never seen again.

The prospectors were waiting for Chuck at a remote location just south of Bathurst Inlet up near the coast. He apparently got there and they loaded the Fairchild with everything prospectors carried, including dynamite, dynamite caps and gasoline for the air hammers they used to drill rock. It wasn't as though McAvoy wouldn't have known his way, but for some reason the party vanished. We finally figured that either something went wrong with the engine and they went down, eventually going through the ice before anyone could find them, or that something blew up while they were in the air and everything was in such small pieces that nobody could find them.

We spent quite a bit of time searching for McAvoy and his party but when he didn't show up on the surface of a lake, which we figured he would, we feared the worst. The guys who knew the North, like McAvoy, were always pretty well on track. The most they would be off were perhaps five miles because they knew how hard they would be to find if they wandered too far off course. McAvoy would want to be easy to find, but he was never found.

Then, in 1962, I spent over 130 hours looking for Ken
Stockall. Max, as usual, paid for every bit of it.

Ken was a good pilot and a very ambitious guy. He
worked for us for a couple of years, but quit in 1959 to
start Ptarmigan Airways, Ltd. with a partner by the
name of Les Mullins. Ken and Les had one airplane to
start with and within a year or so they had a couple
more, all small Cessnas. Ken was one of those real
driver types, and once he had his own outfit there was
nothing that could keep him from flying. He was a driver
that just kept going too long and that may have been the
trouble on September 29.

Some of the most beautiful but rugged and remote
acreage on earth is located 400 miles to the west of
Yellowknife in an area called the Nahanni River country,
and old Henry Busse, the only good photographer we
had in town back then, decided he wanted to take some
pictures in the Nahanni area on September 29. Henry
had wonderful photographs of northern lights and all
kinds of night photos of the effects of the midnight sun
in the North Country. His photos had appeared in a
number of Canadian and U.S. magazines and he sold a
good many of them out of his shop. Henry and two men
from Giant Yellowknife Mines, Victor Hudson and
Gerhart Geortz, hired Ken to take them on a photo excursion into the Nahanni River country.

The Nahanni River country is intriguing because a
number of people — mostly bush pilots, prospectors and
trappers — had disappeared into the Nahanni and never
turned up again. The territory was full of canyons with
dead ends that could prove deadly to a tired or preoccupied or inexperienced pilot. The South Nahanni River
itself wasn't very big but it was a wild mountain river
with dozens of tributaries.

Ken Stockall was not inexperienced, but for whatever
reason he failed to return or report in and his partner,
Les Mullins, asked Jim McAvoy to take him over to the
Nahanni in McAvoy's Cessna 185. They spent all of Sep-

tember 30 looking for Ken and on October 1, 1962, the RCAF was called in to conduct an official search. Because Ken had been one of our pilots, Wardair contributed both an Otter and a Beaver to the search effort and the first thing we did was check out the South Nahanni River valley. We not only flew the river, we walked it in areas where we could land. I figured we might pick up some evidence of where they had been, such as empty film boxes or some other clue, but we didn't find a thing.

A number of search aircraft landed a mile or so above Virginia Falls on the South Nahanni and searched the entire area on foot. Then we went to a place on the river called Rabbit Kettle Lake because it had a couple of interesting rock formations that I thought Henry might go out of his way to photograph. It was about a half-mile trek across a creek and through a bunch of deadfalls to get over to the formations, and we worked our way over in the hope of finding some sign. The formations were a pair of huge limestone dishes, each about half a city block in diameter, that stuck out of the earth. I had never seen anything like them before or since. They had water flowing out of them, over the edges, and it was like a swamp all around them. But there was no sign of Ken.

We spent more time on the ground than in the air that first week and my eyes were so tired they almost fell out of my head at night. After a week we thought the surface possibilities had been exhausted so we started straight air searches, flying up into all of the Nahanni's tributaries where valleys would quickly become narrow canyons and you had to be very careful you could get high enough or turn around before being trapped in a dead-end. As it turned out, that's exactly what happened to Ken. He had flown up into a blind canyon and didn't get turned around soon enough.

The wreckage of Ken's Cessna 185 wasn't spotted until the next summer. It was lying on the floor of a

blind canyon near the headwaters of the Ram River
about 25 miles to the north of the area we had been
searching. The bones were there along with Ken's bill-
fold but the remains must have been eaten by a wolverine.

Ken Stockall was not only a fellow pilot, he was a good
friend. The search for Ken consumed hundreds of hours
by as many as five aircraft at one time. But no one
searched as long or as hard as we did. I was sure, just
so sure I was going to find him. He left behind a wonderful wife and five young children. Ken reminded me of
Max because when he was flying for himself he was always pushing the outer fringes. This time he had
pushed his luck too far.

I also remember during the war years when a couple
of DC-3s took off within a couple of hours of each other
and became lost on what were supposed to be routine
flights from Fort Nelson up to Watson Lake along the
Alcan Highway. It was late in the fall and Bounce Weir
was my copilot in the old Lockheed 10. A heavy snowfall
and low ceiling forced us to put down at Fort Nelson. It
was time for supper, anyway, and the procedure for
getting into Lake Watson on instruments was very odd
to the point of deciding in favor of landing at Fort
Nelson. There were little stations at Smith River and
Tesland between Fort Nelson and Watson Lake, but they
didn't have landing facilities for the Lockheed in the
event we would need to put down because of the weather.

I told Bounce we would sit tight overnight at Fort
Nelson until the weather cleared and that's exactly what
we did. The next morning, however, we were informed
that the two DC-3s were missing and we agreed to do a
search on our flight to Whitehorse, which was another
250 or more air miles northwest of Watson Lake. We
didn't see anything out of line during our flight to
Whitehorse. Meantime the RCAF and everyone else who
flew the run became involved in the search for the two
aircraft.

As it turned out, one of the DC-3s went down only about six miles out of Watson Lake across the Francois River from the landing strip. The aircraft apparently stalled out as it was turning into the landing strip and it went in straight enough to kill the crew up front. The DC-3 impacted in the trees and that saved the two guys in back. The two men, an old cook and an air force corporal, could hear aircraft taking off from the Watson Lake landing strip. The only problem was that each man had a broken leg, so they decided to stay with the aircraft. Within half an hour the wreck was covered with snow.

After a couple of weeks the two men were getting low on rations and they decided they wouldn't be found unless they took matters into their own hands. The aluminum ration containers were about three or four feet long, just about right for sliding a busted leg across country in the snow. Each man lashed half a container to his broken leg and they slowly began making their way toward the Watson Lake landing strip. After a time they reached the Francois River, and although it was frozen solid it had very steep banks. The men struggled for the better part of a day and were only able to make it across the river and halfway up the river bank on the other side.

About this time a fellow by the name of George "Del" Dalzell was flying a Norseman for the RCAF into Watson Lake when he spotted a peculiar set of tracks up the river bank. Del had been flying in the bush for years and he circled to get a closer look as a matter of routine. He discovered the two men from the DC-3 and quickly landed, got them aboard the Norseman, and brought them in. Over the years there were stories about these two guys using engine cowlings for toboggans and the Mounties finding them, but it was a bush pilot who saved them.

As for the other DC-3, it hit the first high mountain on the west leg out of Fort Nelson. It was rumored to have a

payroll on board but I don't think that was true. All
aboard were killed and the wreckage wasn't found for a
couple of years. As it turned out, the aircraft was spotted by a member of a hunting party aboard a charter
flight out of Yellowknife.

The pilot of the charter was a young man named Max
Ward.

CHAPTER SEVENTEEN

TIME TO CALL IT QUITS

"By 1969, the year I made my second trip to the pole, Marie's condition was worse than ever and it was really starting to wear on me. I was finding fault with everything and everybody, including Wardair and Max."

There were many more suicides in Yellowknife than there should have been for the small population we had. The suicides would always happen around the end of winter and the beginning of spring, which to me was crazy. Just when you're ready for another beautiful summer, these people would kill themselves after a winter of too much booze and not enough sunlight. I guess the North Country does that to some people. It drives them to drink and worse.

Marie's depression started four or five years after our move up to Yellowknife in 1955. I still don't know if you can blame it on the North or if there was something else that might have caused it no matter where we lived. There's no doubt in my mind, however, that my being away on long trips was as much to blame as anything. Like the time I spent three days up at Banks Island in that igloo. It was that sort of thing that must have driven Marie around the bend.

I would go out on a trip and plan to be back the next day. Then I wouldn't come back and Max would come up with some kind of story that I was safe somewhere and everything was perfectly all right, which was usually the case. But the uncertainty of not knowing whether Max was just giving her a line would drive Marie crazy. The wives of the other pilots would try to give Marie some support, but it wasn't much help because their husbands weren't disappearing nearly as often as I was. Being the chief pilot, I was taking the most chances. I was always the first in or the farthest out before other aircraft would follow. As Marie's depression worsened, it became increasingly difficult for me to leave on these trips. She was so erratic taking care of the boys, and sometimes she wouldn't go shopping or even leave the house to go out among other people when I was gone.

At first I really didn't know how to handle Marie's bouts of depression and I would only make matters worse by fighting back. After a time I found that all a person can do is walk away. Fighting was the worst thing I could have done because there isn't one argument in the world that will do any good at all. Fighting only provokes violence and Marie would throw things when she got mad, anything at all that she happened to have in her hand.

The fighting and the depression and my being gone so much were also taking a toll on the boys, especially Christopher, our oldest. He began hanging around with a bad crowd and doing drugs. I figured he was such a bad example for the other two boys that either he was going to straighten out or get kicked out. I warned him of this a couple of times and the third time he came home after being out all night I had his clothes piled up by the front door. I said, "That's it. You're out. You've pulled this stunt once too often and we've got two more boys to think of. If you want to go on drugs, go on drugs, but you're not coming back to this house!" So, at 18, Christopher left and simply disappeared. Marie never forgave me for that.

Charles stayed pretty much in line and left home to go to vocational school in Edmonton after completing his schooling in Yellowknife. He took a two-year business course and then went on to a job. That left Joel home alone with his mom and it had to be very hard on the little guy. Marie's depression became so bad that I finally took her to Edmonton a couple of times to see some psychiatric specialists, but she was convinced they were trying to poison her and she wouldn't take her medication.

In 1967, the year of my first North Pole landing, Max purchased four more Bristol Freighters for Wardair's northern operation. The Bristols had been military aircraft and they were being converted for civilian use at Bristol's factory at Weston-super-Mare in England, just south of the city of Bristol. It would be my job, as chief pilot, to go over to England and fly the first Bristol across the Atlantic to Edmonton, where it would be registered, and then up to Yellowknife. I decided this would be the perfect opportunity for Marie and me to have a real vacation away from everything and Max was kind enough to provide us with passes on British Airways so we could see some of Europe. We left for England a full two weeks before the Bristol was scheduled for pickup.

Marie was in much better spirits during our trip and it was almost like old times. We flew from England to Genoa, Italy, then rented a car and drove to Milan where I hoped to find the first of two Italian pilots I had befriended earlier in the year when we were in training together at de Havilland in Toronto prior to accepting our first Twin Otters. The two men were having trouble understanding the technical terms, although they both spoke some English, and after the third or fourth day of classes I asked them if they would like some coaching at night. They agreed and we got to know each other quite well. They invited me to visit them in Italy as a gesture of appreciation.

The first pilot, Peter, was away with his family on a Mediterranean vacation, so we drove west to Turin and found my other pilot friend, Tony. After introducing us to his family and inviting us to join them for supper, Tony drove us back to Milan the next morning and offered to fly us to the resort village of Cortina in the Italian Alps since his flight out would have room for us. We agreed and soon found ourselves in a lovely little inn at the small airport at Cortina up in the mountains.

The inn had comforters filled with down that were very thick but light as a feather. I remember just as if it was

yesterday how Marie and I took such pleasure in rolling
the darn thing over us. Our room, the food, the flowers
and everything were just beautiful. Marie knew enough
German to order our food, although the people spoke
both German and Italian because Cortina is very near
the Austrian border.

Tony came back in a couple of days in his Twin Otter
and flew us to Venice, the city built on islands, where
there are no roads, just canals and thousands of boats.
You never saw so many cats and pigeons in your life, not
to mention cathedrals and statues. The cats would yowl
all night and the pigeons would practically land on you
during the day. Venice, of course, is slowly sinking into
the sea. The hotel we were staying in had water marks
about a foot and a half up, all around the ground floor.
Even St. Mark's Square during the spring high tides had
thousands of feet of boardwalk laid across the square
because the area was under a foot or more of water.
Many of the older masonry buildings have large steel
rods going through the stones with big nuts on the ends
so the buildings are literally bolted together to prevent
collapse. Everything is hauled by boat, of course, and
Marie and I would stand on the high arch bridges over
the canals and watch the boats and gondolas go under
and beep at each other at every intersection. You'd think
there would be more crashes and sinkings, but somehow that never happened very often.

After a few days in Venice the weather turned bad and
we were unable to fly out, so we rented a car and drove
back across northern Italy to Genoa. We became lost
several times, mostly because I preferred to take the
country roads and stay off the turnpikes. Marie and I
were almost killed driving between Milan and Turin.
There are four lanes of traffic and everyone's going like
mad; some even driving at night without headlights, just
with their parking lights on. And when they come to an
intersection in the old part of a city where the buildings
come right up to the corners, they flash their lights and

honk their horns to let you know they're coming. Even my friend, Tony, on the drive over to Milan, had our tiny rental car up to 130 kilometers on the highway. And we were barely keeping up with the traffic!

When we returned to England and Weston-super-Mare to pick up the Bristol, I was told that it would be another five weeks before the aircraft would be ready.

Marie became very upset and said she had no intention of waiting five weeks, that she wanted to get back to Joel. I also knew she was worried sick about riding across the North Atlantic in that Bristol, even though it was the first one we had equipped with hot water to make coffee or bouillon. I told Marie all she had to do was go down the ladder into the cargo hold and put on the water and throw in the bouillon. But she just couldn't see how in the world she was going to climb up and down the ladder and spend any time at all alone in the 39-foot cargo hold with nothing but spare parts for company.

I put Marie on a plane headed back home and waited out the five weeks in England. My copilot on the flight back in the Bristol was just a kid, but a good one, and I thought he could go down into the hold and make us something hot to drink. It turned out to be such a lousy trip, however, that we never really got anything hot to drink other than what we had in our thermoses to begin with. We didn't do much eating, either, and during the 32 hours it took to reach Edmonton my sleeping was only little naps, maybe 20 minutes every eight hours or so while the copilot took over for a bit. Our flight took us from Weston-super-Mare up over the North Atlantic to Reykjavik, Iceland, and then over to the west coast of Greenland where we landed at Søndrestrømfjord, which was an airstrip used during World War II. From Greenland we were scheduled to land at Iqaluit on Frobisher Bay at the south end of Baffin Island, but the weather was bad and we went on to Churchill and then to Edmonton where I had the Bristol licensed to Canadian standards. All in all it wasn't too bad a trip and proved to be a real picnic compared to the Bristol delivery that I made in November of the same year when the weather was really terrible.

Before taking off from Weston-super-Mare in the second of our four Bristols, I was warned that we might encounter heavy icing out over the North Atlantic. They said there wouldn't be much use in trying a lower altitude and that I should turn around and head back to northern Ireland if we ran into it.

Out over the Atlantic we had no choice but to fly in the overcast since we didn't have oxygen and we couldn't go any higher than we could stand for very long, about 12,000 feet. The tops of the clouds were way above us, reaching as high as 18,000 feet, and there was no hope of maintaining that kind of altitude. About a hundred miles out of Iceland the ice really began to build up despite the Bristol's weeping de-icer system or perhaps because of it.

A glycol mixture would flow back over the wings and tailplane of the Bristol from a series of small perforations near the leading edges and this would help keep the ice from building up. The trick was to release the glycol before you ran into heavy ice because the system was not designed to dislodge it. The de-icer seemed to be working for a while, but gradually the ice began to build up faster than the glycol could handle it. The glycol would go about two-thirds or three-quarters of the way back on the top side of the wing and then stop flowing as it encountered a ridge of ice along the length of the wings. As the ridge grew in size, like an ice dam on the roof of a house, it distorted the airflow across the surface of the wings.

About 80 miles out of Reykjavik, much as I hated to, I turned back and started to descend. Over the ocean, with good barometric readings, you can get down fairly low and I kept letting down. We were down to about 600 feet on the altimeter when we started seeing the nasty old North Atlantic through the breaks. I finally let down to 400 feet and I'll be darned if we didn't start to lose the ice.

I turned the Bristol around and headed back toward Reykjavik at low altitude. It was pouring rain when we touched down, but we made it through the worst ice conditions I had ever experienced.

When we finally arrived at Edmonton many hours later I went nose-to-nose with a funny old inspector who insisted on checking all 51 crates and pieces of equipment listed on my manifest. The problem was I had thrown out a 400-pound spare wheel before taking off in England because I was a little overloaded and that left me a piece short on the manifest, which he started to lecture me about.

"Look here," I said, "You can stay in the belly of this Bristol and do all the checking you want for as long as you want, but I've been awake for almost 40 hours and I'm going to bed!" He signed the papers and left.

By 1969, the year I made my second trip to the pole, Marie's condition was worse than ever and it was really starting to wear on me. I was finding fault with everything and everybody, including Wardair and Max. The fact we operated for so many years in the North with no real hangar, just those nose hangars shoved over an engine when we were working one, was becoming a real sore spot with me and I was constantly after Max to give us a hangar. Max, of course, was busy trying to build up the southern operation and he had every cent and all he could borrow invested in that. He couldn't build a hangar for us, he said, and he didn't.

That did it. I finally told Max I was giving up. Quitting Wardair.

Marie needed medical help and I just refused to keep on flying aircraft that were being maintained out in the cold. That's what I told Max, that we've all worked hard to make the northern operation go but this was the end of the line. If Marie hadn't been so sick and we had a decent hangar, I probably would have stayed and flown a couple more years. But it just got to be too much. We returned to the farm in St. Cloud in late 1969 where I basically grounded myself.

CHAPTER EIGHTEEN

JUST ONE MORE FLIGHT

*"In all the years I've been flying, this was the
closest thing to actual flight that I had ever
experienced. You don't fly high or fast in an
ultralight; you sit out in the open and play the
wind like an eagle."*

Despite the fact he was alone and in failing health when
we returned, Dad moved out of the farmhouse into a
small cottage on the other side of our driveway so Marie,
Joel and I could have the house. I went to work for Como
Machine, where I had worked in the early 1950s, and
spent the next couple of years trying to make a living and
trying to help Marie. At first she agreed to go to a psychiatric health center, but she couldn't get it out of her
mind that they were trying to harm her and she refused
further treatment. Joel was now a teenager and becoming
impossible. He could get anything from Marie by being
nice to her for a few minutes and the next minute they'd be
fighting and throwing things. I never knew what was
going to happen because Marie's moods could change
so quickly.

After we had been home about five years I read an ar-
ticle about lithium, a new "wonder" drug that had dramatically helped some people suffering from manic
depression. Much as I hated to pick something out of a
magazine and go to a doctor with it, that's exactly what I
did because I was desperate. The doctor was skeptical
and prescribed lithium with considerable reluctance. There
was a very dramatic turnaround for a little while. But the
lithium wore off, just like all of the other drugs Marie had
tried, and she refused to increase the dosage because there
could be serious side effects. I really couldn't blame her,
but from then on it was just a steady downhill thing.

Even on a good day Marie had a difficult time getting along with most people, including members of her own family. She would even fight with her mother. Marie would go over to see her with perfectly good intentions, but the first thing you knew she would be back without one good thing to say about her own mother. And her mother was a lovely old lady. I got along really well with her. Then there were people Marie was always fond of, like my sister Mary or Len Wickert, my sister Marge's husband. Leonard was definitely one of her favorites. And she liked my brother Jim, too, until the day she said Jim deliberately tried to tip her out of a boat. That ended it for Jim. She didn't like him from that day on just because he happened to rock the boat while she was standing up.

The disappearance of our oldest son, Christopher, was something Marie thought about constantly. She was always trying to find out the latest rumors of his whereabouts. We had heard Christopher was working on drilling crews in British Columbia and later he let us know in a roundabout way that he was attending a diesel mechanic school. But we never heard from him directly and often we would hear that he was in trouble. Drill guys are some of the toughest, roughest characters in the world, and it troubled us to no end that he might be one of them. Joel lived at home and Charles always kept in touch with us on a fairly regular basis, but Christopher...

Our phone rang one evening after we had been back in St. Cloud a few years and for some reason or another I answered it. It was Christopher.

He was so apologetic about being gone for so long and asked if there was any way he could come back. I said there sure was. "All you've got to do is come back and you're home," I told him.

Christopher didn't come back right away, but he and a buddy stopped at the farmhouse a few months later on their way to jobs in Ontario. He only stopped for a few hours because they were anxious to get to their jobs.

Christopher looked so ratty and awful when he came through that I thought, holy smokes, I hope he feels better than he looks. But the poor guy was so apologetic and felt so bad about all of the worry he had caused, just as he had told me on the phone. We didn't hear from Christopher for several months, but the job in Ontario apparently didn't work out so he and his friend dropped in again on their way back west. He had no intention of staying home and never did, which was fine with me as long as he stayed in touch.

Christopher returned to British Columbia and got married at some point although he never said anything to us about it at the time. Just before Christmas in 1977 I received the most wonderful letter from Christopher. He told us he had married, and that he and his wife, Lynda, had a baby daughter, Tanya. Again he asked for forgiveness, saying he had been confused, angry and even selfish. I couldn't believe it. We were so happy to have him back, with a wonderful wife and granddaughter, too!

I honestly never thought Christopher was going to pull himself out of the hole he had dug for himself. But he did. Now, you couldn't have a better son, no two ways about it. He's a good husband and a good father and I couldn't be more proud of anyone than I am of him.

While I was keeping busy in retirement trying to earn a few dollars at the machine shop and watching after Marie and Joel, Max at last had decided to plow some money into Wardair's northern operation. He built a $1.5-million hangar in 1975, which was much bigger than any hangar I ever wanted, and purchased two of de Havilland's new Dash 7 aircraft. The Dash 7 was a beautiful airplane with four turbo-prop engines mounted on a high wing, much like the smaller Twin Otter, and good S.T.O.L. capability. It could carry 50 passengers or five tons of freight.

The first Dash 7 was received in May 1978, and Max decided to name the aircraft after me in a christening ceremony at de Havilland's Toronto facilities. Max had been naming most of his big charter jets after famous Canadian bush pilots, but this was the first aircraft in the northern fleet to be named. Marie and I were the honored guests of Wardair at the ceremony and it was Marie who actually christened the C-GXVF *Don Braun*. Like the North Pole landing, it was another special moment of my life and I was so happy that this time Marie was able to play the starring role in it. Within two months, the *Don Braun* carried Britain's Queen Elizabeth and Prince Phillip on a leg of their 1978 Canadian tour.

Wardair took delivery of the second Dash 7 a year later, but the northern operation was proving too costly and Max pulled the plug on it in October 1979. The northern operation out of Yellowknife, where it all began, sadly became history.

Everything, it seemed, was changing or becoming history. The old farm where we lived really wasn't much of a farm at all by the mid-1970s. Parcels of the property were being sold to developers and what were once my dad's fields were now streets lined with houses filled with children as the population of the St. Cloud area was booming.

Around 1980 the new trust company that was handling Wardair's pension funds wrote to me with all kinds of questions about how much I had earned during my years of service and, of course, I didn't know. I had never written any of that down and I didn't have the slightest idea. I was one of those guys that never kept track of how much I earned, only how much — or how little — I had in the bank. Anyway, I answered what I could and left the rest of the form blank and sent it in.

The folks at the trust company wrote back and said under the circumstances they needed more information or they couldn't continue to send me my monthly pension. I wrote, "Fine, for that measly $112 a month, keep it!" on the back of their letter and returned it. I also told them I didn't have the information and that they could check with the company, which they did.

As it turned out, neither Max nor Wardair's vice president at the time, George Curley, knew that several of us old-timers had retired with only a small monthly pension. Years earlier Max had given me, George Bell and a few others blocks of shares in Wardair just before it went public in 1967. They were only worth about 25 cents a share at the time, so I threw them in a drawer and promptly forgot about them. Those shares eventually became worth a considerable amount and I guess Max and George Curley never gave much thought to our pensions because of the stock.

I continued getting my $112 a month, and then a few months later on a trip to Max's fishing lodge on Redrock Lake 200 miles north of Yellowknife, Max and George Curley approached me the first evening there. They wanted to know why I had retired without saying anything about the pension.

"Well, if you recall, I retired four years early because I was mad at you for not building a decent hangar for the northern operation and I had to get Marie out of the North because something had to be done about her mental condition. That's why," I told them in a fairly straightforward way.

Max reminded me about the block of stock and then said he had rectified the pension situation, and I would now get two-thirds of the pension that I would have received if I had retired at regular retirement age. So I started receiving $750 a month, which amounted to around $630 U.S., depending on the rate of exchange at the time. After all those years, it was real nice of Max to do something like that.

I like to think it's because Max appreciated how much I helped make the northern operation so well-oiled that he was able to start working on his bigger plans for Wardair out of Edmonton and eventually Toronto. But I only helped because I know Max would have made it no matter what. I honestly thought for a time that Max would resent my quitting, but he never did. He's always shown just the greatest regard, even inviting me up to his fishing lodge every year.

I helped Max build his original fishing camp at Red-rock Lake back in the mid-1960s. It was nothing more than a tent camp where Max could take the people who were helping him out at Boeing, some of the engineers and sales people. I took in the timber framing material in the Bristol for three or four tents, each about 20 by 24 feet. One tent served as the main lodge and had plexiglass windows and an extension on it for a kitchen. Max likes to kid me about bringing in the frames. I knew where they were supposed to go but when I got up there with the Bristol that spring the only decent place we could find to land was a couple of miles down the shore-line from where Max had planned the camp. Every time I go up to Redrock Max insists I either forgot the location or was determined to put the camp somewhere else. He had to move all the material to the campsite by snowmobile.

Each spring Max would go up to Redrock and stretch the tents back over the frames to get the camp ready for another season of fishing and entertaining. He'd have the camp open for only about six weeks because the summer was so short. I've been up there when it snowed in July.

Then Max got a bee in his bonnet about establishing a permanent camp at Redrock where he could put his guests up in warm buildings built on rock with a beauti-ful view out over the lake and not have to worry about the weather. It took him a couple of years to get all the plans formulated in his mind, but once he did, it went up fast. He flew in all of the building material, furniture and diesels, making at least 150 trips with the Twin Otter. A Yellowknife contractor — Reg Lafleur — performed miracles of construction. Max always calls Reg "the mas-ter builder." He began with a large lodge with double-glass windows and a freestanding fireplace in the middle. The main dining room alone must be 30 by 40 feet. Reg then put up other buildings — guest sleeping quarters, a woodworking shop, storage buildings and a powerhouse with three diesel generators.

Best of all was Max's choice of a site for his new camp, on a point of rock 50 feet or so above the lake and about three miles from the old tent campsite. The view of Redrock Lake and the fact his lodge now rested on the rock above the lake soon had Max and everyone else calling this beautiful retreat, simply, Rockhaven.

Actually, the rock around the lake isn't all that red. It's called red rock because the south face of it is covered with a red shale and that's apparently what the early explorers first saw. So they called it Redrock Lake and it stuck.

Up until he sold Wardair in 1989, Max and his top people continued to entertain business associates by getting them away from everything up at Redrock to relax. Even in retirement Max is always inviting up friends that he had gotten to know over the years — lawyer friends and government people that had helped him out, along with judges and doctors and members of his family, of course. Most of all, though, I think Max enjoys the company of his former Wardair people up at Rockhaven. He frequently invites the top people who worked with him but he is always kind enough to invite me and some of the other Wardair old-timers every so often to swap stories and do a little fishing in between.

Rockhaven can accommodate plenty of guests, so I never really know who's going to be up there until we fly in. Each visit I always look forward to the possibility that someone I particularly respected or enjoyed working with might come along. As I've said before, Max's choice of people at Wardair over the years sometimes left a lot to be desired. But he made great choices, too. Like George Curley, probably one of the best men Max ever hired. A real brain. And there's the attorney Max stole from Boeing, Tom Spalding. Jimmy Maguire was another top pick, at least in my book. He was tenacious as hell and always hung on to something until he got it, usually another aircraft for Max's fleet. Bob O'Hara, our base manager at Yellowknife, was tops. But I always thought Max was kind of lucky when he picked men like these because he picked so many duds.

In recent years Max has really gone out of his way to keep in touch with me, even dropping by St. Cloud in his private plane just to check up on me and visit. His friendship means more to me than I can ever say or express in a book. It's special, not just because we go back to the very beginning of Wardair and even before that to the Snare River project after the war, but because Max knows he can count on me to be straight with him. In all the years I've never been shy about telling Max what's on my mind and I like to think he appreciates and respects that.

I am always amused by the way some people treat Max. He's got friends who are rich and famous, people in high places, but many are afraid to ask him anything.

One day I was sitting with a group of such people and someone wondered how Max felt about a particular matter. I said why don't you ask him? "Oh, never!" They would never think of asking Max. So I said I'll ask him. "Oh, you wouldn't do that!"

I said you bet I would, and I did. In all my life I never hesitated to ask Max whatever needed to be asked, and if he wanted my opinion he got it. But these folks respected him to the point where they wouldn't dare ask him anything or tell him what they really thought, only what they thought he wanted to hear.

This was never more evident than the time Marie and I were invited by Max to be special guests at a ceremony in Toulouse, France, in November 1987 when Wardair received the first two of some 12 brand new A-310 Airbuses Max had ordered. Wardair at long last had received permission from the government to start scheduled service in 1985 and Max needed more aircraft almost immediately. He leased three A-300 Airbuses from South Africa, arranged for the 12 new A-310s and also put in an order for 16 McDonnell-Douglas MD-88s for delivery in 1989. Everyone at Wardair was so excited by this rapid turn of events that the entire trip to France and back was one big party attended by so many Very Important People, or people who thought they were important, that Marie and I felt very ill at ease.

The reason we were invited along, of course, was Max's decision to name one of the two Airbuses, C-FHWD, the *Don Braun*. Now there would be two of my namesakes in the air, the beautiful Dash 7 in the North and a high-tech jet airliner called an Airbus flying everywhere else. I was just about speechless when Max told me of his intention to put my name on the nose of an Airbus and to this day I can never thank him enough for all of the courtesies this good and thoughtful friend has shown me in recent years. We flew back to Canada on the Airbus and I remember being so darned proud for Max and for Wardair.

As it turned out, however, neither of the aircraft kept their names for very long. Max reluctantly sold Wardair for $250 million in May 1989 after agonizing over the decision for many months. That decision, in my opinion, closed the chapter on one of the great stories in the history of commercial aviation.

Sometime in the early 1980s, Marie started to talk about changing her name back to the name she was baptized with, Maria. There were two more Marie Brauns in St. Cloud and she just couldn't stand that. There were two other Don Brauns, too, which didn't bother me at all. But one of them was married to one of the other Maries and that was too much for my Marie. Her legal name had been Marie since childhood, but she decided to change it back to her birth name. I never liked Maria and told her so, but she went through all the legal steps to change it and I didn't say another word if that made her happy. I will always think of her as Marie until the day I die.

Because of Marie's condition we didn't spend as much time socializing with our St. Cloud relatives as I would have liked. Marie would sometimes surprise me, however, and agree to go to one of the many family gatherings on the Braun side. It was the doggonedest thing because she usually ended up having a really good time, but then the depression would return and she'd find fault with everybody and that was that. I like nothing better, of course, than sitting around with a Scotch and visiting with my brothers and sisters and all of our other relatives. Sometimes I would go on my own, but not often, and I would always return early for Marie's sake.

My life in retirement actually seems busier than it ever was during my years with Wardair up at Yellowknife. In the summer there are endless hours in the garden. Marie and I would pull weeds together without so much as a word between us, somehow knowing what needed to be done. She's gone now, but I still find great pleasure in tending the garden and pulling weeds that I am almost too blind to see. In the fall you may find me down by the river sawing wood on a rig I set up using an old Ford Model A engine, and in the winter I spend hours in my machine shop doing odd jobs for people. In recent years I find myself giving more talks on Yellowknife, Wardair and the North Pole landing to school children, senior citizen groups, newspaper reporters and radio talk show people. It never ceases to amaze me how much people like to hear about bush pilots and the North Country. I've also joined a bowling league, restored a bright red 1958 MGA British sports car and bought myself a motorcycle, a Kawasaki 650 road bike.

The Kawasaki was quite a smooth machine compared to the old Henderson that I rode in the 1930s. In 1988, at the ripe old age of 75 and with my vision starting to go, I decided to take a cross-country trip on the bike because I didn't think I'd be able to do it too much longer.

I made it from St. Cloud to Dallas in just over two days, and that included driving through a three-inch rainfall in the Kansas City area. Cy Nolen, one of Marie's brothers who lives in New York state, met me in Dallas. We drove a car to San Pedro Necta, Guatemala, and left it with a Maryknoll priest, then returned to Dallas by air a few days later. I made it back to St. Cloud on my Kawasaki 650 without incident, only to be greeted by lectures from my younger brothers and sisters on what a dumb stunt I had pulled. Marie took note of the relatives' reaction and a year later joined me in pulling a similar stunt.

I'll never forget the stir Marie and I created in 1989 when we rolled into the Braun family reunion at Green Lake on my Kawasaki. All the Braun relatives get together every other year for a week and they come from all over the country, as many as a hundred of them by week's end. Green Lake was only a 50-mile trip over country highways from St. Cloud, and with Marie aboard as my navigator I didn't have too much trouble finding the resort despite being half blind. But you would have thought Marie and I were a couple of delinquent teenagers the way we were taken to task. Here we were, a couple of 76-year-olds, being lectured to by relatives all younger than us!

That motorcycle excursion was worth every bit of the guff we took, however, because it was just about the last real outing Marie and I had together. She died a little over a year later, October 4, 1990.

Despite all the difficulties, Marie and I were close in our own way. Thank goodness for my three boys and their wonderful wives and my granddaughter, Tanya. They have filled my life with so much happiness since Marie passed on. Charles married and he and his wife, Marilyn, are expecting their first child — my second grandchild. They are also living in British Columbia, in Victoria, not too far from Christopher and Lynda. Then there is Joel and his bride, Jackie. They live right here on what remains of the old farm property, in that basement house Marie and I built into the hillside overlooking the river in 1949 after returning from the North the first time. Jackie has been the greatest blessing in my old age. She keeps house for me, pays the bills, sees to it that I eat properly and even gives my hair and beard a proper trim. With Jackie around I don't dare miss taking my medication or I never hear the end of it. She runs a tight ship and I love her for it.

Up until about 10 years ago, around the time I turned 70, I had done very little flying since leaving Yellowknife and even my license had expired. During the past 10 years, however, I've been back in the air in a fragile little thing that doesn't require a pilot's license. It's called an ultralight.

I had read about ultralights but had never seen one until a chance encounter one sunny afternoon out at the St. Cloud airport. As I watched the darn thing, which is nothing more than a small glider with a tiny motor and tricycle wheels, I was determined to give it a try. I received the proper instructions, put on my old motorcycle helmet and a pair of goggles, then took off. In all the years I've been flying, this was the closest thing to actual flight that I had ever experienced. You don't fly high or fast in an ultralight; you sit out in the open and play the wind like an eagle.

My first solo ended with a rather bumpy landing, however, and this eagle was treated for a dislocated hip and several bruises. Still, I was hooked.

In less than a month I was back up, flying just above the treetops out over the Mississippi River and the old farm. I bought an ultralight and then decided to go into the business, selling the contraptions and giving instructions on how to fly them. By the mid-1980s I had a small hangar and eight or ten ultralights at a grass airstrip near Clearwater, a few miles south of St. Cloud. Most of my customers and students were relatively young men from the area and I've become a good friend to many of them. They know they are always welcome to stop by the farmhouse and visit about their latest exploits, and they often do just that.

The last few years my eyesight has been failing to the point where I can hardly see the pins when I'm bowling, so I've sold the ultralight business and I'm just about ready to ground myself for good. The last time up I did okay until it came time to land and the only thing I could make out for sure was the roof of the hangar. I used it as a reference point and made it in, just as I had in snowstorms or bad weather years ago in the North. The old Arctic Fox, however, is now a half-blind 79-year-old with a bad heart and a pacemaker, and the prospects of one more flight are growing dim.

Next summer I'll be well into my 80th year, but just maybe I'll be able to make one more flight. My inspiration is a particular verse in a song by a Canadian singer I really like, Rita MacNeil, and it's on a tape my kids gave me. I listen to that song nearly every day. It's called "Moment in Time" and the verse goes like this:

> You fly where the eagles fly;
> you dance with the stars at night;
> you reach with all your might
> for your moment in time.

If I don't make one last flight next summer, I guess it's okay. I've flown with the eagles and danced with the stars. The more I think about it, I've been blessed with more than my fair share of moments in time.

FINAL LOG ENTRY:
A PERSONAL REFLECTION

I never had much of a philosophy of life and I never planned anything at all.

A person should plan ahead further than I ever did. Maybe then I would have had more of a goal in life than just flying. But flying was the only thing I ever wanted to do. My life was nothing more than hard work and being lucky enough to be in a job where I really enjoyed what I was doing. When you think about it, very few people have the opportunity to go through life doing what they like.

As for money, I was never too interested in making any. With Max starting up Wardair and my getting into the business with him so early, I probably worked as hard for Wardair's growth as anybody else. But I was more interested in the business being a success than I was in making a lot of money. It shows, too, because I never made any money. Max's friendship over the years, however, is payment enough.

Flying for Wardair also gave me the opportunity to make the first landing of a wheeled aircraft at the North Pole, and it's the one accomplishment in my life that I'm most proud of. Taking that old Bristol in without preparation was a little risky and just a bit harebrained, but I was very proud of the fact we got in there safely.

I'm also real proud of my family.

Each day, now, I find myself thinking more often than not about my three boys and their good wives and how well everything has turned out. I really didn't have too much to do with that. Marie is the one who should get all the credit. But I sure do appreciate my boys now, I tell you. You don't realize what you've got until awful late in life sometimes.

I just hope that when I'm gone people will remember me as an honest and fair person, even though I know sometimes I wasn't. And that my family will remember me as someone who tried his best to be a good father and husband, although I know sometimes I failed.

Well, I guess that about sums it up.